Environment, Technology and Sustainability

Looking at the concept of sustainable buildings, this text covers the available technologies and techniques for establishing a suitable environment within buildings while minimising exploitation of scarce energy resources.

Taking a holistic view, this book explains environmental influences on buildings and moves on to outline principles of design, considering the influence of any one set of choices on other areas – the balances and trade-offs required to be a successful building designer.

The book logically runs through the topics, including coverage of:

- principles of climate design
- wind flow around buildings
- thermal comfort
- solar energy
- energy systems in domestic buildings
- lighting design and daylight principles
- acoustic design
- environmental impacts of buildings
- climate change and building design.

Offering design examples at the end of each section, the book concludes with four deeper case studies for observing theory in practice.

Tailored to courses in architectural technology and architecture, this extremely helpful guide will steer students through architectural engineering and building surveying modules as well.

Steve Sharples is Professor of Environmental Design and Sustainability at the University of Sheffield, UK. He was previously Head of the School of Architecture, Technology and Environment at Sheffield Hallam University, UK.

Hocine Bougdah is Principal Lecturer in Architecture at University College for the Creative Arts at Canterbury, UK

Technologies of Architecture
Editor: Joan Zunde

Technologies of Architecture is an introductory textbook series providing a coherent framework to the architectural design process in a practical and applied way. This series forms an essential suite of books for students of architectural technology, architecture, building surveying and construction.

Other titles:
Volume 1: Integrated strategies in architecture
Joan Zunde and Hocine Bougdah

Volume 2: Environment, Technology and Sustainability
Hocine Bougdah and Stephen Sharples

Volume 3: Materials, Specification and Detailing
Norman Wienand

Volume 4: Practice, Management and Responsibility
John Hickey

Volume 5: History, Performance and Conservation
Barry Bridgwood and Lindsay Lennie

Technologies of Architecture
VOLUME 2

Environment, Technology and Sustainability

Hocine Bougdah and Stephen Sharples
with Peter F. Smith

Illustrations by
Hocine Bougdah, Stephen Sharples
and Joseph Deane

LONDON AND NEW YORK

First published 2010
by Taylor & Francis
2 Park Square, Milton Park, Abingdon, OX14 4RN

Simultaneously published in the USA and Canada
by Taylor & Francis
270 Madison Avenue, New York, NY10016

Taylor & Francis is an imprint of the Taylor & Francis Group,
an informa business

Typeset in Univers by Keyword Group Ltd
Printed and bound in Great Britain by MPG Books Ltd., Bodmin

Every effort has been made to ensure that the advice and information in this book is true and accurate at the time of going to press. However, neither the publisher nor the authors can accept any legal responsibility or liability for any errors or omissions that may be made. In the case of drug administration, any medical procedure or the use of technical equipment mentioned within this book, you are strongly advised to consult the manufacturer's guidelines.

British Library Cataloguing in Publication Data
A catalogue record for this book is available from the British Library

Library of Congress Cataloging in Publication Data

Bougdah, Hocine
Environment, technology, and sustainability / Hocine Bougdah and Stephen Sharples.
p. cm. – (Technologies of architecture)
Includes bibliographical references and index.
1. Sustainable architecture. 2. Architecture–Environmental aspects. I. Sharples, Stephen. II. Title.

NA2542.36.B68 2009
720'.47–dc22 2008046859

ISBN10: 0-415-40378-2 (hbk)
ISBN10: 0-415-40379-0 (pbk)
ISBN10: 0-203-87840-X (ebk)

ISBN13: 978-0-415-40378-8 (hbk)
ISBN13: 978-0-415-40379-5 (pbk)
ISBN13: 978-0-203-87840-8 (ebk)

Contents

Introduction

Peter F. Smith

Buildings are responsible for the largest share of energy use and carbon emissions, hence their prominence in the sustainability debate. There are two evolving crises which will bear hard on the construction industry. The first is the accelerating pace of climate change; the second, the growing uncertainty about the security of supplies of fossil fuels.

Climate change

The fourth Assessment of the Inter-governmental Panel on Climate Change (IPCC) produced in 2007 went further than the previous report in stating that there is a 90 per cent probability that humans are implicated in forcing climate change. Since then, there has been a discernible increase in the level of anxiety regarding climate change and one of the reasons is the wider awareness of the significance of so-called 'tipping points'. The key tipping point indicator for climate change is the concentration of atmospheric carbon dioxide. At present concentrations of CO_2 are about 383 ppm and increasing at 2–3 ppm per year and rising. The tipping point would be when the concentration of carbon dioxide reaches 450 parts per million (ppm), accompanied by a 2°C rise in average temperature. There is general scientific agreement that this concentration would signal a steep change in the rate of global warming and associated climate change. Mutually reinforcing feedback systems will gather momentum, leading rapidly to a situation which is irreversible – in other words, runaway global warming driven largely by the heat trapped in the atmosphere. It could mean that there is less than 15 years in which to halt the rise in CO_2 levels.

Research at NASA's Goddard Institute for Space Studies concludes that further global warming of 1°C defines a critical threshold, beyond which there are likely to be changes that will make Earth a different planet from what it is now. Earth would be the hottest it has been for a million years and another decade of business as usual carbon emissions will probably make it too late to prevent the ecosystems of the north from activating runaway climate change. Other studies, at the Tyndall Centre for Climate Change, University of East Anglia, concluded that the loss of the Greenland ice sheet may now be inevitable, leading to a sea level rise of 7m. Similar occurrences are happening in Antarctica, the sub-Arctic regions, such as Siberia where melting is occurring three times faster than the global average. This is leading to huge releases of methane, which is 23 times more potent in greenhouse warming terms than carbon dioxide. In the UK, storm surges look like being one of the most important threats resulting from climate change. The Thames estuary is being designated as a location of the highest risk from storm surges to the coasts of northern Europe up to 2080.

The view of scientists is that the UK must achieve a 70 per cent cut in greenhouse gas emissions by 2030 and 90 per cent by 2050 if irreversible climate change is to have any chance of being avoided. This would mean stabilising emissions within four years and cutting them by 9 per cent per year thereafter for the next 20 years. Time is of the essence. One calculation is that, if serious action is delayed to 2020, it would mean that counter-measures to prevent runaway climate change would have to be seven times more stringent than if implemented immediately. The Stern Report of 2006 by economist Nicholas Stern estimated that it will be 20 times more costly to deal with climate change impacts in the future compared to tackling them now.

All this places considerable pressure on the demand side of energy, dominated as it is by the built environment, since energy is the prime forcing agent behind climate change. In addition, conventional energy has its own problems.

The profile of energy

Energy demand

The demand for energy continues to rise steadily in the industrialised countries. In the developing world energy demand is rising almost exponentially due to double digit economic growth. Consequently, energy demand is outpacing gains in energy efficiency. The World Energy Council estimates that by the end of this century primary energy demand will be more than three times the current level. However, even since this assessment was made, the International Energy Agency now believes there will be an even greater rise in associated CO_2 levels due to the increased use of coal in place of gas and the commissioning of new coal fired power stations – in China, for example, two new plants are commissioned every week. Economic developments in countries such as China, India, Russia and Brazil (which between them account for 70 per cent of the world's economic growth) will have an enormous impact on energy demand and climate change if left unchecked.

Energy supply

It is believed that reserves of conventional oil have already passed their peak, called predictably 'peak oil', and will be nearly exhausted by 2040–50, with gas following in 2060–70. This is another tipping point, namely the stage at which demand starts to outpace the discovery of new reserves. As reserves move down the bell curve and guarantees of supply become increasingly uncertain, not only will there be considerable price volatility but also an extension of the oil wars which are already under way. However, this disturbing scenario may be avoided. This is because it is clear that fossil fuels must be virtually abandoned long before they are exhausted if the world is to avoid catastrophic climate change. The Tyndall Centre believes that the only scenario that avoids dangerous climate change over the long term is the minimum emissions scenario, which allows for about one quarter of known fossil fuels to be used (about 1,000 GtC out of 4,000–5,000 GtC). This scenario allows for a small increase in global emissions to 2025, followed by a steady linear phasing out by 2200. Because the UK has high emissions per capita the implications for the UK would be a need for an immediate, significant and on-going programme of cuts in emission. The Tyndall Centre thinks that if all conventional and non-conventional fuels are expended, the outcome will be a concentration of CO_2 of 1,000 ppm by 2100 and possibly over 5,000 ppm by 3000. The consequences could be:

- Global and regional warming more than quadrupling after 2100 to as much as 15°C.
- Sea levels rising by 11.4 metres. For London it could be 13 metres since isostatic change is already causing London to sink 2mm per year.
- Abrupt climate change events could occur like the complete disappearance of Arctic sea ice causing North Atlantic seas to heat up 8°C accompanied by UK land temperature increases of up to 5°C within 20 years.
- Abrupt climate changes can occur many decades after emissions have ceased – the 'sleeping giant' in the climate system.
- Ocean pH levels will fall dramatically as seas become more acidic, threatening marine life, especially plankton. This would have major implications for the rest of the marine ecosystem.

The assumptions behind the Tyndall study are said to be 'conservative'. This means that climate changes could be even greater if climate systems turn out to be more sensitive to the level of greenhouse gases. Only by reducing emissions to zero by 2200 can dangerous climate change be avoided.

All this makes it obvious that extreme actions are urgently needed to reduce CO_2 emissions. In the front line of the campaign to prevent the world crossing the 450 ppm Rubicon are the professions involved in shaping the built environment – both new-build and existing. It may seem extravagant to suggest that these professionals are key players in the current drama of the planet. However, they are not only responsible for producing buildings to the highest environmental standards; they are also in a position to influence those who commission buildings. It is often at the commissioning stage that high eco-ideals are dismissed. This reasoning, and the stark warnings described previously, set the scene for this book, which provides a detailed, design-orientated approach to the technologies of environmental architecture. Although sustainability in the built environment extends beyond the issue of energy use, the importance of low and even zero energy design has never been greater. The book proposes a series of approaches that would enable building design students to consider low energy strategies. After all, a kilowatt-hour saved is infinitely more beneficial to the planet than a kilowatt-hour generated from even the greenest of renewables.

Peter F. Smith, University of Nottingham

Part 1
Buildings and climate design

Chapter **1**

Principles of climate design

Introduction

Winston Churchill said 'We shape our buildings, and afterwards our buildings shape us'. The reverse is now probably true for climate – it has shaped human activity, and now human activity is shaping the climate. Historically, human activity and development have always been inextricably linked with climate. Many of the great ancient cities and civilisations developed in benign climates that were conducive to social, cultural and scientific development. Some civilisations, such as the Mayan, are also thought to have died out due to changes in their local climate. Figure 1.1 shows how a mean outdoor air temperature contour of 21°C linked the sites of many ancient cities.

One of the most basic human activities linked to climate is building to provide shelter from adverse external climatic conditions. Consequently, the study of the interactions between buildings and climate – building climatology – is as old as the concept of shelter itself. Early civilisations demonstrated a deep understanding of how built form could work with the prevailing climate to create habitable and comfortable internal environments. Caves were an early form of shelter which offered summer cooling and protection from wind, rain and snow. The Greek, Xenophon, in 400 BC, described the design and orientation of openings to provide natural heating and cooling in buildings. The Roman architect Vitruvius, in the first century BC, included in his famous *Ten Books on Architecture* advice on passive solar design and natural ventilation – indeed, the Romans passed sun-right laws to protect the solar access of existing buildings.

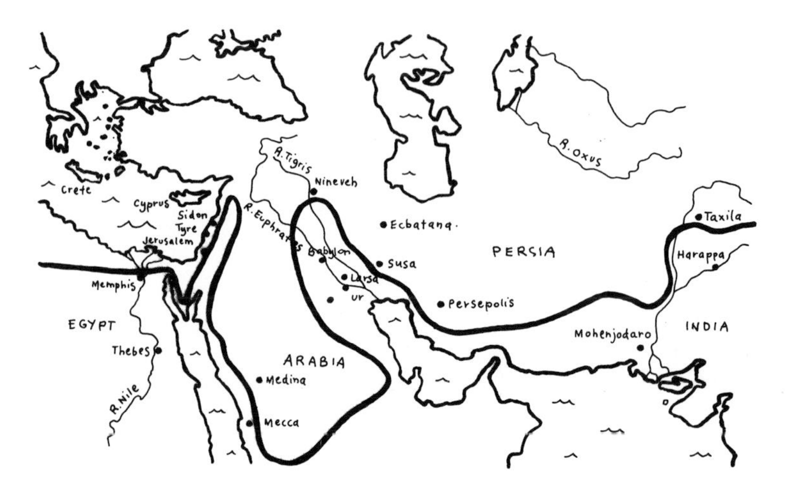

1.1

Although other factors (social, religious, cultural and economic) have been important, there is no doubt that climate has played a major role in shaping traditional vernacular architectural forms around the world. It was only in the early twentieth century that developments in structural design, materials technology and building services enabled tall buildings to be constructed of glass and steel with internal environments that could be decoupled from their external climate. A typical example of a climate insensitive structure, Mies van der Rohe's Seagram Building in New York, is shown in Figure 1.2.

1.2

Such buildings tended to have high levels of energy consumption to maintain comfort. Concerns over fuel costs, environmental impact, sustainability and occupant health have led to a renewed interest in climate-sensitive building design. Many of the techniques that were intuitively learnt in the past are being re-visited and applied today in low energy, sustainable and environmentally-aware buildings. This section will consider some of the basic principles of climatic design and describe some of the ways in which a site's microclimate can be used to improve the environmental performance of a building and the comfort of people located in and moving around the building. Climatic analysis techniques will be introduced and examples presented of some contemporary architectural responses to climatic design. The section is divided into three chapters. This chapter will describe how global climate types are categorised and consider how traditional architectural forms have responded to these climates. Chapter 2 will discuss some specific climatic elements (sun, wind, rain and snow) in terms of how they affect building design. Chapter 3 will explain how climate information can be applied in terms of site planning and bioclimatic analysis and will conclude with some case study examples.

Basic elements of climate

Climate (from the Greek word *klima* meaning *inclination*) describes the long term atmospheric conditions observed at a site. Weather is the individual short term (hourly or daily) observations of climatic features. The major weather elements of interest in architecture are:

- Dry bulb air temperature (°C) – thermal comfort, heating and cooling
- Relative humidity (percentage) – thermal comfort, condensation, mould growth
- Precipitation (rain, hail, frost and snow) – drainage, loading, damage
- Wind speed and direction (m/s) – energy, ventilation, comfort, loading
- Sunshine hours – indication of solar availability
- Solar radiation (W/m^2) – indication of solar energy options

In order to standardise weather measurements around the world similar procedures are followed in most countries. Air temperature and humidity are measured in a Stevenson Screen (Figure 1.3), which is a white, shaded and ventilated box raised 1.2m to 1.6m above the ground. Precipitation is collected in a ground buried container whose rim is just above ground level (to avoid collecting run-off water). Wind speed and direction often use a cup anemometer and vane placed on a mast 10 metres above open ground or at an effective height of 10 metres above surrounding buildings. A wind rose shows the annual frequency and distribution of wind speeds and directions. Sunshine hours are measured using a solid glass sphere called a Campbell Stokes Sunshine Recorder. The sphere is typically 100mm in diameter and focuses sunlight on to a wax chart that scorches to show the daily duration of the sunlight. In the USA the Marvin Sunshine Recorder is more commonly used. Solar radiation measurements are made using a solarimeter, which consists of a blackened thermopile housed under a protective glass dome. As the thermopile absorbs the solar radiation its temperature increases and an electrical signal proportional to the heating effect is recorded.

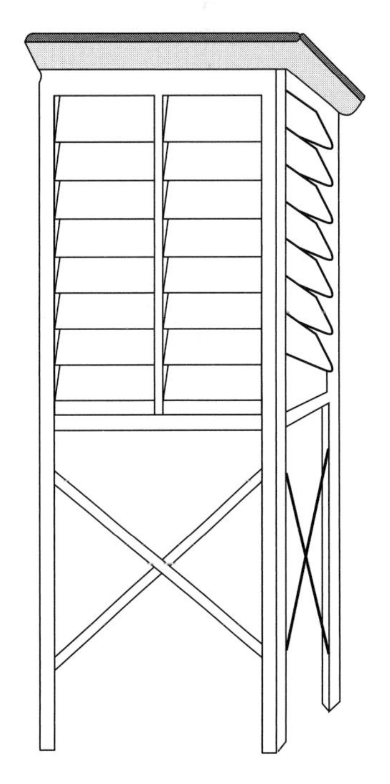

1.3

Representative climate data for many locations can be freely found on websites such as those given in the webliography on pp. 47–48 (www.weatherbase.com and www.climate-zone.com) at the end of the section. Commercial climatic software, such as Meteonorm, provides an enormous database of weather information as well as the possibility of creating weather files for sites where no weather records have been kept.

Climate classification

World climates, as studied by meteorologists, display a wide range of complex characteristics and variations. For building design purposes it is possible to make use of a simplified version of the climate classification system initially developed by Köppen in the early 1900s. This simplification divides the world's climates into four basic types: polar/cold, temperate, hot dry and hot humid. Figure 1.4 shows these climate zones.

Polar / cold climates

This type of climate is typically found at high latitudes above 55°. The key shelter problem in polar / cold climates is providing thermal comfort against the extreme cold. Average minimum air temperatures in winter may be below –15°C, with the lowest temperatures dropping below –40°C. In the summer temperatures will not rise above 10°C. The coldest temperature ever recorded was –88°C at Vostock in Antarctic. Strong winds can add to the chill factor. Perhaps surprisingly, polar regions are dry, and may have similar levels of precipitation to those found in desert areas.

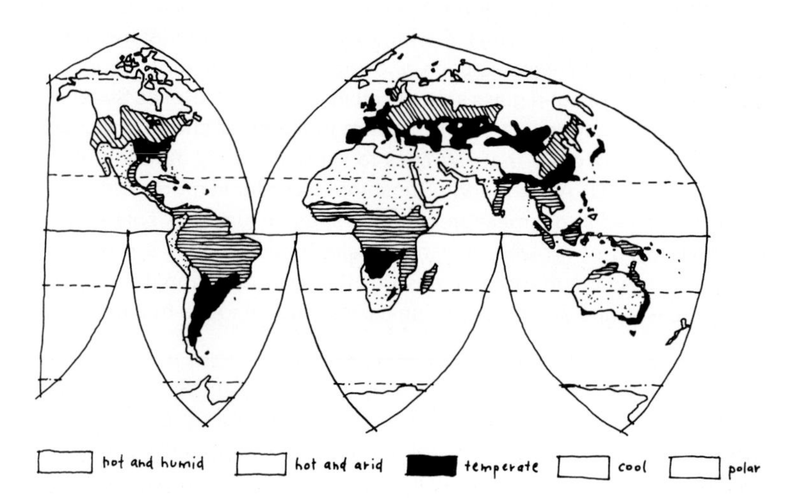

1.4

Temperate climates

This type of climate is usually found at latitudes between 30° and 55°. The main shelter issue with temperate climates is coping with the seasonal variations. This leads to potential overheating problems in summer but overcooling issues in winter. In the summer air temperatures may average 25°C but then drop down to as low as –15°C in winter. Humidity levels are not normally a problem. Precipitation may occur at any time of the year.

Hot dry climates

This type of climate is usually found at latitudes between 20° and 35°. The main shelter issue is overheating. Mean summer temperatures are around 25°C but can reach a maximum of 45°C. Clear nocturnal skies can cool temperatures down as low as –10°C. The hottest temperature ever recorded was 58°C in Libya in 1922. Relative humidity is low and precipitation is very low. This lack of moisture, together with strong seasonal winds, can make wind-borne sand storms a major problem.

Hot humid climates

This type of climate is usually found at latitudes between 0° and 25°. The main shelter problems are overheating and oppressively high humidities. Day time temperatures do not normally exceed 35°C, but night time temperatures will often not drop below 20°C. Relative humidities are very high, reaching 80 per cent in some months. Rainfall is frequent and occurs as heavy falls, typically in short, intense spells. There is little seasonal variation in the climate, apart from rainy seasons such as monsoons. A comparison of the four climate types is given in Figure 1.5

Traditional climatic design

> Primitive man often builds more wisely than we do, and follows principles of design which we ignore at great cost.
>
> (Rapoport (1969))

This observation reflects the fact that traditional forms of shelter were built by the people who were going to inhabit them. An iterative process of trial and error meant that only those designs that succeeded in

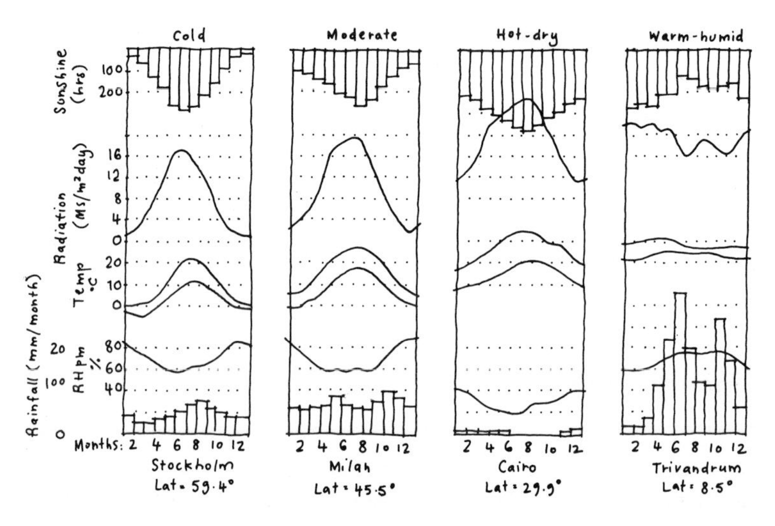

1.5

reaching a compromise between comfort, durability and buildability survived to become the traditional architecture of that area. All traditional architectural solutions for the creation of shelter have addressed the issues of moderating the prevailing external climate with the building's form, orientation and construction materials. These materials had to be local, naturally available and require little processing – an approach which is mirrored today in the way that many eco-buildings try to reuse and recycle local building materials.

Traditional design for polar / cold climates

For polar and very cold regions the key aim is to minimise heat loss from external surfaces. The ratio of internal volume to exposed surface area is an important parameter. Geometrically, the sphere or hemisphere has the highest value of this ratio, and so it is not surprising that the most famous traditional form of shelter in polar regions is the dome-shaped igloo (from the Inuit word *igdlu* meaning *house*), see Figure 1.6.

1.6

The domed construction is also very stable structurally and presents a smooth aerodynamic shape to the polar winds. Snow is the only major building material available. The snow blocks used to make the igloo contain trapped air and act as a good insulator. They typically measure 900 mm long by 450 mm high and 150 mm high and are laid in a continuous spiral from floor to roof. Openings are kept to a minimum and entrances are located away from prevailing winds or linked to the living

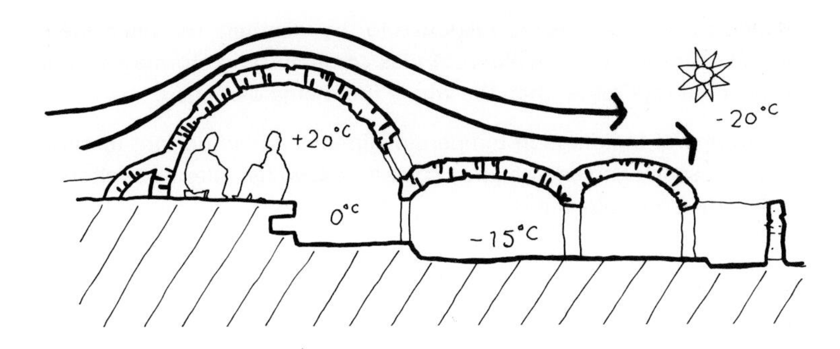

1.7

area via a tunnel. Inside the igloo snow platforms are covered with insulating fur skins. Heat from lamps and people slightly melts the internal snow surface and this refreezes to give a coating of ice that acts as a barrier to air infiltration. Ventilation is provided by a very small opening in the roof. The effectiveness of igloos as shelter is demonstrated by a study of air temperatures inside and outside the igloo by Cook (1996) – see Figure 1.7.

Cold climate areas outside the polar regions are able to support the growth of vast forests and so timber is the key traditional building material. Heavy wooden structures with small openings are used in the construction and the form is compact. Roofs are covered in shingle, turf or logs and have a low pitch to encourage snow to lie evenly. The snow layer, particularly when freshly fallen and not compacted, acts as a good insulator and stops heat escaping through the roof. Figure 1.8 shows a typical cold climate building.

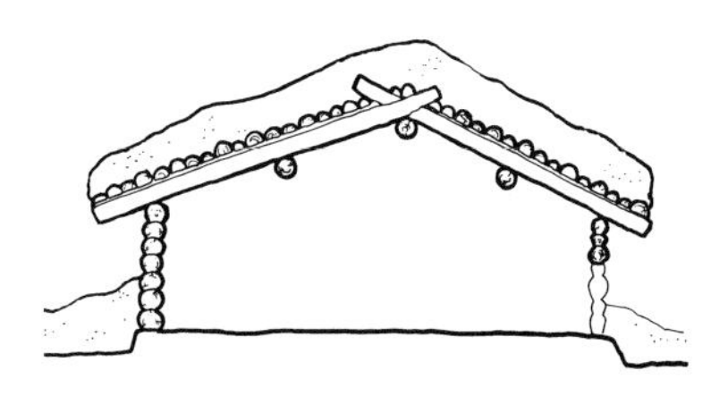

1.8

Traditional design for temperate climates

The milder winters and warmer summers of temperate climates mean that traditional buildings are freed from the need to have a compact, low surface area form. Openings can be larger and orientated to enjoy solar gains in winter, spring and autumn. Provision must be made for shading of the openings in summer to avoid overheating. This may be in the form of an overhanging roof, which will also be pitched to allow rain to run off. The thermal capacity of the building is normally high so that day time heat gains can warm internal spaces at night. Temperate climates vary from warm Mediterranean type temperate climates to cool Northern Europe temperate climates and so the range of architectural solutions is quite broad. For warm climates adobe / rammed earth walls and thatched roofs were a traditional design (Figure 1.9). In the UK, which has a wet and windy temperate climate, the use of tiled

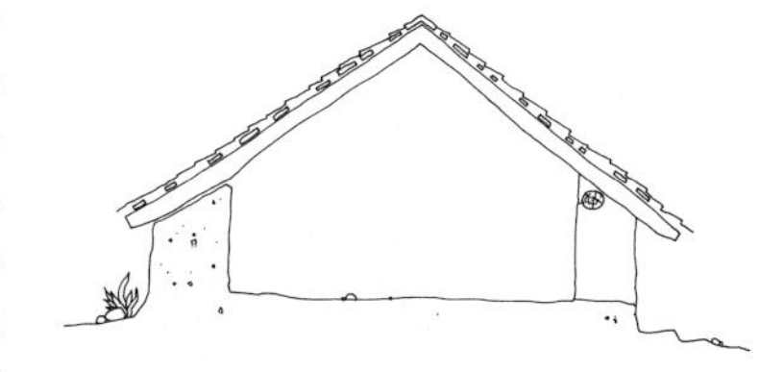

1.9

pitched roofs is a sensible response to the weather. The pitch helps with the run-off of rain while roof tiles come away in storms as small parts of the roof rather than the whole roof being damaged.

For groups of buildings in temperate climates it is important to allow sufficient spacing to ensure good solar access whilst offering sheltering protection from cold winds.

Traditional design for hot dry climates

For hot dry climates the overriding requirement is to try and moderate the very high external air temperatures and intense solar radiation levels. The use of thermally massive walls and roofs is the key design response. They help retard and reduce the flow of heat through the fabric by several hours, keeping rooms cooler during the day and providing background heat during cold nights. External surfaces are often painted white to reflect solar gain whilst at night the painted surfaces (particularly the roof) can effectively radiate heat to the night sky. Window and door openings are kept to a minimum, both to reduce solar gain and the ingress of wind-blown sand. Roofs are flat for several reasons: first, there is very little precipitation and so drainage is not a consideration. Second, the roof is the building surface that is most exposed to the high sun and so needs to have the minimum surface area for solar absorption. Finally, if the roof has a parapet it can be used at night as a thermally comfortable sleeping area. Given the harshness of the prevailing external climate it is not surprising that one of the most successful traditional desert architectural solutions – the courtyard house – creates a sheltered and shaded space by looking in on itself. The main thermal elements in a courtyard house are shown in Figure 1.10.

The key thermal element is the courtyard itself. This will often contain a pool of water and some vegetation to cool the air held within the courtyard by evaporation and transpiration. The walls of the courtyard offer shade and thermal mass to regulate the heat flow in to the living spaces that adjoin the courtyard. Openings in the walls provide a means of controlling the air flow through these spaces. The courtyard house operates under three diurnal thermal regimes (Figure 1.11). First, at night radiation from external surfaces to the clear skies cools the air in the courtyard. This cool air is relatively 'heavy' and lies in the courtyard (chilling the surrounding surfaces) and flows in to the surrounding rooms. This cooling effect can last until the afternoon of the following day. For the second thermal regime, which operates from around midday, the courtyard floor absorbs the heat from the high sun and warms the air, causing it to rise and create a chimney effect which draws relatively cool air through the house. In the third phase, from late afternoon, the sun is lower and shading is created in the courtyard.

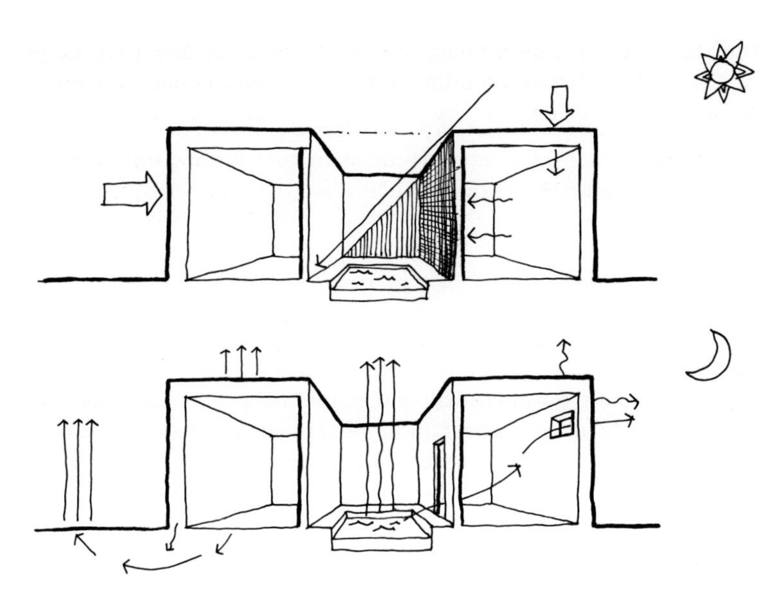

1.10

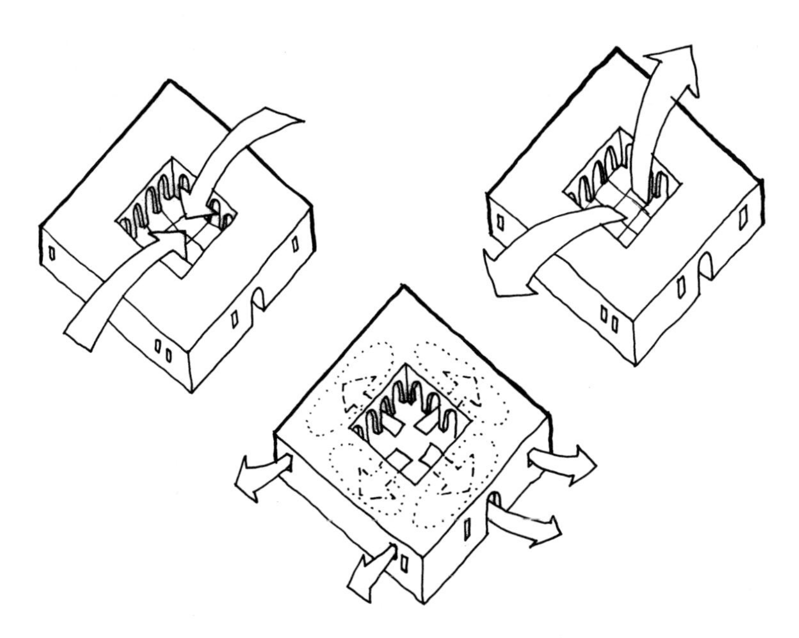

1.11

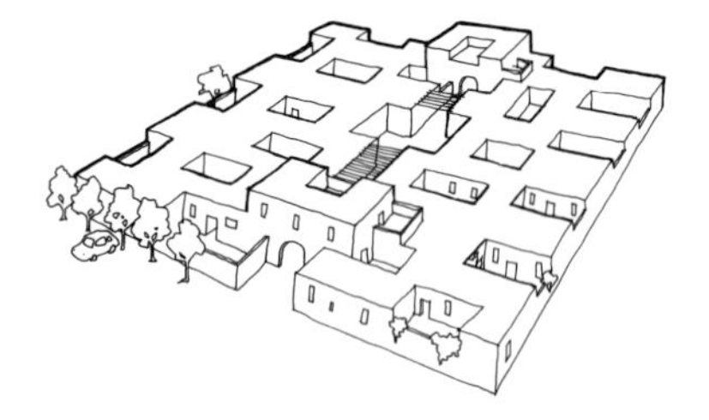

1.12

This, together with the cooling effects of the water and vegetation, begins to cool down the air prior to the night cycle commencing again.

Buildings in cities with hot dry climates are often positioned close together along narrow streets to provide mutual shading from the sun and hot, dust-laden winds (Figure 1.12).

Traditional design for hot humid climates

For hot humid climates the key environmental requirements are to alleviate the effects of very high humidity, solar gain and heavy rain. The daily temperature range is small and so thermal mass is not desirable as it will simply retain the heat throughout the day and night. The only non-mechanical way to reduce the thermal discomfort from high humidity is through the promotion of air movement. Consequently, traditional architecture in this climate consists of very lightweight structures with large openings. In some instances the walls are removed altogether, leaving the roof supported on poles. The floors are slotted and raised above the ground to encourage air flow. This arrangement also offers protection from insects and flooding and provides a reservoir of cool, shaded air below the floor. The roof has a steep pitch for rain run-off and large overhangs to provide solar shading and to drain the heavy rains away from the house. The roof is traditionally made from vegetation, such as banana leaves, which provide a porous structure to allow warm air to escape through the top of the building. This vegetation soon rots in the humid conditions but is easily replaced. In fact, the whole structure is made from the local plant materials supplied by the tropical jungles (bamboo, vines and grasses). The lack of tools and metal fixings means that the buildings are put together using skills more aligned to weaving rather than construction. Figure 1.13 shows a typical construction.

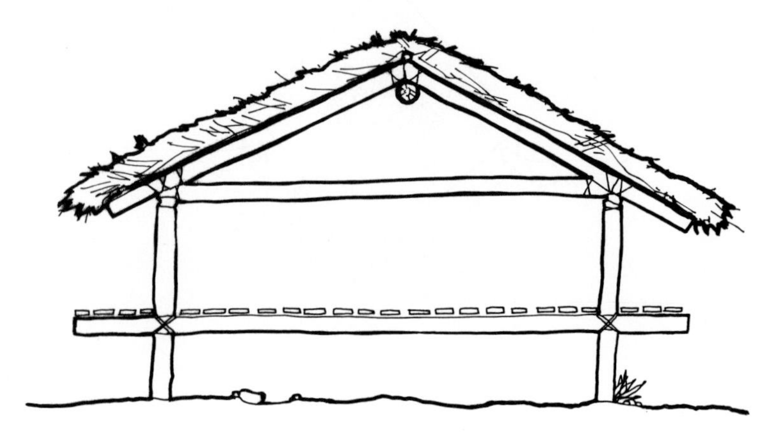

1.13

The buildings are normally single storey and shallow in plan to encourage the maximum amount of airflow. It is also important that groups of buildings do not shield each other from any winds and so they are positioned in a staggered and widely spaced configuration that faces the prevailing wind direction, as shown in Figure 1.14.

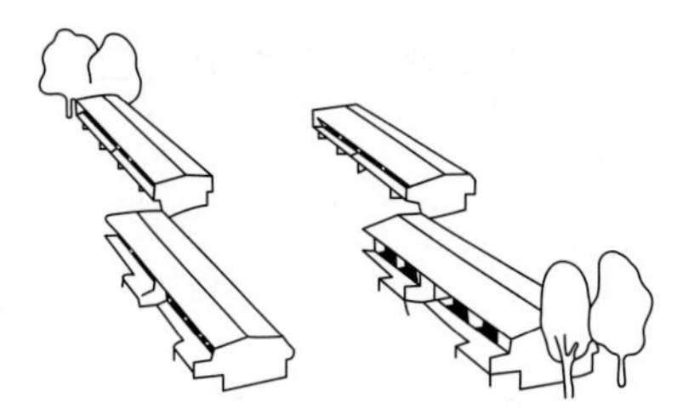

1.14

Architectural design and climate change

One good reason for understanding the traditional interactions between climate and buildings it that it can give guidance to how future designs might be developed to adapt to climate change. If the summers of the 2080s in London may be as hot as the summers in southern Europe today then what aspects of vernacular Mediterranean design may be used in future UK architectural and environmental developments? If flooding may become a more common feature of twenty-second-century Britain then how have countries historically at risk from flooding, such as the Netherlands, planned and designed their built environment? Because the patterns of climate change impacts on the built environment are uncertain and long term then the most sensible approach to future building design is to make buildings as adaptable as possible – a strategy discussed by Roaf *et al.* (2005). It is ironic that issues relating to climate change, thermal comfort, energy and sustainability may mean that building design in the future will have to look at and learn from the traditional architectural responses to climate of the past.

Chapter **2**

Solar principles in climatic design

Introduction

The sun is the origin of most of the world's energy sources; it drives all of the planet's weather systems and makes it possible for life to survive on Earth. It is not surprising that ancient civilisations worshipped the sun as a god. The sun can be used to bring similar benefits (energy, microclimate and well being) to people, buildings and the spaces around them, but to do this requires some awareness and planning on the part of the designer. The main considerations include:

- Thermal – the sun can provide useful heat gains in spring, autumn and winter but may create overheating problems in summer; solar radiation can be used with solar collectors to produce hot water and with photovoltaic panels to generate electricity for buildings.
- Visual – sunlight shining in to a room can increase illuminance, enhance colours and textures and provide visual interest as shadows move and light levels vary; problems may arise from glare and overheating.
- Biological – how the sun moves around a site, and the areas of light and shadow created, are important for plant growth, landscaping and external recreational areas; places where the sun rarely reaches are prone to be cold, damp and uninviting.
- Structural – the heat and high ultra violet (UV) components in solar radiation can have physical and chemical impacts on timbers, plastics, paints and fabrics, causing weathering, fading and structural movement. UV is particularly serious where light sensitive exhibits, such as pictures and tapestries, may be exposed to sunlight
- Psychological – many people, particularly in developed countries, may spend up to 90 per cent of their time indoors. Sunlight provides a link with the outside world and can produce a sense of well being in occupants of a building.

The sun and the Earth

The sun is a nuclear fusion reactor located approximately 150 million kilometres away from Earth. This is not only a reassuringly long distance away at which to have a nuclear power plant but also means that the solar energy that reaches Earth is actually the result of nuclear energy. The Earth moves around the sun, performing a complete orbit in approximately 365¼ days (which is rounded to 366 days approximately every fourth or leap year). The Earth is also rotating about its own axis, taking around 24 hours to complete one rotation. This axis of rotation, through the North and South Poles, is not at right angles to the plane of orbit around the sun but is inclined at 23°27′ (~23.5°) to the normal to this plane. The importance of this tilt is that it is responsible for the seasons and the changing positions of the sun at different times of the year. For half the year (March to September) the northern hemisphere is tilted towards the sun, with the longest day occurring around 21 June (the summer solstice). From September to March it is the southern hemisphere that is tipped towards the sun, with the longest day around 21 December (the winter solstice). During spring and autumn the rotation axis is nearly at right angles to the orbital plane, giving rise to a day and night with near equal lengths each of approximately twelve hours (hence the name *equinox*). The spring event takes place around 21 March (the spring or vernal equinox) and for autumn it is around 21 September (the autumn or fall equinox).

From an analysis point of view any solar studies only need to be carried out on the days of the summer and winter solstice and the equinoxes to see the full range of sunlight and shade that will be experienced at a location.

Solar geometry

Although the Earth revolves around the sun it is conceptually much easier to visualise that the Earth is stationary and that is it the sun that is moving across the sky in an arc from east to west. The shape of this arc will vary with latitude and time of year.

A basic requirement of using the sun in design is to know at any time where in the sky it will be with respect to a site and the buildings on that site. Because this is a three-dimensional situation two co-ordinates are required to locate the sun's position in the sky. The angle between the horizon and the sun is called the *solar altitude* and varies from 0° when the sun is just rising to 90° (the zenith) when the sun is directly overhead. If a line from the sun to the Earth was projected vertically downwards on to the horizontal plane then the angle between this projected

Table 2.1 Solar altitude at noon for different locations and times

Latitude	*Summer solstice 21/22 June*	*Vernal and autumnal equinox 20/21 March 22/23 September*	*Winter solstice 21/22 December*
90°N	23.5°	0°	– 23.5°
66.5°N (Arctic Circle)	47°	23.5°	0°
60°N	53.5°	30°	6.5°
50°N	63.5°	40°	16.5°
23.5°N	90°	66.5°	43°
0° (Equator)	66.5°	90°	66.5°
23.5°S	43°	66.5°	90°
50°S	16.5°	40°	63.5°
60°S	6.5°	30°	53.5°
66.5°S	0°	23.5°	47°
90°S	– 23.5°	0°	23.5°

line and south is called the *solar azimuth*. It will vary from 0° to 180° east of south and 0° to 180° west of south.

The maximum solar altitude at noon for a latitude of θ° N is given by

Summer solstice: $90° - \theta° - 23.5°$
Equinox: $90° - \theta°$
Winter solstice: $90° - \theta° + 23.5°$

Table 2.1 shows the values of the maximum noon solar altitudes for different latitudes in the northern and southern hemisphere. There are many tools for calculating solar angles, such as the shareware package given in online sources. Most environmental modelling packages, such as ECOTECT, calculate solar angles as part of their analysis (see http://squ1.org/wiki/SolarPosition calculator_Hourly).

From a design point of view it is useful to be able to convey the position of the sun at any time with respect to a building's façade in plan and elevation drawings. For plan drawings the sun's beam is projected vertically down on to the horizontal plane and the angle between this projected line and the perpendicular to the façade is called the *horizontal shadow angle (HSA)*. For elevation drawings an imaginary line is drawn from the sun parallel to the façade of interest. This line will intersect a plane perpendicular to the façade and the angle this intersection point makes with the horizontal is called the *vertical shadow angle (VSA)*. It is apparent that to size solar shading devices for windows it is necessary to know these angles. Paradoxically, the horizontal shadow angle is used to size *vertical* shading devices whilst the vertical shadow angle is needed for *horizontal* shading devices. These angles are normally calculated in software packages as part of a shading calculation.

Solar time

Historically, the apparent movement of the sun across the sky was the basis of keeping time. A solar day is the interval between two successive passages of the sun across a fixed point (for example, due south). Due to perturbations in the Earth's orbit around the sun and in its rotation about its own axis a solar day is not fixed at 24 hours. Instead, it fluctuates by up to ±15 minutes over a year, making solar time an imprecise way of time-keeping. When dependable clocks and watches were developed in the seventeenth century a fixed day of 24 hours based on mechanical rather than solar movements was adopted. However, from a design point of view solar time has the advantage that the sun's position in the sky is symmetrical about its position at solar noon when the sun is due south (in the northern hemisphere). This makes it easier to produce design charts and perform solar shading/ access analyses. Consequently, except for very rare occasions when shading or sunlight is required for a building at a specific clock time, then using solar time is perfectly acceptable for most solar analysis design purposes.

Solar analysis techniques

There are four basic approaches to solar analysis in design:

- *Paper-based techniques* use table, charts and overlays to determine solar angles and sun paths.
- *Model-based techniques* use scale models under real skies or in a laboratory to visualise shadow patterns and solar ingress.
- *Site-based techniques* use optical means to show how the sun will move around the site.
- *Computer-based techniques* use calculation and visualisation to produce both numerical values and graphical images of sunlight and shade both around and within buildings.

Although computer-based techniques have come to dominate solar analysis studies there is still a place for the use of models and site-based tools.

Paper-based solar analysis techniques

Charts and tables of solar altitude and solar azimuth angles were widely used before computers enabled the geometric calculations that describe solar geometry to be performed simply and quickly. Tables of altitude and azimuth angles for any site can be readily found from many software packages. It is possible to project the sun's paths either horizontally or vertically. The circumference of the chart represents the horizon and the centre of the chart is zenith of the sky dome.

Diagrams show the sun paths for different times of the day and year. The shape of the sun paths will vary with latitude. There are many ways of projecting the sun's path on to a flat surface, but the most commonly used is called a *stereographic* projection. Figure 2.1 shows a stereographic or horizontal sun path diagram. To extract information on solar altitude and shadow angles it is necessary to either integrate an angular protractor in to the chart or place a transparent protractor over the chart at the time and day of interest.

It is also possible to project the sun's path vertically and this perhaps gives a better sense of the sun's motion across the sky. Figure 2.2 shows a vertical sun path diagram for latitude 52° N. To produce vertical sun path charts for any location see http://Solardat.uonegon.edu/AboutSunCharts.html.

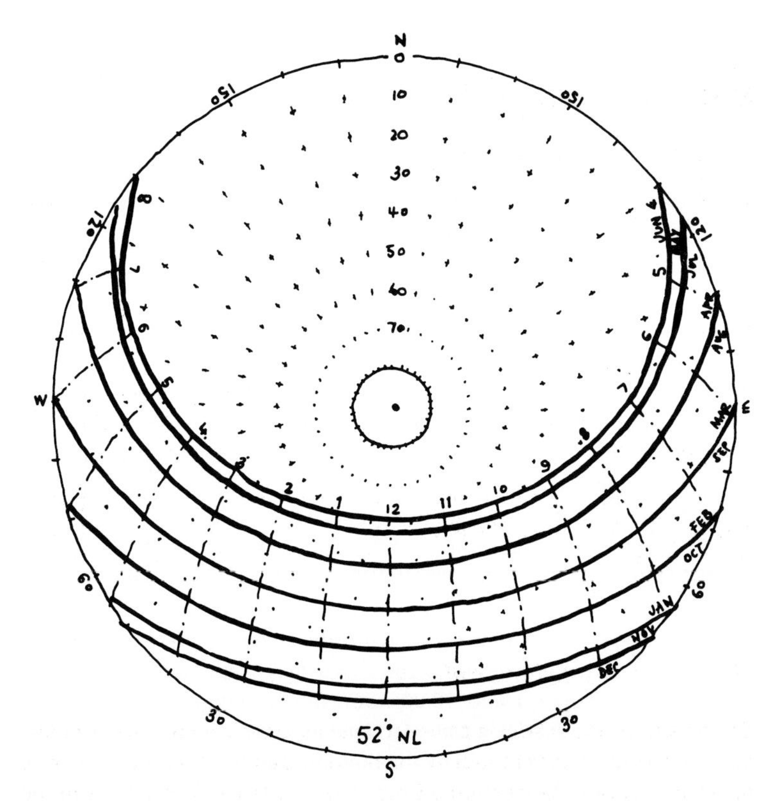

2.1

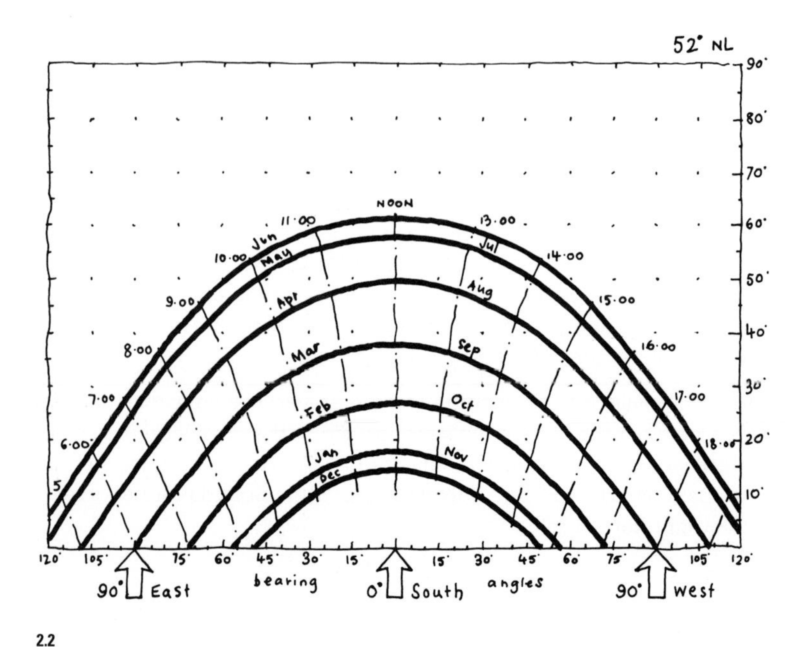

2.2

Model-based techniques

These techniques are very useful as a model of the building and its surroundings will often have been created as part of the design. Most of these model-based techniques are very easy to learn and can provide a detailed understanding of sunlight and shade patterns both within and around a building. A basic system is called a *heliodon* and will involve a lamp (to represent the sun) which moves up and down a vertical scale to simulate the time of year. The building model is placed on a table (to represent the Earth) which can be rotated to give time of day and tilted to represent the latitude of the site. White paper is fixed to the table and the model is then positioned on the paper, the surface tilted (for example, for London it would 52°) and then the lamp is slid to the required date. 21 June is at the top of the scale, the equinoxes in the middle and 21 December at the bottom of the scale. The sizing of the components is based on the geometry that the angle between the June and December lamp positions and the centre of the table when horizontal is 23°27′ and –23°27′ respectively (northern hemisphere – reversed for the southern hemisphere). The lamp/scale represents due south (northern hemisphere) and 12.00 noon on the table should point in this direction. The model is placed to face the way it would on the actual site and the shadows created by the building can be recorded at several times during the day either by drawing around the shadows or by taking a photo (flash should not be used as all the shadows will be lost).

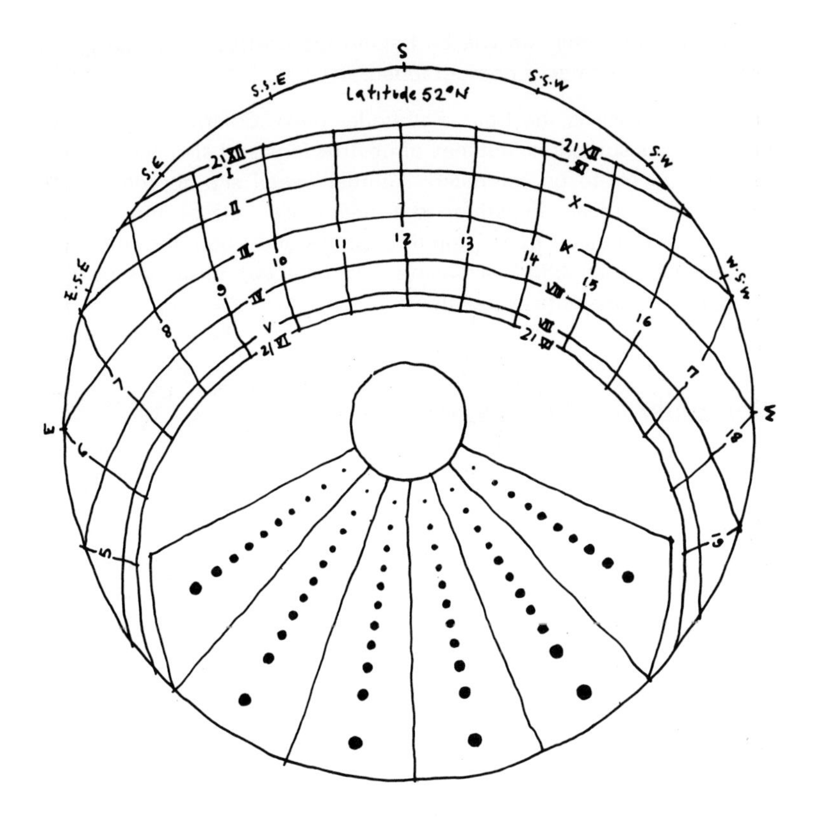

2.3

Details on how to build this cheap, but very effective, solar simulation tools are given in the book by Lechner (2001). A striking modification to the heliodon is to use three primary colour lamps for the equinox and solstice positions. This configuration creates simultaneously three shadow patterns around the building in different secondary colours for the three times of the year.

Site-based solar analysis techniques

One of the best ways of appreciating how the sun will move across the sky at a site (and when it will go behind existing obstructions such as other buildings and trees) is to go to the site with an optical visualisation tool. The TNO insolation meter consists of a plano-convex lens placed over a horizontal sun path diagram for the latitude of the site. The lens superimposes the images of the surroundings on to the sun path curves and wherever a sun path line crosses an image of an obstruction then the sun will be behind the obstruction (Figure 2.3). These images are easily photographed.

A related device is the Solar Pathfinder (www.Solarpathfinder.com) which shows sun paths, outlines of obstructions and also allows solar radiation levels to be estimated. Another useful site approach is to transpose a vertical sun path on to a sheet of clear plastic and produce a solar site evaluator. By looking through the sheet both the sun paths and the site's obstructions are visible. Lechner (2001) describes the construction of a solar site evaluator.

Computer-based techniques

Most energy simulation software and many CAD packages now come with some form of solar assessment. This may range from simply showing shadow patterns to detailed solar radiation levels on different surfaces for solar energy applications. Very advanced packages, such as Radiance, enable photorealistic images of sunlit spaces to be generated.

Chapter **3**

Wind flow around buildings

Introduction

Any building in the natural environment will be subjected to the forces of the wind. These forces may be used constructively to enhance natural ventilation, remove indoor pollutants and provide thermal cooling in buildings. Alternatively, the wind can act destructively, and this 'wind loading' may take a few tiles from a roof or destroy whole groups of buildings. This chapter will focus on the nature of wind forces on buildings and the particular problems associated with wind flow around tall buildings.

Nature of wind flow: the atmospheric boundary layer

As the wind flows over the Earth's surface the wind speed is slowed down by the frictional elements on the surface (sea, soil, trees, buildings, etc.). This frictional drag effect decreases with distance above the surface until at some height the friction effect is lost altogether. Consequently, wind speed will increase with height above the ground and the higher a building then the more severely it will be subjected to wind forces. This region is called the *atmospheric boundary layer* (ABL), and its depth will depend on the scale of the surface roughness. For open country the depth may be only one or two hundred metres, but in cities the depth may be half a kilometre. Figure 3.1 shows schematically the nature of the ABL for different terrains.

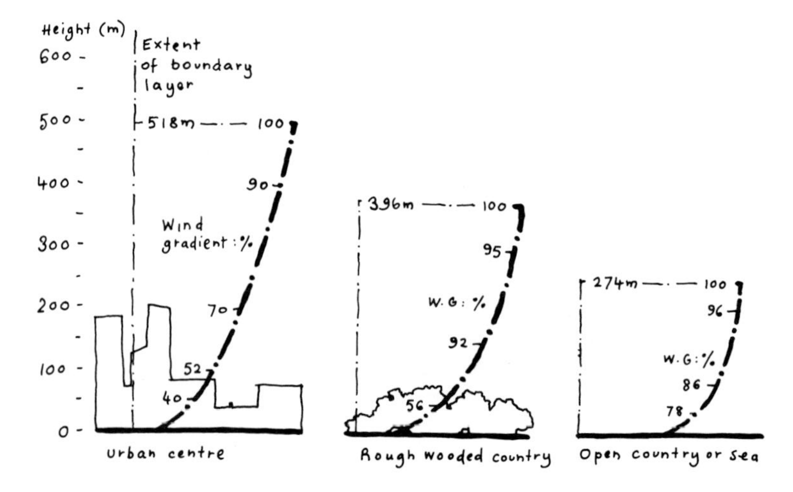

3.1

The generation of wind forces

When the wind encounters a façade of a building then the dynamic force of the wind is converted in to a positive or pushing pressure on that façade. At the same time some of the wind is deflected over and around the building. At the roof and wall edges the air flow is accelerated away from the building and creates negative or sucking forces in these areas. Air flowing down the windward façade reaches the ground and is deflected upwards where the oncoming wind then spins the air in to a rotating spiral called a *vortex*. This phenomenon can be experienced when walking towards a tall building – the wind may be behind you as you approach the building but as you get closer you will feel the wind blowing in to your face. Accelerated flows at the sides of a building and vortex action at the front of a building can create dangerous conditions for pedestrians. On the leeward or sheltered side of the building (the *wake* region) there is a much weaker region of negative pressures. Figure 3.2 shows these flow features.

The arrangement of positive pressure wind forces on one side of a building and negative or suction pressure forces on other sides is helpful for natural ventilation as fresh air is driven in and stale air is sucked out. However, if these wind forces are too strong then building damage may occur. Some features of a design may make a building more susceptible to wind damage. These include lightweight construction (such as a steel frame covered in thin cladding panels), flat or low pitch roofs, elements protruding above the roof line (such as chimneys or ventilations stacks), rows of buildings forming a channel through which the wind can accelerate and tall buildings in low rise developments. Although it would be natural to assume that most wind damage occurs from things being blown over by positive forces it is, in fact, the negative

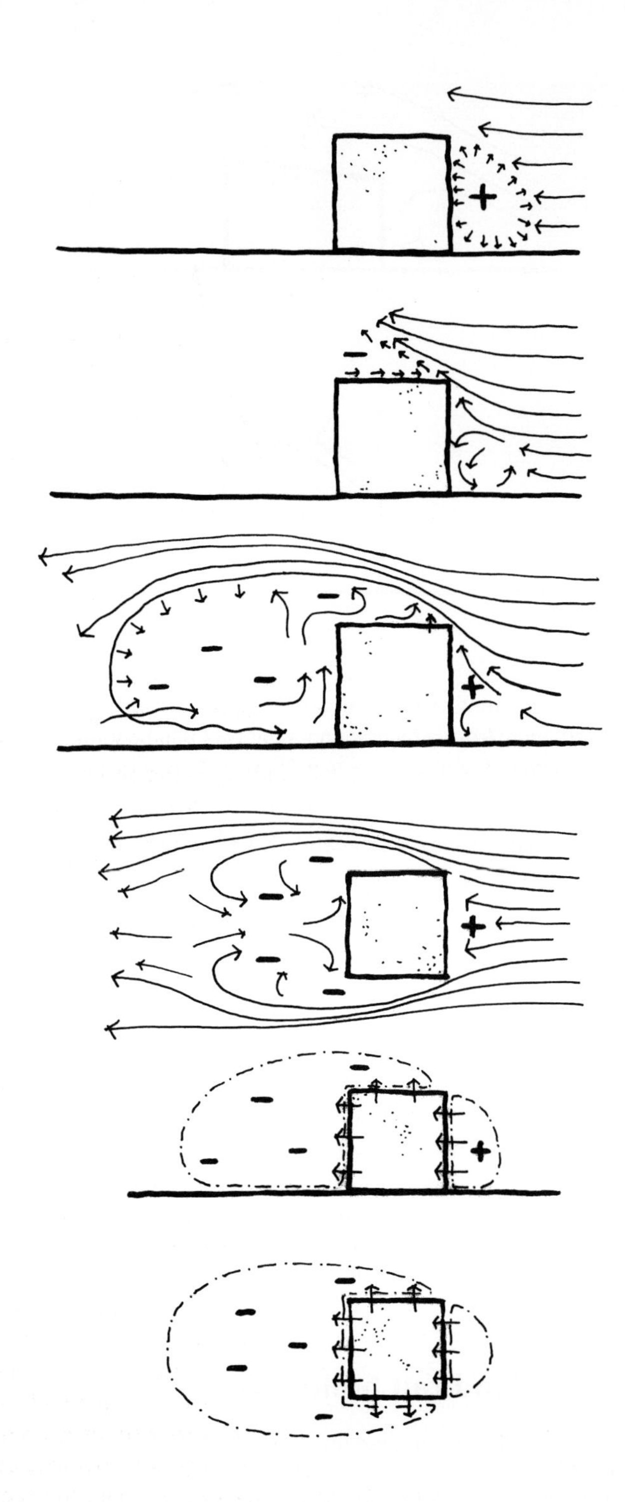

3.2

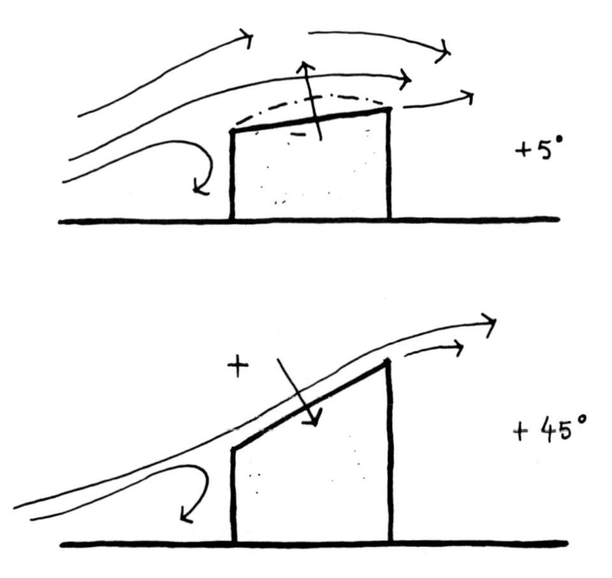

3.3

or suction forces that have the bigger impact. Cladding elements tend to be pulled away from a façade and a flat roof will be lifted off whilst a pitched roof will stay in place – see Figure 3.3, which shows the flow and forces over a 5° and 45° pitch roofs.

It is possible to get a sense of negative wind forces by two simple demonstrations. In the first demonstration two long, narrow strips of newspaper (representing two rows of buildings) are held hanging down 150mm apart just below head height. Blowing down the space between the strips will cause them, counter intuitively, to come together. This occurs because as the air leaves the ends of the strips it creates areas of negative pressure (or suction) that pulls the strips together. For two rows of inflexible buildings this might result in windows or cladding panels being removed from the façades. For the second demonstration the end of a spoon is lightly held and the curved surface of the spoon is placed under a flow of water from a tap. It might be expected that the water flow (representing the wind) would push the spoon (representing a flat building façade) away. However, because the flow separates from the flat surface and creates a negative or suction force then the spoon is pulled in to the flow – just as some cladding might be pulled from a building.

Wind flow and tall buildings

Some of the worst wind-related building problems occur at the base of a tall building, particularly when the building is surrounded by much lower buildings. The wind flow patterns in urban areas are significantly

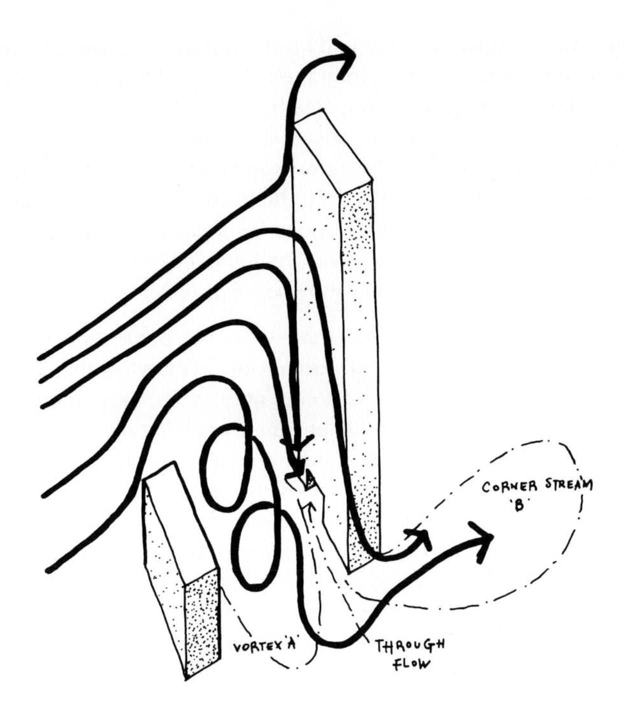

3.4

altered as the tall building deflects high speed winds down to ground level where they can create unpleasant conditions for pedestrians and do damage to surrounding low rise buildings. In front of the building the flow becomes the vortex mentioned previously. The accelerating flows at the edges of the building create curved areas of unpleasant buffeting winds called a *horse shoe vortex* (because of their shape in plan). These problems are exacerbated if there is a smaller building upstream of the tall one – this traps the vortex created at the base of the tower. Also, if there is an opening through the bottom of the tall building, such as a road or walkway, then winds will be accelerated through this space and create possibly dangerous conditions at ground level. Figure 3.4 shows these features.

The area affected by increased ground level wind speeds from a tall building is significant, stretching radially around a site a distance approximately equal to the height of the building.

Assessing wind flow problems

The areas around the bases of many tower blocks were often landscaped and planned as places for office workers to sit at lunch-time. This approach suggests that the designers of the time were unaware of the wind flow problems that would be created by the towers. In order to assess whether a tall building might produce wind flow problems there are two main factors to consider – the height of the tall building and the average wind speed at the site. Extensive analysis of building-related wind flow problems by the Building Research Establishment in the UK (BRE 1994) enabled a design chart to be produced. This chart gave the probability of a pedestrian wind speed level above 5 m/s (the limit for safety) being produced for a given building height or average wind speed. A version of this chart is shown in Figure 3.5.

The BRE analysis suggested that there were few complaints for combinations of building height and speed that lay on or below the 10 per cent probability curve. Conversely, complaints were very common for combinations at or above the 20 per cent probability curve. Wind speed data for the UK can be found at online sources such as that given in www.bwea.com/noable. Where problems are likely to occur then a more detailed analysis could be carried out using a wind tunnel. A wind tunnel is a fan arrangement that produces wind flow over building models. Wind tunnels range in size from small (around 4m long), low velocity (up to 5 m/s) systems suitable for simple flow analysis to large (over 20m long), high velocity (up to 25 m/s) arrangements that can investigate flows in complex urban areas. Figure 3.6 shows the basic arrangement of a low velocity wind tunnel.

A fan draws air in through a bell mouth entry and flow straightening tubes help to reduce turbulence in the flow. Slats or roughness

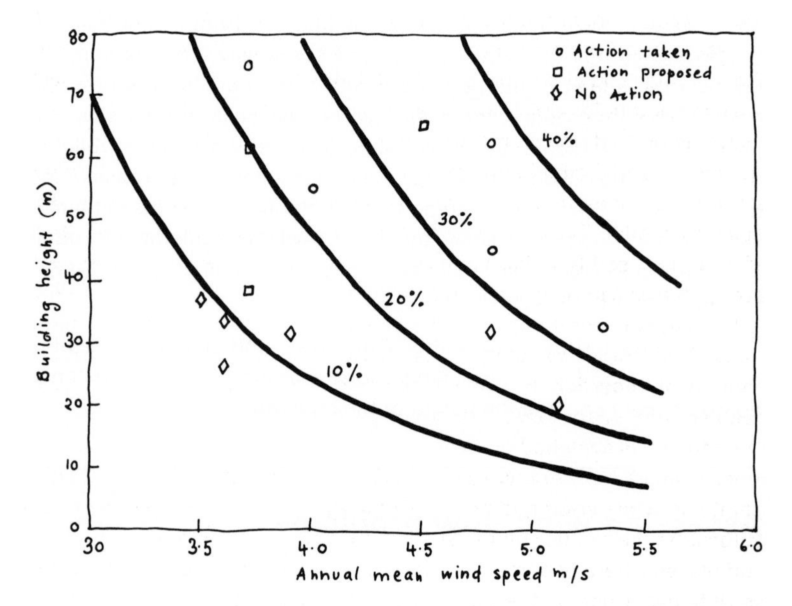

3.5

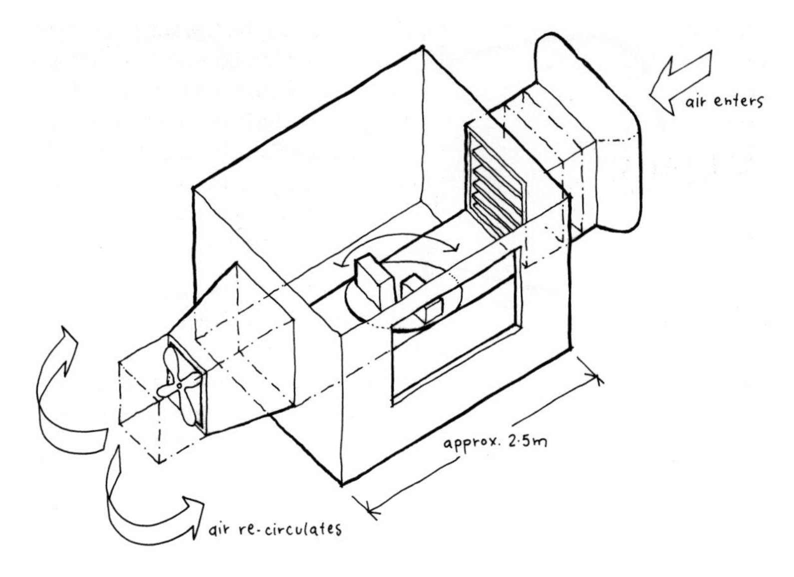

3.6

elements on the tunnel floor then alter the flow to create a velocity gradient profile to mimic the atmospheric boundary layer. The wind blows over building models that are placed on a turntable which can be rotated to create differing wind directions. A viewing window allows flow phenomena to be observed. Three basic flow phenomena are of interest – the pressure forces generated on the surfaces of the models, the air speeds around the models and the air flow patterns created between the buildings and at ground level. For the pressure forces hollow models are used and holes drilled in the surface are connected, via tubing, to a manometer that measures the pressures created by the wind. Air speeds around the building are measured by a very small sensor called a hot wire anemometer, which can be located in spaces around the building model. Typically, wind speeds will be measured before and after a proposed building is placed in the existing building layout. Air flow patterns can be visualised in several ways. The most obvious way is to generate non-toxic smoke and let it flow between the building models. General flow patterns can be observed and captured with a camera or recorder. For pedestrian level flows granular substances such as sand or semolina can be spread around the models before the wind tunnel is switched on. Areas of high wind speeds will be revealed where the grains are blown away. An alternative to this is to mix dayglo paint and white spirit and pour the liquid on to a thin metal sheet prior to locating the models on the sheet. The tunnel is run for about an hour and places where pedestrian wind speeds are high will cause the white spirit to evaporate and remove the paint from these areas. Running the tunnel for this length of time allows the paint to dry and the plate can

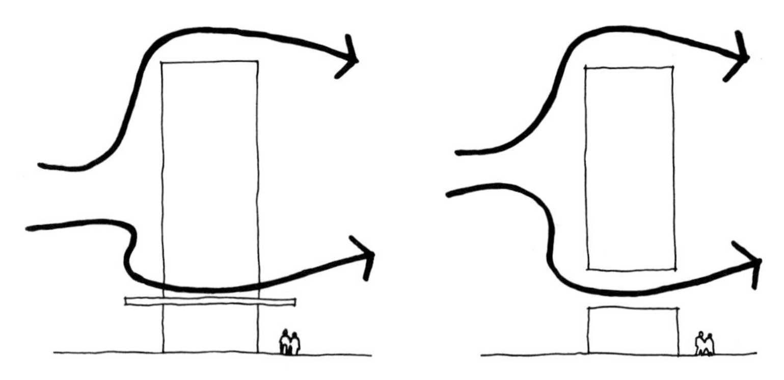

3.7

be removed to be photographed. Finally, a recent development is the use of a very powerful computer based technique called Computational Fluid Dynamics or CFD. This allows the air flow patterns around buildings to be calculated and, more interestingly, visualised as either an image or an animation.

Controlling wind flow problems from tall buildings

The key wind flow problem generated by tall buildings arises when high level winds are deflected down to ground level and create turbulent, high speed conditions. The best way of solving this problem (apart from not placing tall buildings in pedestrian areas) is to intercept these downward flows before they reach the ground. This can be done by either constructing a canopy around the building at the height of the first or second floor or by creating a very large opening through the building at the same sort of height (through which the downward flows will be diverted). Figure 3.7 shows these solutions. Obviously, these measures may only finish up redirecting wind problems to surrounding areas.

Some of the key design stage actions to avoid or reduce wind flow problems include the following:

- Tall buildings should not be located in pedestrian or low rise areas.
- The entrances to buildings should be placed on the sheltered leeward side and away from building corners where accelerated flows occur.
- Canopies should be put over pedestrian walkways in the vicinity of tall buildings.

Chapter **4**

Microclimate, site planning and bioclimatic design

Introduction

The prevailing climate at a site, and the nature of the site itself, are important considerations at the initial stages of a building design. Both parameters can be used to improve the environmental performance of the building and its surroundings (for instance, by allowing good solar access) and indicate where precautions should be taken to protect the building and its surroundings (for example, by sheltering from cold winds). This chapter will consider how site factors and site planning can affect the local environment and influence the design of a building.

Microclimate

The long-term weather conditions, or *macroclimate*, for a region are derived from the accumulation of day-to-day observations made at meteorological stations, as discussed in Chapter 1. Historically, most meteorological stations have been located close to airports or in open fields – that is, far away from the towns and cities where most buildings are constructed. Therefore, it is unlikely that the very local *microclimate* data for a specific site will be available. Marked climatic variations can take place over distances of only a few kilometres, due to the factors identified below, and so it is useful to understand how local features may influence the microclimate of the site as opposed to the macroclimate of the region. The four main factors influencing the microclimate of a site are:

- urban heat island – buildings, traffic, surfaces absorbing solar radiation, less vegetation
- topography – altitude, slope, orientation, nearby hills and valleys
- terrain surface – type of surface (natural/man-made)
  – form of surface (water, soil, colour)
- vegetation and obstructions – hedges, trees, walls, buildings

Urban heat island effects

Cities will typically be 2°C to 5°C warmer than the surrounding countryside with night-time temperatures, in particular, being higher because of thermal storage in the city's building fabric. The lower levels of vegetation and areas of open water in city centres reduce potential cooling mechanisms. Milder winters reduce heating demand but this is balanced by possible thermal stress and air pollution impacts in summer. Some of the main considerations for mitigating the impact of urban heat islands on the microclimate of cities are:

- the use of light coloured building finishes to reflect away more solar radiation;
- the use of green roofs to reduce temperatures;
- the creation of open green spaces with grass, trees, fountains and lakes;
- the reduction traffic levels.

Topographic effects

Air temperature decreases by around 10°C for every 1,000 metres increase in altitude. Higher levels of precipitation are experienced on windward slopes; sunrise is later and sunset earlier and cooler air temperatures are experienced in valleys than on the tops of moderate hills (particularly after clear, calm nights). It is obviously very important to know the orientation of the site. In the northern hemisphere south facing slopes offer much better access to solar energy and daylight then level and north facing slopes – a south facing slope can receive up to 100 times more solar radiation that a north facing slope.

The main considerations for using topography to enhance the microclimate are:

- taking advantage of any south facing slopes (northern hemisphere);
- providing adequate spacing to avoid overshadowing;
- building on leeward facing slopes for best protection from prevailing winds;
- building mid-way up any slope rather than at the top or bottom.

Terrain surface effects

Different soil types affect the microclimate due to their different thermal capacities and conductivities. Light, sandy soils heat up rapidly in the day but cool quickly at night, whereas heavy clay soils show a much slower thermal response. Natural surfaces such as grass will heat up much less during a sunny day than man made surfaces such as concrete and tarmac. These different thermal responses can be utilised in landscape design to create comfortable external spaces for day or night use.

Large bodies of water tend to produce lower land air temperatures in the summer but higher temperatures in the winter. Strong sea breezes are created by the sea–land temperature differences, creating winds blowing onto the shore in the day and off the shore at night. The main considerations for using ground surfaces to enhance the microclimate are:

- the use of thermally heavy surface materials to warm up any external play or sitting areas;
- the use of natural ground cover such as grass and water to cool summer air temperatures close to buildings;
- the use of light coloured ground cover to reflect winter sun and daylight into buildings and on to walls;
- the use of darker coloured ground cover or banked ground beneath windows to reduce reflected solar heat gain in summer.

Vegetation / obstruction effects

The major effects of vegetation and obstructions are on solar shading and wind speed and direction. Deciduous trees and plants can provide solar control in summer and solar access in winter. However, they will not offer much protection from cold winter winds. The correct choice of vegetation and planting orientation around buildings can help reduce energy losses and improve outdoor comfort. For example, if sheltering by vegetation can reduce the incident wind speeds on a building by 50 per cent then the infiltration energy losses from the building can be reduced by as much as 75 per cent. Fabric transmission losses can also be decreased – the U-value for double glazing in exposed conditions is 3.2 W/m^2K compared to a sheltered location value of 2.8 W/m^2K (a 14 per cent reduction). The main considerations for using vegetation to enhance the microclimate are:

- the use of vegetation and neighbouring obstructions for winter wind protection;
- the use of vegetation and neighbouring obstructions to provide summer shade, but vegetation should be chosen that will allow good levels of solar penetration in non summer months;
- the use of vegetation to increase exposure to summer breezes by channelling flows allows rows of trees and hedges.

Optimising the microclimate of a site

It is apparent that the microclimate of a proposed building site will be influenced by a large number of parameters which cannot necessarily be controlled or altered by the designer. These include: the prevailing climate, the choice of site, the form of the site, the surrounding land, any retained buildings, the established road network and any planning restrictions. A designer may be able to influence features such as: the orientation and spacing of buildings, the internal layout of rooms, the materials and thermal response of the buildings (glazing areas, insulation, thermal capacity), the location of open spaces, the provision of gardens and the landscaping of the site to provide shelter planting and suitable ground surfaces (grass, paving, water). For many microclimate schemes the two main aims are to maximise solar access to the site and buildings and to control the wind flow around and through the buildings.

Solar access

People enjoy having high levels of sunlight and daylight in and around their buildings, and so good solar access should be considered an important design parameter and be provided for those periods when it will be most appreciated. This will usually be in the spring, autumn and winter in Northern Europe. In summer the solar access should be controlled by shading (either natural or man-made). The obvious first step in a solar access site analysis is to identify how the sun will move across the sky at different times of the year and for what periods it might be obstructed by existing site feature. Site layout is the most important

Table 4.1 Minimum spacing to achieve solar access

Slope	*21 December*	*1 March*
1:10 slope, south facing	18.1m	12.8m
Level ground	24.4m	15.7m
1:10 slope, north facing	38.6m	21.2m

factor influencing solar access, and so a good starting point is to determine appropriate north/south spacing of the buildings to avoid overshadowing with respect to the site's orientation, latitude and slope. As a general rule in winter months a building will cast a shadow approximately two to three times its own height. Typically, spacing will need to be greatest at higher latitudes; even a small south facing slope will help to reduce the spacing whilst a north facing slope requires a very large separation. Table 4.1 shows the necessary spacing between two 7m high buildings at latitude 50°N to avoid overshadowing for level ground, a 1-in-10 slope facing south and a 1-in-10 slope facing north – note the near doubling of spacing required for the north facing slope. Designing for solar access on 21 December (northern hemisphere) is too restricting (due to the shortness of the day and the low probability of much sunshine at that time) and 1 March is often chosen as the basis for assessment.

Computer simulations or model studies on heliodons (see Chapter 2) can help establish the right spacings for a group of buildings on a particular site. It is also desirable to orientate one glazed façade to face within ±30° south (northern hemisphere). For adequate daylighting the obstruction angle between the top of one building and the normal to a point 2m above the ground on an adjacent building should be less than 25°. Landscaping can have a big impact on the solar microclimate. The use of 'hard' landscaping elements such as paving slabs and stone will provide thermal mass storage for daytime solar radiation that can be released in the early evening to enhance the air temperature either inside buildings or in sitting-out areas. 'Soft' landscaping, particularly trees, offer solar control in summer, solar access at other times (if deciduous) and will cool air through evaporation from their leaves. Evergreen trees can also provide shelter from the wind. Some of the main design implications for good solar access are:

- allowing buildings to have wide, south facing fronts;
- placing the tallest buildings on the north side of the site;
- orientating any terraced buildings to run along east–west roads;
- placing detached buildings on NE–SW running roads;
- using low pitched roofs;
- running as many road lengths as possible within ±15° of east–west;

- plant coniferous trees to the north and deciduous trees to the south of the site (northern hemisphere).

Controlling wind flow

For many parts of the world the wind will provide welcome cooling breezes in summer but unwanted cold air flows in winter. Therefore, in trying to design for wind microclimates it will often be necessary to develop a combination of site strategies. Helpfully, wind directions will often change dramatically between summer and winter – for example, in the UK most summer winds come from directions between south-west and north-west whilst in winter the coldest winds come from between the north and north-east. Therefore, a key piece of information is a wind rose for the site from the nearest weather station (see Chapter 1). Some hints may be provided by the site itself, especially in rural areas. The patterns of tree and hedge plantings around old buildings will often have evolved to provide shelter from the coldest winter winds. Landscaping the spaces between buildings offers the most aesthetically pleasing way of controlling the wind microclimate. The landscaping works best when it is incorporated in to the design at an early stage, in conjunction with the layout of the building development. Trees, bushes, walls, fences and ground profiling can all contribute to provide wind barriers that are called *shelter belts*. Shelter belts can be major elements at the edges of a site and smaller features between individual spaces or buildings. Their orientation may be dictated by the prevailing wind direction or by the coldest wind directions.

The performance of shelter belts is effected by four parameters: porosity, shape, height and length. Porosity is the percentage of gaps in the shelter belt. Paradoxically, a solid obstruction such as a wall is a less effective down wind barrier than one containing some openings. This is because of the high levels of turbulence created downstream of the obstruction when the wind suddenly strikes a solid obstacle. Figure 4.1 shows the effect of porosity on wind speeds either side of a barrier, indicating that a medium porosity obstruction (40 per cent to 50 per cent porosity) gives the best overall sheltering performance.

The shape of a shelter belt will depend upon whether it is trying to provide shelter from a predominant wind direction or a range of directions. Figure 4.2 shows the shapes required for winds coming mainly from the west and from any direction between west, north and east.

The height of a shelter belt determines the potential depth of the wind shadow created behind the barrier – the taller the barrier the longer the shadow. However, to achieve the maximum size of shadow the width of the shelter belt must be significant, otherwise wind will simply flow around the ends of the barrier. The width of a shelter belt needs to

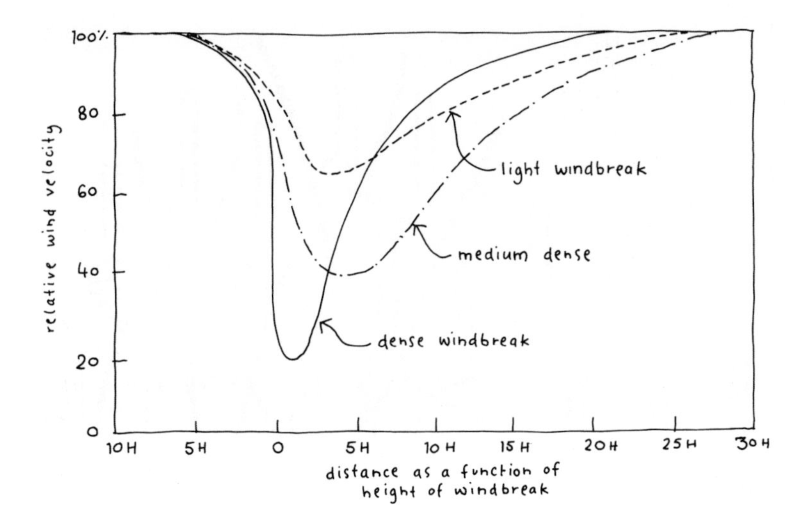

4.1

be 11 to 12 times its height for maximum shadow depth. Increasing the shelter belt beyond this width has little impact on wind shadow depth. There is obviously potential conflict between vegetation providing shelter from the wind and it restricting solar access. The suggested compromise is that the distance between a building and a southerly shelter belt should be 3 to 4 times the height of the barrier Figure 4.3 suggest the scale of this layout.

Bioclimatic design

Bioclimatic design refers to an architectural approach that tries to utilise the prevailing microclimate to enhance natural thermal comfort and thereby reduce energy requirements. The environmental components of thermal comfort discussed in Part 2, Chapter 6 (dry bulb temperature, mean radiant temperature, relative humidity and air speed) can be equated to microclimatic elements (external air temperature, solar radiation, relative humidity and wind speed). It is possible to represent these microclimatic influences on a chart that shows how combinations of these parameters combine to provide a zone of thermal comfort for building occupants. This approach is possible when there is a close link between the occupant and the microclimate. This will obviously occur for outdoor conditions but also happens for passively heated and cooled buildings with lots of solar gain through windows and natural ventilation through openings. The first design chart to show

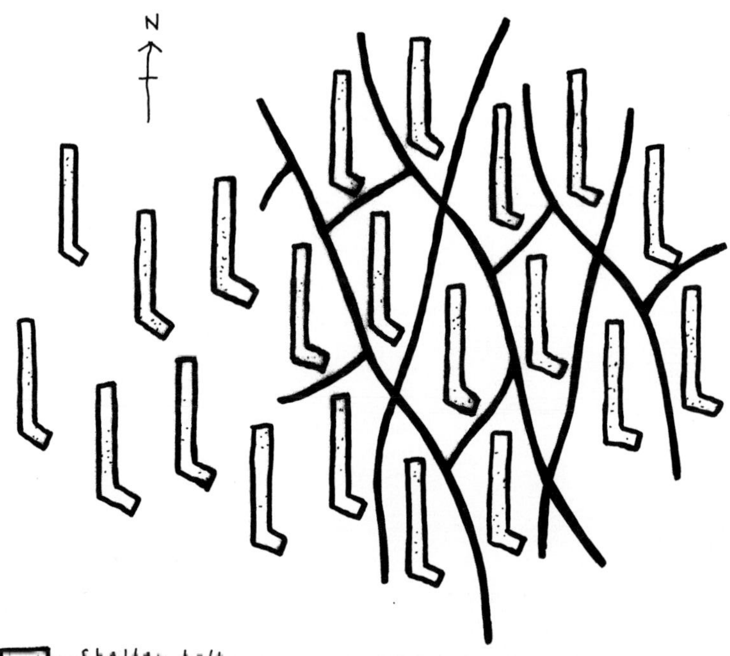

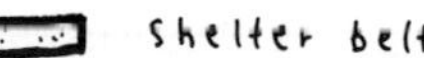

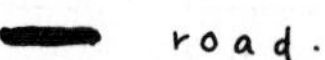

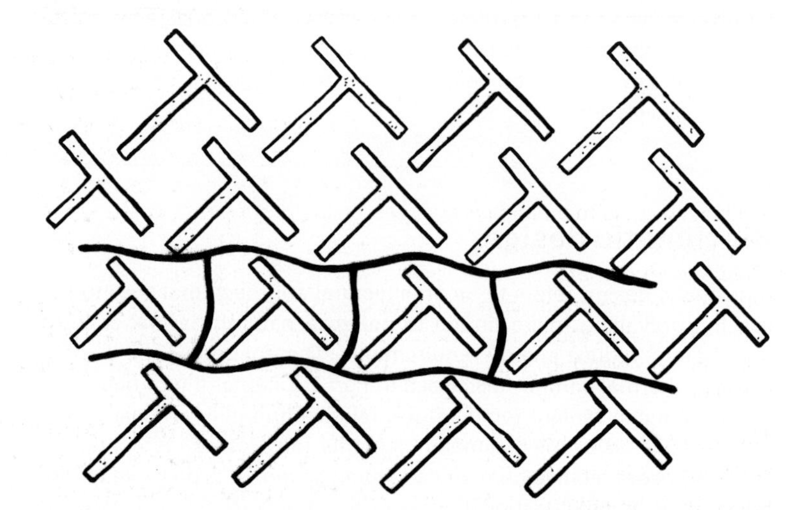

4.2

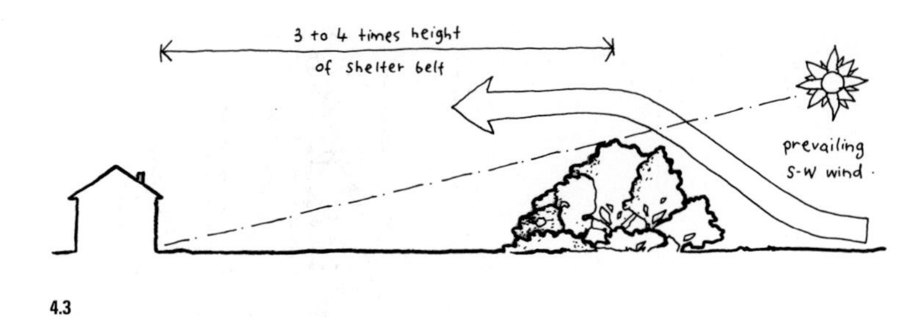

4.3

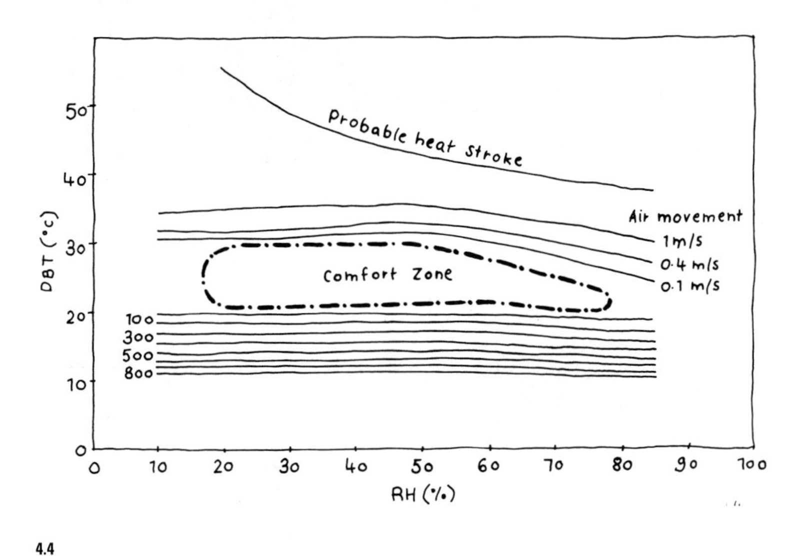

4.4

links between climate and comfort was called the bioclimatic chart and was developed by Olgyay and described in his 1963 influential book *Design with Climate*. The chart was expressed in terms of air temperature and relative humidity but also had lines representing the impact of wind speed and radiation. Figure 4.4 shows an example of this chart for a person wearing 1 clo performing a sedentary activity in a warm climate.

The comfort zone shown in Figure 4.4 is for a person in a shaded room with negligible air movement. If the prevailing external conditions were a dry bulb temperature of 15°C and 50 per cent RH then the person would not be experiencing thermal comfort as these co-ordinates are outside the comfort zone. To produce comfort the chart shows that at the 15°C, 50 per cent point the person would need to receive approximately 400W/m^2 of radiation to achieve comfort. This could be achieved by allowing this amount of solar radiation to shine on the person through a window. Conversely, for a DBT of 35°C and RH of 50 per cent

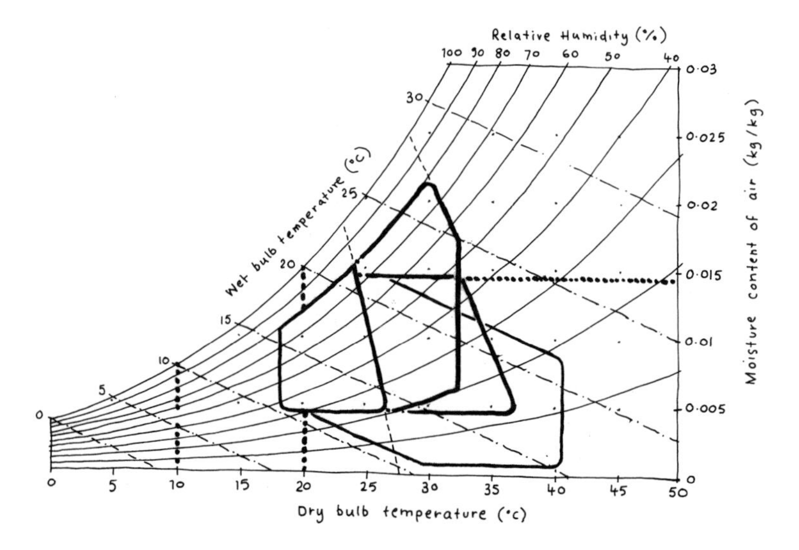

4.5

overheating would occur in the space. To achieve thermal comfort now the chart shows that the person would need to be exposed to an air movement of approximately 1.0 m/s in the room. Givoni (1973) developed a different type of bioclimatic charts for use in buildings when detailed weather data is available. The standard psychrometric chart is used as the basis of the Building Bioclimatic Chart that indicates what passive procedures might be incorporated in to a design to produce comfort. A version of the chart is shown in Figure 4.5.

Numbered zones on the chart suggest different bioclimatic heating and cooling design strategies for producing indoor thermal comfort. Zone 5 is the shaded comfort zone which represents the combinations of dry

Table 4.2 Bioclimatic design strategies for different zones

Zones on chart	*Bioclimatic design strategies for comfort*
Zones 1, 2	• restrict conductive flows • restrict infiltration • promote solar gain • minimise external air flows
Zones 6, 8	• promote natural ventilation
Zones 3, 15	• restrict solar gain
Zones 8, 10, 11	• promote evaporative cooling
Zones 7, 10	• promote radiative cooling
Zones 12, 13	• restrict conductive heat flow • will need air conditioning

and wet bulb temperatures that will give thermal comfort. To use the chart, hourly values of dry and wet bulb temperature for a site are plotted for representative months of the year. The zones that the temperatures cluster in indicate what strategies should be adopted. Table 4.2 shows what actions the zones represent.

Although the charts described above are quite general and simplistic in their advice one of their benefits is that they can help designers who may be asked to build in an unfamiliar climate or country. The charts give an early design stage indication of the basic bioclimatic strategies that should be adopted at different times of the year.

Part **1**

Bibliography

BRE, *Wind around Tall Buildings*, BRE Digest 390, BRE (1994).

Cook, J. Architecture indigenous to extreme climates, *Energy and Buildings*, 23, 277–91 (1996).

Givoni, B. *Man, Climate and Architecture*, Van Nostrand Reinhold (1973).

Lechner, N. *Heating, Cooling, Lighting: Design Methods for Architects*, 2nd edn, John Wiley & Sons (2001).

Olgyay, V. *Design with Climate*, Princeton University Press (1963).

Rapoport, A. *House Form and Culture House Form and Culture*, Prentice Hall (1969).

Roaf, S. Crichton, D. and Nicol, F. *Adapting Buildings and Cities for Climate Change*, Architectural Press (2005).

Webliography

www.bwea.com/noabl/ (accessed 28 March 2008).

www.climate-zone.com (accessed 28 March 2008).

www.meteotest.ch/en/mn_home?w=ber (accessed 28 March 2008).

http://solardat.uoregon.edu/AboutSunCharts.html (accessed 28 March 2008).

http://www.solarpathfinder.com/ (accessed 28 March 2008).

www.squ1.com (accessed 28 March 2008).

http://squ1.org/wiki/SolarPositionCalculator_Hourly (accessed 28 March 2008).

http://www.susdesign.com/sunangle/ (accessed 28 March 2008).

www.weatherbase.com (accessed 28 March 2008).

Part 2
Buildings and low energy design

Chapter 5

Energy in buildings

Energy consumption

One of the previously stated objectives of this book series is to promote a holistic and integrative approach to building design with a view to encouraging the adoption and development of sustainable principles. Energy is the biggest single resource that affects both human existence on the planet and the future of the planet itself. Energy use plays a major part in our daily existence. Energy is used to keep us warm, drive our cars, make the products we use and go about our lives. This section will discuss energy use in buildings in order to identify ways in which it can be reduced if not altogether dispensed of whenever possible.

Energy consumption is on the increase year on year. In the UK, the 2001 energy consumption reached a level higher than in any other year over the last 30 years. Needless to say, any increase in energy consumption is associated with increased levels of carbon dioxide emissions that contribute to global warming. Official statistics of the United Kingdom Department of Transport and Industry show an increase in overall energy consumption by 13 per cent since 1970 and 11 per cent since 1990. The same statistics show some changes in the pattern of energy consumption by various sectors of the economy. In 1990, industry contributed towards 30 per cent of primary energy, with the domestic, transport and services sectors coming at 29, 25 and 16 per cent respectively. The consumption figures for the 2001 census had changed. While energy consumption for transport and the services sectors has seen little change, remaining at 26 and 18 per cent, the domestic sector registered 31 per cent of energy consumption overtaking industry, which contributed with 25 per cent. In terms of energy consumption by fuel type, similar changes were recorded between the 1991 and 2001 census. Coal and petroleum had seen a drop in use from 31 and 37 per cent respectively in 1990 to 17 and 32 per cent in 2001. Over the same period, the use of natural gas went up from 24 to 40 per cent. The changes in energy consumption by sector and energy use by fuel type can be summarised in the following points:

- An overall increase in primary energy from 213.6 to 237.7 million tonnes of oil equivalent.
- A shift in the fuel use from coal to gas, which meant a slight reduction in carbon emissions (around 5 per cent).
- An increase in domestic energy use.
- The servicing of buildings takes the lion's share of energy consumption. Space heating, on its own, now accounts for some 40 per cent of total energy use.

These trends and the built environment are important to building designers and professionals. It is worth taking a closer look at energy use in buildings.

Energy use in buildings

The provision of various comfort and commodity related services to buildings, is an energy intensive process. By 2001, the domestic sector was responsible for 30 per cent of energy use, compared to transport 34 per cent, industry 22 per cent and the service sector 14 per cent. Except for the transport sector, other economic sectors account for most of their energy use as buildings related. Space heating alone accounts for 40 per cent of non-transport energy consumption. When combined with hot water, the figure amounts to 53 per cent of all non-transport energy consumption. This also amounts to 82 per cent of domestic use of energy and 64 per cent of commercial use in 2000.

Although these statistics are only applicable to the UK, none the less, they give an indication of relative energy use by sector for a typical industrialised economy.

Carbon dioxide

The figures for energy use would not have been an issue if, and only if, there was an infinite supply of fossil fuels and that energy use has no impact on the environment. However, even the most hardened cynic would agree that resources are rapidly depleting and that global warming is not mere scaremongering. Although it is not the intention here to present the arguments for the effect of climate change, it would help put the issue of energy use in context if some data are to be quoted. According to data from a UK government department the rise in sea level between 1834 and 1984 varied from 20cm in Aberdeen to around 38cm in Sheerness and Liverpool. Over the same period, global temperatures in terms of annual average have risen by more than 1°C. These figures seem to be borne out by the trend of carbon dioxide in the atmosphere. According to data from the Mauna Loa Observatory in Hawaii (see:http:www.cmdl.noaa.gov/ccgg/trends), carbon dioxide levels as of January 2007 stand at 383 parts per million (ppm). This figure represents 0.0381 per cent of the earth's atmosphere by volume or 0.057 per cent by weight. The trend for carbon dioxide concentration in the atmosphere follows a steady increase that is mirrored by an increase in global fossil carbon emissions. In the case of the UK, there has been a reduction in CO_2 emissions by 5.6 per cent between 1990 and 2004. This is still below target in order to reach the UK government target of 12.5 per cent reduction below 1990 levels by 2008 to 2012. Beyond this, the government is committed to cutting carbon dioxide emissions by 20 per cent by 2020, 60 per cent by 2050 and 80 per cent by 2100, compared to 1990 levels in order to achieve stabilisation of atmospheric carbon dioxide. Various strategies are needed to achieve a sensible reduction in carbon dioxide emissions. These include energy efficiency in use and conservation as well as the use of 'clean' or renewable energy sources.

Renewable sources of energy

Around three-quarters of the UK energy use is derived from fossil fuels. Although the size of these reserves at global level can be debatable, their depletion and effect on climate are something that even the most cynical person would agree on. Renewable sources of energy include solar, wind and wave power as well as biological sources such as wood, from sustainably managed forests, and fuels derived from crops. The discussion in Part 3 of this volume will extend to combined heat and power, as a recovery method, and heat pumps.

Solar heating using collectors that convert solar radiation into energy for both space and water heating is a well proven technology, provided the availability of the sun is not an issue. Collectors consist mainly of black surfaces (to increase absorption) that are glazed (to trap the heat) and insulated (to reduce heat loss) and have a suitable orientation. The heat is passed on to a medium (water/air) that circulates it to a hot water store from which hot water is used when required. The effectiveness of solar heating systems depends largely on the climatic conditions (solar availability, sky conditions). In the UK, the effectiveness of solar collectors varies between 2 and 13 per cent. This percentage represents the proportion of solar radiation incident on the collector that is effectively delivered as useful heat. Although this energy is useful, it is not cost effective for middle and northern European climates. Some applications may not require heat at high temperatures, as in the case of swimming pools. In this case, the system can be simple, with no need for insulation or glazing, which makes it relatively cheap and cost effective.

The use of photovoltaics is another application that relies on harnessing the energy of the sun. Photovoltaic, commonly known as PV, cells work on the principle of converting some of the incidental solar radiation into an electric current. There are two main types of cells available; either single silicon crystals or amorphous silicon deposits onto a substrate. The former is more expensive but with improved performance. The latter costs less and has lower efficiency. Given the climatic conditions of the UK, there are two inherent problems with PVs. The first one is the need for storage of excess output at times of high levels of solar radiation. The second one is the need for backup power at times of low solar availability. A way of overcoming this is to have grid-connected systems, which generate electricity and trade it in and out with the grid. At present the economic argument for PVs is not yet strong, given their low efficiency and high costs. The future however is likely to see changes to both costs, through market take up, and efficiency through continuous research and development.

The use of wind energy is not new. For centuries, the energy of the wind was used to move sailing boats and power windmills to pump water or grind flour. Nowadays wind energy can be harnessed to drive turbines that generate electricity. The effectiveness of windmills to generate power depends mainly on the availability of wind. The theoretical power extracted from wind is given, approximately, as five-eighths of the product of, the swept area of the turbine multiplied by the wind speed cubed. In practice, this is likely to be reduced by a third, due to mechanical and electrical losses. As is the case with all naturally driven systems, the effectiveness of a wind turbine is dependent on the level of exposure to wind. For comparison purposes, a wind turbine in Cornwall would produce 11 times as much energy as the same one on an urban site in London. Most wind turbines are designed to operate at speeds between 5 and 15m/s. Even at the lowest speed, the energy generated is of the same order of magnitude as that extracted by solar collectors. Although, most wind farms in the UK, at present, are located in remote areas where access to the national grid is difficult, onshore generation from wind farms is on the increase and seems to offer the potential to generate up to 30 per cent of current electrical energy demand.

The principle behind the release of energy from hydroelectric generation is similar to that of wind (in both cases, a fluid is being moved). In this case however, there is far more concentration of that energy, given that the movement of water takes far more energy than the movement of air. With this in mind and given the advances in low-cost controls, hydroelectric generation offers a potential for a renewable source. At present this is under-exploited in the UK.

The use of wood as a fuel is not something new. For centuries people burnt wood for heating, and in many parts of the world they still do. Modern wood-burning stoves can be efficient to use and offer a sustainable alternative to fossil fuels. Wood derived fuels, such as wood pellets, are also available. Not only they can be used as an alternative to fossil fuels, but they also make use of a waste product. Wood could be thought of as a bio fuel. This word is used to designate any fuel that is derived from recently living organisms or their metabolic by-products. This definition can include agricultural products (corn, soyabeans, flax seed, rape seed and sugar cane), biodegradable outputs from industry, agriculture, forestry and household waste. In some industrialised countries, food is cheaper than fuel when compared by price per joule.

Chapter 6

Thermal comfort and indoor air quality

The provision of comfort remains one of the primary objectives of the design and creation of the built environment. Comfort is a state of mind that is informed by the environmental conditions, the level of control that occupants have over them as well as some psychological factors. The complexity of the issue does not excuse designers to overlook it. In the pursuit of sustainable developments, the Vitruvian principles of firmness, commodity and delight would still be the criteria against which the design is to be judged. Research into thermal comfort falls into two categories. The conventional heat-balance approach puts more emphasis on the environmental conditions surrounding the body. The relatively recent adaptive comfort approach has been gaining in popularity. It gives more weight to people's actions to adapt and change their environments. The following section will discuss the two approaches to thermal comfort.

Heat balance comfort model

From a physical point of view, thermal comfort relates to the body's balance between heat gains produced by the metabolism and heat losses to the surrounding environment. The heat needs to be dissipated at a rate appropriate to keep the body temperature constant at around 37°C. Both the heat production by metabolism and heat dissipation by various processes are dependent on a number of factors. The rate of heat emission from the body is related to the activity. The greater the level of activity, the more heat is given off. It is also related to the body size (or surface area) and the age of the person. The average metabolic rate is likely to decrease with age. For a typical adult female engaged in similar activities, the output would be around 85 per cent of that of male.

The body's sensation of its surrounding environment and the way it reacts to it at various levels of activity is closely related to the type of clothing worn. Clothes provide thermal insulation for the human body. Different types of clothing provide different levels of insulation and require different levels of comfort temperatures. A scale of insulating values of various clothing systems has been developed. This is based on the *clo-value* where 1 clo-value represents 0.155 m^2 K/W of thermal insulation. Whether our bodies are likely to secrete sweat or shiver at a given temperature and level of activity depends on the clothes we wear. This can be made use of to define different comfort conditions for different parts of the same building where people are likely to engage in different activities. For instance a staircase where, the level of activity increases, would not need to be heated to the same level as the interior of the building, if any. The diagram in Figure 6.1 shows the relationship between activity, clothing and comfort zone for an average male. It is believed that on average females prefer slightly higher temperatures than males for the same conditions of clothing and activity.

Heat loss from the human body is mainly by convection, radiation and evaporation during perspiration and respiration. The lack of conduction heat loss is due to the fact that there is minimum contact between the human skin and the outside environment. The various temperatures in the room would affect different components of the heat exchange between the body and its surrounding environment and hence the body's thermal sensation. The surface temperatures in the room would affect the radiant heat loss from the body. When taken as an average of all surface temperatures in the room, this temperature is known as mean radiant temperature, and often gives a good indication of the level of thermal sensation likely to be experienced by the room occupants. On the other hand the temperature of the air in the room would affect the heat loss by convection as well as the sensible heat loss during respiration. Another aspect of air temperature that is relevant to comfort is the temperature gradient, particularly the vertical gradient. A difference in air temperature of 3°C between head and toe is likely to cause the body some discomfort. The movement of air in a room has a direct effect on the convection heat loss from the body. As the air movement increases, its cooling effect is accompanied by the sensation of draughts, which the body finds uncomfortable, particularly around the neck, forehead and ankles. This is particularly a problem when combined with excessive radiant heat loss such as that for a person seated near a window (Figure 6.2). Relative humidity in the air affects heat flow from the body. Its effect is more significant in hot humid climates than in temperate ones as the increase in relative humidity would make it difficult for the body to lose heat by evaporation of sweat and reduces the ability of the body to cool itself by other processes as the air temperature is already high and makes it difficult to

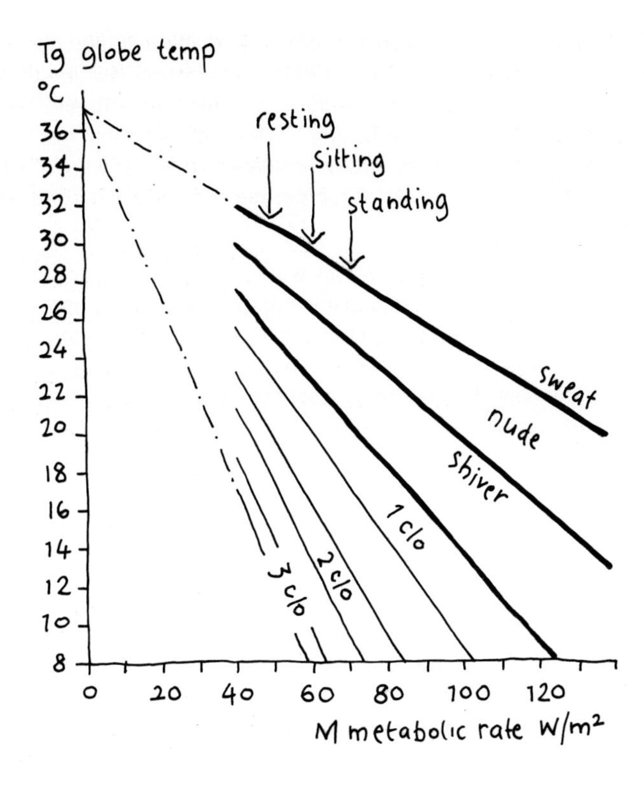

6.1

exchange heat by either convection or radiation. Despite the criticism levelled at it, the heat balance model for comfort has managed to make the various processes involved in the physical and physiological aspects of thermal comfort well understood. The main criticism remains the inability of the model to recognise the effect of occupant lead control over certain aspects of the internal environment and the body's willingness to accommodate environmental changes beyond the narrow environmental parameters used, provided that the change is gradual.

Adaptive comfort model

The rise in popularity of environmentally conscious approaches to design has demonstrated the inadequacy of the old heat balance model with its narrow range of environmental conditions to naturally ventilated buildings. By contrast the *adaptive model's* starting point is that people do not react passively to their environmental conditions but take action to make themselves comfortable. This statement seems to

6.2

be backed up by research work (Baker and Sanderson 1996). According to published research (de Dear 1999), 'satisfaction occurs through appropriate adaptation to the indoor climatic environment'. Other research work by de Dear and Brager (1998) suggested that in field surveys thermal responses in naturally ventilated buildings were more tolerant of a much wider range of temperatures than in air conditioned buildings.

Proponents of the adaptive model will argue that it gives a better chance to naturally ventilated and low energy buildings to work as their occupants would tolerate more changes to the internal temperatures as long as the change is not too fast, not outside normally expected limits and occupants can do something about it. This will no doubt have an effect on the development of future comfort standards that are more sympathetic to low energy strategies and at the same time allow occupants time and opportunity to adapt to and change their environments to achieve comfort.

Indoor air quality

Although indoor air quality has always been a concern for architects, the reader may be forgiven for wondering why the topic is being discussed as part of low energy design strategies. The last few decades has seen an increase in environmental awareness and a move towards low energy, low impact design approaches. Concerns for energy conservation have led to low ventilation rates and higher levels of air tightness in buildings. At the same time new pollutants are finding their way into the indoor air by means of equipment, cleaning chemicals and furnishings. This is particularly a problem for commercial, industrial and public buildings. Such pollutants include ozone from photocopiers and printers, volatile organics from paints cleaning materials and furnishing. These will add to any previously known to be present pollutants already in the outside air coming in. An increase in pollutants coupled with a decrease in ventilation would result in lower indoor air quality. Another reason for architects to be interested in the topic is that some of the pollutants in the air are from burning fossil fuels. If energy use in buildings is reduced through careful design, the levels of pollutants in the air will be reduced.

Indoor pollutants, whether originating outside or inside need to have their concentration controlled. In terms of design standards, there are as yet no agreed limits for all these pollutants. This makes it difficult to give a definition to what may constitute a suitable air quality. In the absence of any design standards, the best approach from a designer's viewpoint is to reduce the incidence of pollutants by careful specification, provide for removal of pollutants at source and design for enough fresh air to dilute them. Even in terms of ventilation rates there are no internationally agreed standards. In the UK, the CIBSE recommends a ventilation rate of 8l/s person for office interiors in the absence of smoking. The American standard, as set by ASHRAE recommends 10l/s person for offices with some smoking.

Energy flow in buildings

The thermal performance for which the building fabric is designed depends primarily on the geographical location and climatic conditions of the site in which the building is situated. Different climatic regions around the world would require different approaches to the design of the building fabric in order to achieve internal comfort conditions. A building located in a cold humid climate would be designed mainly to keep the heat in. On the other hand, a building in a hot arid climate would be designed mainly to keep the heat from the sun out. Although, the principles involved in both heat loss and heat gain are the same, their application to the design of buildings depends on the materials available, the methods of construction to be used and the technology associated with environmental comfort provision that the user has access to. Volume 1 in this series has introduced basic principles of heat and its associated effects in buildings. The following section will discuss various issues relating to both heat loss and heat gain in buildings and the ways these can be dealt with.

Factors affecting heat losses

When the external temperature is lower than the internal one, heat loss occurs by a number of mechanisms. These are illustrated in Figure 6.3 as approximate percentages of total heat losses from an un-insulated house. The diagram clearly indicates that the largest proportion of heat loss (around 75 per cent) is through the building envelope. The main factors affecting the rate of heat loss need to be understood if the designer is to try and minimise heat loss and hence energy used for heating. The main processes involved in the building heat loss are conduction through the building envelope and infiltration through openings (for ventilation) and gaps in the construction.

The level of thermal insulation in a building has a direct bearing on the rate of heat loss from the inside of the building. As the insulating capability of the building is increased, the flow of heat through the building envelope is slowed down. Although all parts of the building envelope need insulating, those elements surrounding high energy input areas of the building are particularly prone to high rates of heat loss given the high temperature difference between the inside and outside.

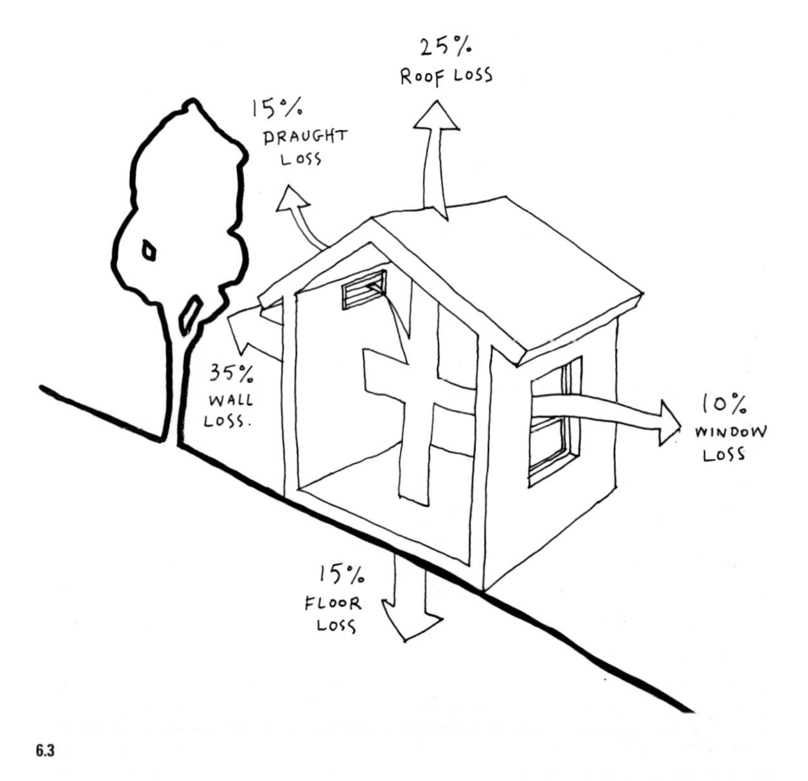

6.3

The area of external envelope is important to the building's energy balance as its size affects the rate of heat loss from the building. The greater this area is, the greater the rate of heat loss and hence the amount of energy used for heating. Compact forms produce the least heat loss for a given internal volume. The other factor that affects the area of external envelope and hence the rate of heat loss is the way buildings are arranged next to each other. Taking the case of various types of dwellings, comparisons would show that the differences in terms of exposed envelope are significant. A semi-detached house would have 81 per cent of exposed envelope compared to a detached one. A terraced house would have even less external surface area (63 per cent of that for a detached house). A middle storey flat would get about a third of external area compared to the detached house. This comparison assumes the same floor area for all dwellings.

A proportion of the energy used in providing heating, hot water and other comfort services is wasted. The design of the services can both minimise these losses and recover some of the wasted energy. Hot gases passing up flues for instances can be made use of to heat the building if the flue is located on the inside instead of the outside. Heat recovered from warm air leaving the inside of the building, when ventilated out, can be re-used by mixing it with incoming cool/cold air. Such systems which, in the past existed in large scale industrial or commercial applications can be found today for small domestic applications. Known as mechanical ventilation with heat recovery they can be used to increase energy efficiency in buildings.

Some buildings are not occupied all the time during the day and week. For such buildings, the control of heating systems needs to be in tune with the occupancy pattern. A building which is used only during the working hours would need to have the heating system switched on some time before the occupants arrive in order for the background temperature to rise enough to reach comfortable levels. By the same token, the heating system needs to be switched off some time before the end of the working day to avoid wasting heat long after the occupants have gone. Times for switching on and off depend mainly on the type of the building fabric (whether lightweight or heavyweight) and the response of heating system.

Apart from heat loss through the external envelope, buildings are likely to lose heat due to the continuous movement of air between the inside and outside of the building. This movement is either intended as a means to ventilate the building or incidental due to the presence of gaps and small openings in the building fabric. Such a movement of air is generally referred to as infiltration. For both ventilation and infiltration, warm air leaving the inside of the building will take some heat with it. As warm air is replaced by cold air from the outside, extra heat input is imposed on the heating system in order to bring the cold air to a comfortable level. Heat loss due to ventilation is not necessarily a big issue, as (a) the need for ventilation surpasses the desire to save some energy and (b) the process is more or less under control. The rate at which heat is lost due to infiltration, on the other hand needs to be minimised if not eliminated by means of sealing any gaps that may appear in the building fabric, as a result of poor workmanship.

Chapter 7

Reducing heat loss

Statutory requirements

A closer look at heat loss from a building will reveal that the conduction heat loss through an element of the building envelope is the product of the thermal transmittance (U-value) multiplied by the area of the element and the temperature difference between the inside and outside. The rate at which heat is lost from the inside of the building increases as the level of thermal insulation is decreased. The thermal transmittance coefficient or U-value of a construction is a commonly used measure of insulation. The levels of insulation required under statutory regulations vary from one country to another. In the UK, the statutory requirements for the levels of insulation are stated in Approved Document L of the Building Regulations. Part L1A of the Approved Document deals with new dwellings while Part L2A covers new non-domestic buildings. A summary of the requirements is given in Table 7.1.

Part L1B on the other hand covers work in existing dwellings that are being the subject of refurbishment and Part L2B deals with work in existing buildings other than dwellings. The requirements for those two types of buildings are given as a summary in Table 7.2 and Table 7.3.

The duty of the designer extends beyond that of complying with current regulations. If sustainability is to be promoted through energy efficient design, the levels of thermal insulation used in the building envelope need to be higher than those required under statutory requirements such as the building regulations.

Insulating the building envelope

In external walls, insulation can be installed in one of three possible positions; towards the inside of the wall, towards the outside or within

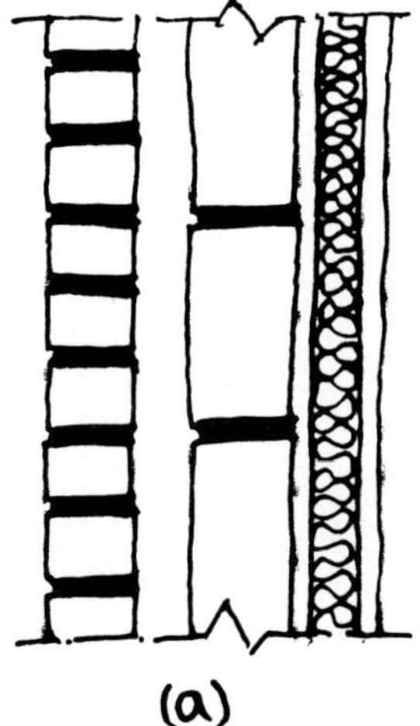

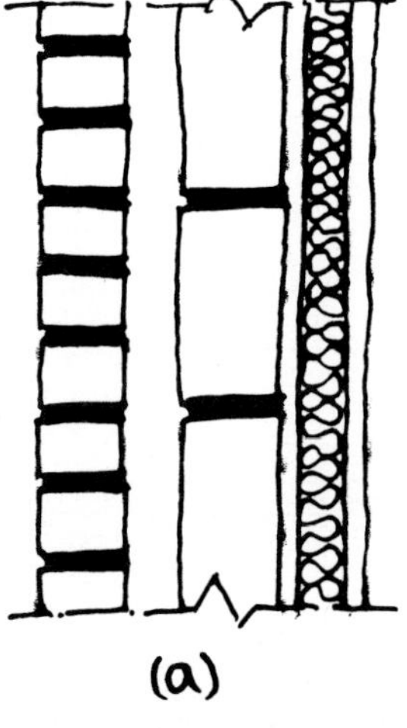

7.1

Table 7.1 Limiting U-values for new buildings – in W/m²K- (BRE 2006)

Element	*Area-weighted average U-value*	*Individual element U-value*
Wall (dwellings and other buildings)	0.35	0.70
Floor (dwellings and other buildings)	0.25	0.70
Roof (dwellings and other buildings)	0.25	0.35
Window/roof light/roof window (dwellings and other buildings)	2.2	3.30
Door (dwellings)	2.2	3.30
Pedestrian door (non-domestic buildings)	2.2	3.00
Large doors (non-domestic buildings)	1.5	4.00
High usage entrance door (non-domestic buildings)	6.0	6.00
Roof ventilator (including smoke vent) in non-domestic building	6.0	6.00

Table 7.2 Standard U-values for new and replacement thermal elements in existing buildings (after BRE 2006)

Thermal element	*U-value of new thermal element in extension*	*U-value of replacement thermal element in existing building*
Wall	0.30	0.35
Floor	0.22	0.25
Pitched roof – insulation at ceiling level	0.16	0.16
Pitched roof – insulation between rafters	0.20	0.20
Flat roof or roof with integral insulation	0.20	0.25

Table 7.3 Standard U-values when upgrading retained thermal elements (after BRE 2006)

Thermal element	*Threshold U-value*	*Improved U-value*
Cavity wall (dwellings and other buildings)	0.70	0.55
Other wall type	0.70	0.35
Floor (in dwellings)	0.70	0.25
Floor (in non-domestic buildings)	0.35	0.25
Pitched roof – insulation at ceiling level	0.35	0.16
Pitched roof – insulation between rafters	0.35	0.20
Flat roof or roof with integral insulation	0.35	0.25

the wall construction. Each of these cases is described below. The construction types discussed in this section are typical, but not exclusive, to the UK. Furthermore, the principles behind them can be adapted and adopted for different construction methods and climatic regions.

Internal insulation in wall construction can be found in both new built and refurbished buildings. In un-insulated masonry cavity walls, internal insulation is added to the inside of the inner masonry leaf, when refurbished, either between battens/channels or as an integral part of the plasterboard (see Figure 7.1a). Though this form of insulation is cheaper than an externally applied one, the risk of both fire and condensation needs to be considered. In the case of refurbishment, the effect of adding internal insulation on the reduction in room size should be borne in mind. Installing the insulation towards the inside of the wall can also be found in timber frame buildings where the insulated frame becomes the inner leaf while the outer leaf is in masonry as shown in Figure 7.1b. A variation on this form of construction is to replace the outer masonry leaf with a weather cladding system as illustrated in Figure 7.2a. For this form of construction, the risk of condensation is even higher. This is usually dealt with by means of a vapour control layer (on the warm side of insulation) and a breather membrane (on the outside), particularly if the weather cladding is not back ventilated.

Having the insulation installed on the outside of the mass of the wall tends to find favour with refurbishment of existing buildings more than newly built ones. In the case of the former, it consists of fixing the insulation onto the outside of the existing wall and either putting rendering over it or applying a cladding system to provide weather protection as is illustrated in Figure 7.2b. Although it can be costly as an add-on, this method of insulation reduces thermal extremes in the building fabric, provides frost protection and prevents cold bridging.

Furthermore, sometimes, it can be the only way to improve the building's thermal performance. Given that refurbishment of existing buildings is central to the sustainability arguments, this method of insulation is particularly useful. However, the designer must be aware of the implications of adding new layers of materials on the detailing around openings and other façade related issues.

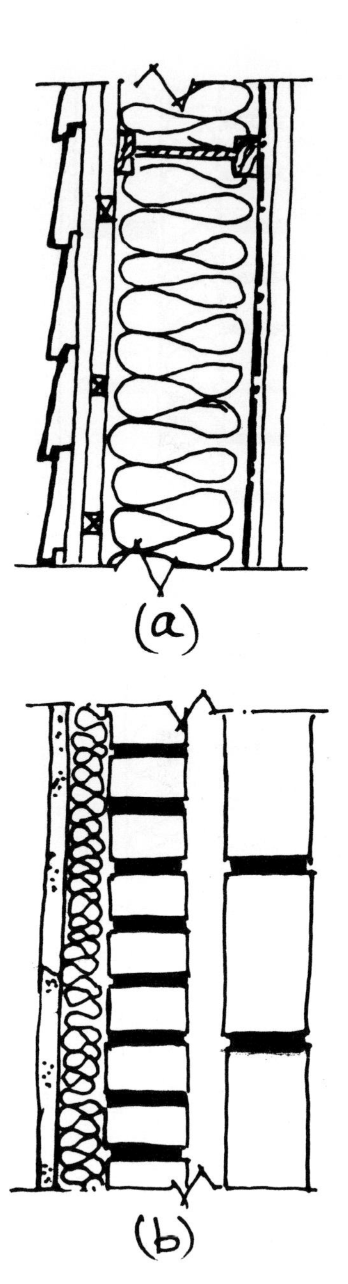

7.2

Cavity wall insulation can be found either as partial or full fill. The first method is commonly used in new build traditional masonry walls where the exposure to driving rain is likely to be high and the outer leaf is not rendered. Under these conditions, a small cavity is left empty to separate the insulation from the outer leaf and stop the rainwater from finding its way towards the inside of the wall. Full fill cavity insulation can be found in both new built and refurbishment work. If the cavity insulation were part of the original design, then the width of the cavity would have been designed to allow for enough insulation. The level of exposure to driving rain would determine the choice of external wall

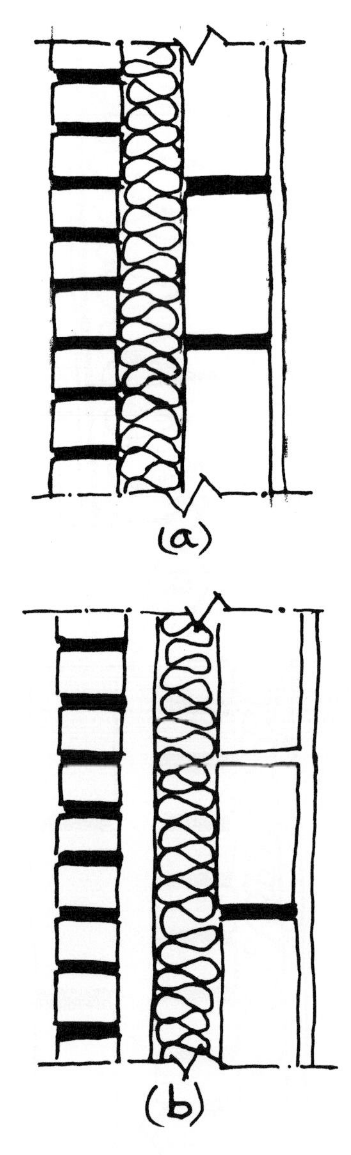

7.3

treatment. This would be either rendered/clad masonry in high exposure areas or facing masonry (brick/stone) in low exposure areas. In the case of full fill cavity insulation as part of an upgrade of an existing building, the cavity fill would take the form of blowing or injecting the insulating material. A variety of insulating materials can be found on the market. The choice however should take into account the environmental impact of such materials. Once again, the rules regarding exposure to driving rain would need to be observed when it comes to external wall finish. Typical cases of cavity wall insulation are illustrated in Figure 7.3.

Roofs are another important part of the building fabric that need consideration with regard to heat loss and thermal insulation. The location of insulation with regard to the other roof components depends mainly on the type of roof, the insulating material and the method of construction.

When pitched roofs are used, the insulation can be found either laid horizontally between the ceiling joists or between the rafters following the roof pitch. The first method of roof insulation is used in new or recent buildings for which the loft space is left uninhabitable and in old buildings that have seen their thermal insulation upgraded without the loft space being converted. This type of insulation comes in the form of rolls of either mineral wool or glass wool. In order to prevent condensation, the roof space needs to be ventilated by means of eave openings (in either the fascia or the soffit) as illustrated in Figure 7.4. Insulation can be laid along the pitch of the roof, between the rafters. Either quilt or board type insulation can be used, although the latter is more practical. The cold side of insulation needs to be ventilated in order to avoid condensation. A ventilation gap above the insulation is used in conjunction with ventilation inlets at the eaves and outlets at the ridge. In high moisture rooms, the use of a vapour control layer on the warm side of

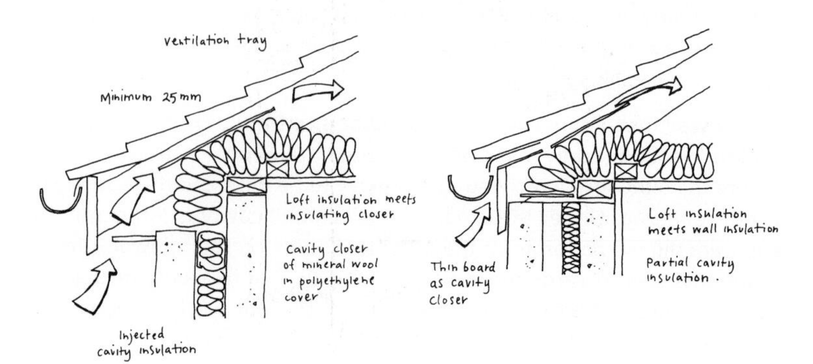

7.4

insulation is advisable. Figure 7.5 shows a typical example of pitched roof with sloping insulation.

In the case of flat roofs, insulation can be found in different locations with respect to the roof deck. In a cold roof construction, the insulation is laid below the deck supported by the ceiling and having a vapour control layer on the warm side. There is a need for a ventilation gap above the insulating layer with inlet and outlet gaps in the eaves similar to those in pitched roofs. This type of flat roof is to be used with timber roof construction only. Figure 7.6 shows an insulated cold roof construction.

In warm roof construction, insulation is laid above the deck. It can be either below the waterproof membrane (sandwich warm roof) or above it (inverted warm roof). If the roof construction is of the latter type, there would be no need for vapour control layer but the insulating material must be water resistant. Warm roof construction can be used with timber, concrete or metal structural deck as illustrated in Figure 7.7.

The continuous but slow improvements to thermal performance standards meant that all new buildings and some existing ones that have

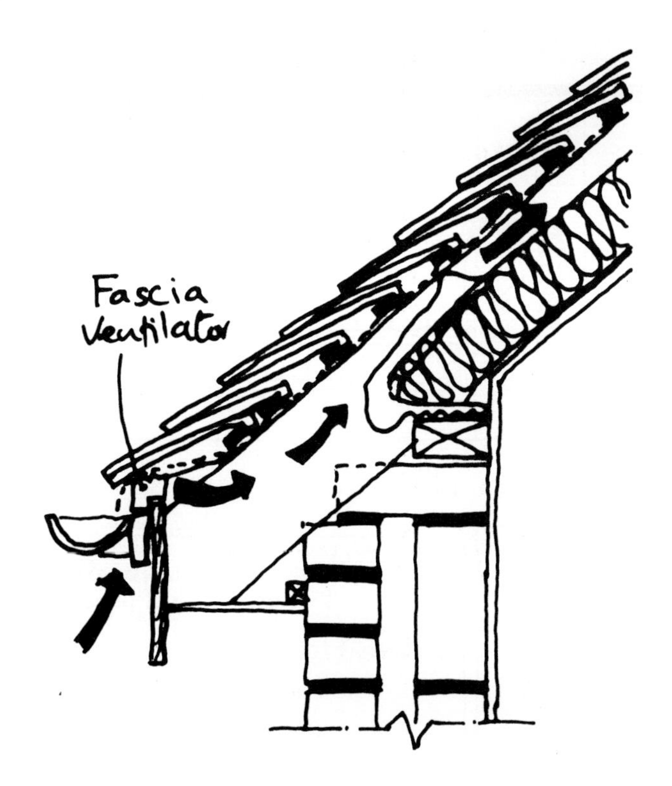

7.5

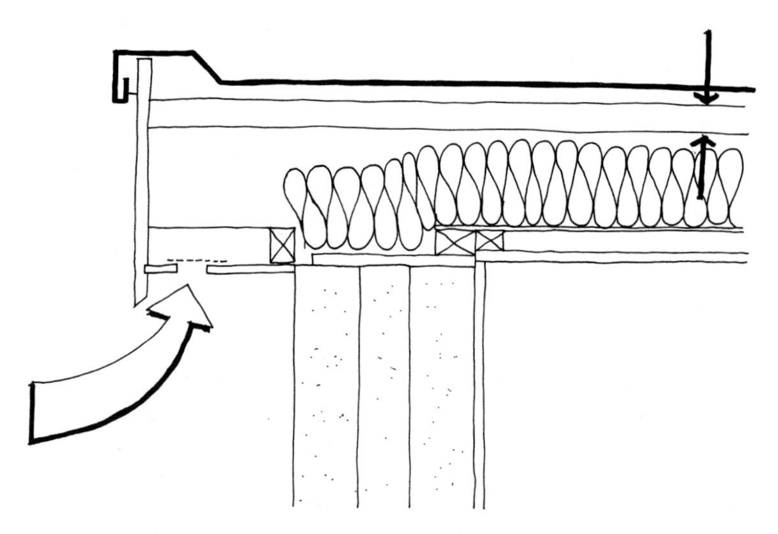

7.6

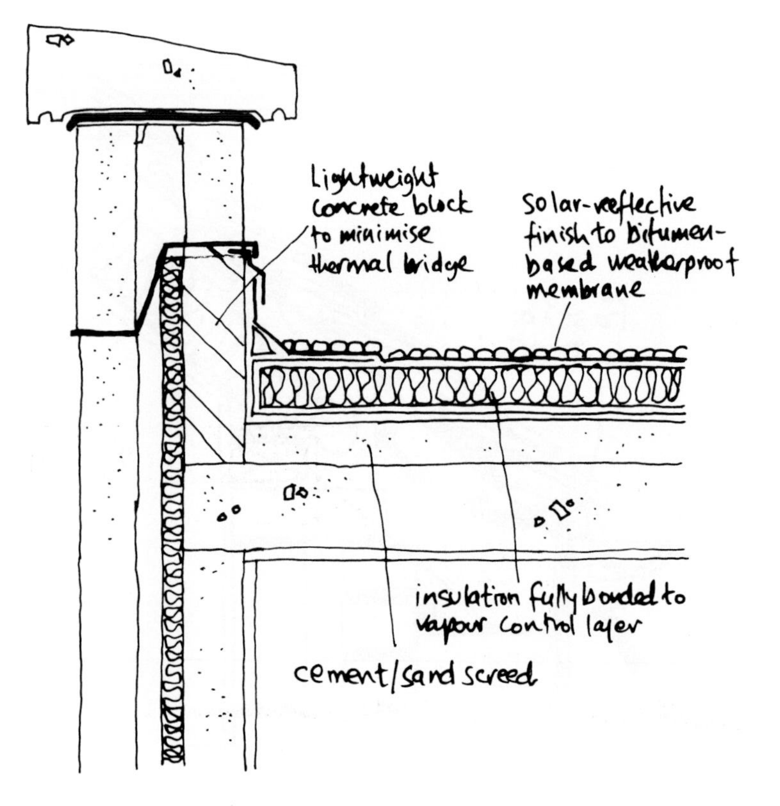
Lightweight concrete block to minimise thermal bridge
Solar-reflective finish to bitumen-based weatherproof membrane
insulation fully bonded to vapour control layer
cement/sand screed

7.7

undergone refurbishment or conversion, have their ground floors insulated to reduce the rate of heat loss. The methods of applying insulation vary according to the type of floor construction and the timing of installing insulation (during as opposed to after construction). In suspended timber floor construction, insulation can be found between the joists in the form of quilt or board as shown in Figure 7.8. This method of insulation can be used in new floors or in refurbished ones if the floorboards are to be removed and replaced. An alternative method to insulating a floor is to place rigid insulating boards above the joists. Such an example is shown in Figure 7.9.

When solid concrete floors are considered, the insulating material needs to be of the board type. If laid below the slab, the board is required to have enough rigidity to resist loading and to be protected from rising damp. Such a floor construction would give a cold floor under the feet. Alternatively, the insulating board can be laid above the concrete deck. In this case, the floor would be warm under the feet. In both cases, the issue of cold bridging at the floor external wall junction needs to be taken into account. These methods of insulation are illustrated in Figure 7.10 and Figure 7.11 respectively.

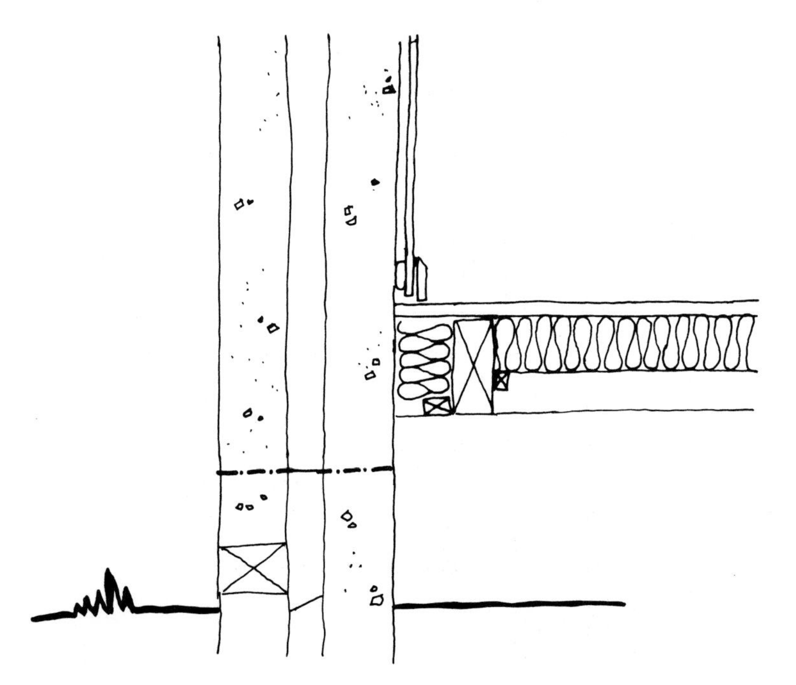

7.8

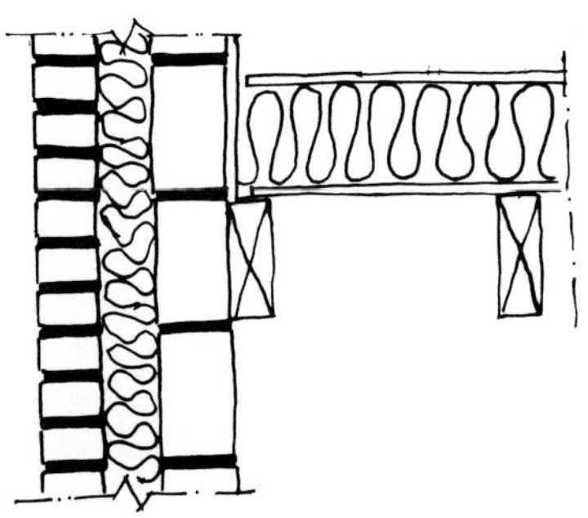

7.9

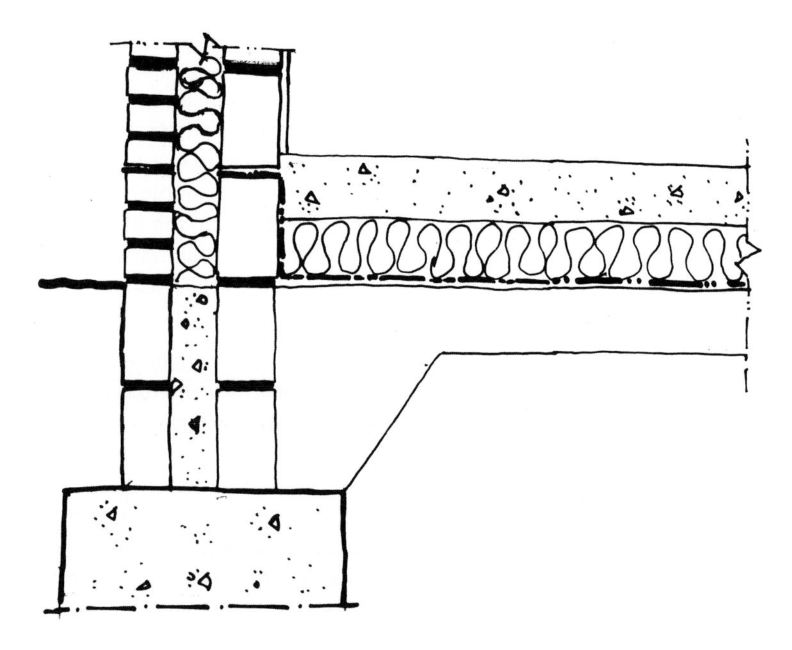

7.10

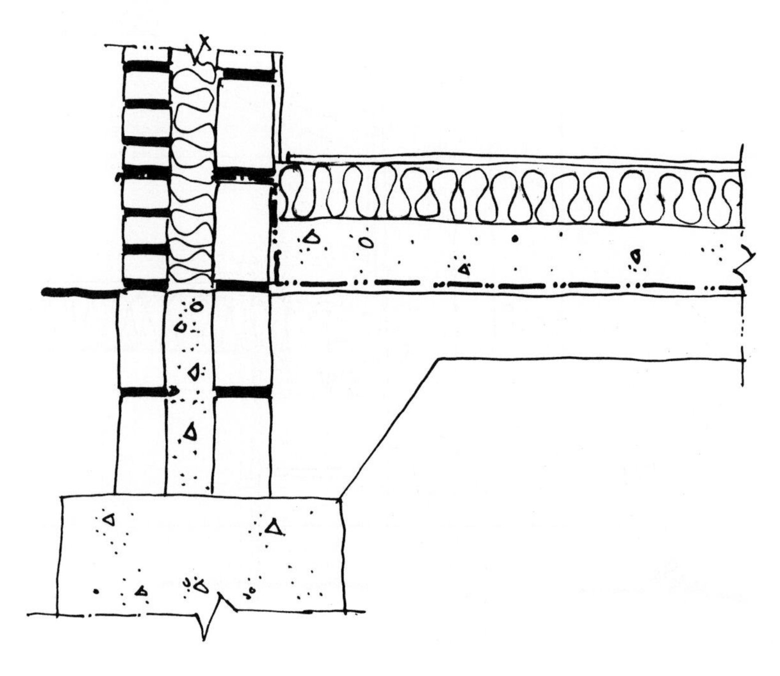

7.11

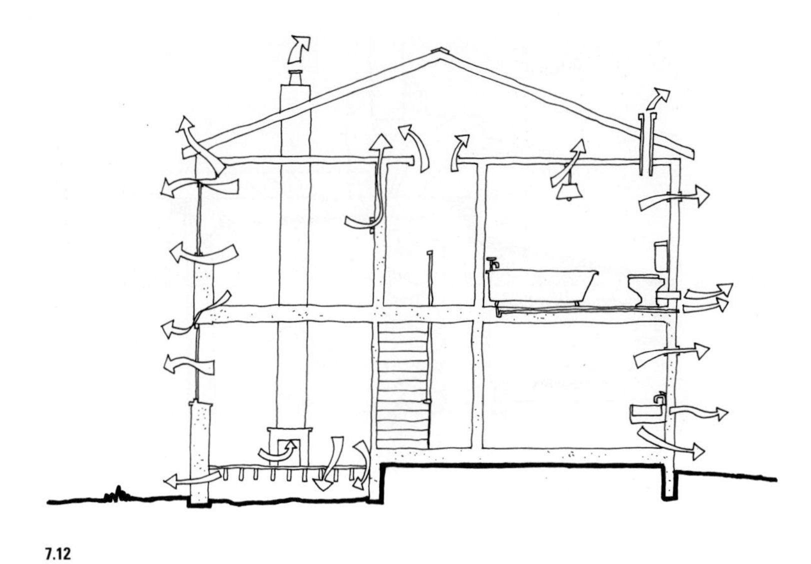

7.12

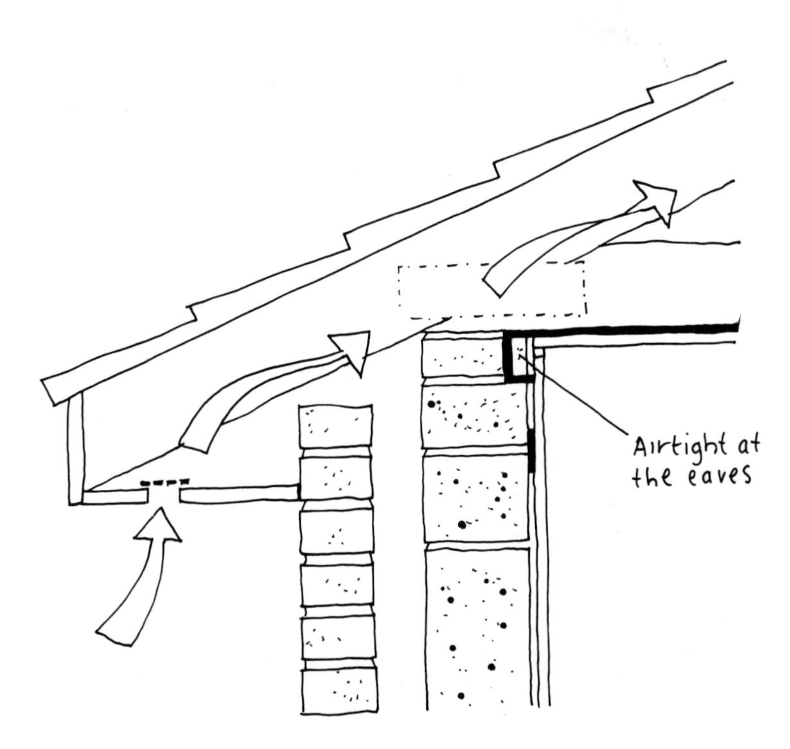

7.13

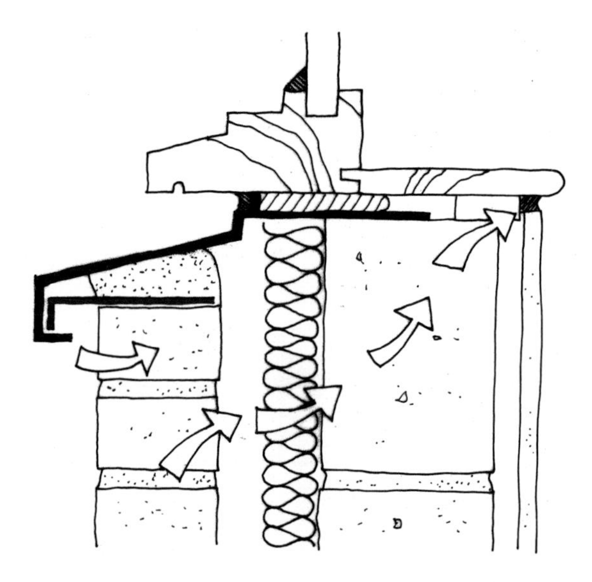

7.14

Air tightness of building envelope

Air leakage through gaps and cracks in the building fabric has been identified as a cause of heat loss. Improving air tightness will reduce air leakage and hence heat loss. In the UK it is now a statutory requirement for new buildings to be built to a certain standard of air tightness. The Building Regulations Approved Documents L1A, L1B, L2A and L2B, which came into effect in 2006, have introduced a new requirement for achieving a reasonable limit for air permeability. This is given as 10 $m^3/(hm^2)$ when measured at a reference pressure difference of 50 Pa between the inside and outside of the dwelling.

To avoid air leakage in new buildings it is necessary to know where leaks are likely to occur. Figure 7.12 illustrate the most common paths for air leakage. For detailed guidance and advice on how reduce air leakage the reader should refer to Energy Saving Trust (2005) and TSO (2002). Two typical examples of sealing around vulnerable areas are shown in Figure 7.13 and Figure 7.14.

Chapter **8**

Maximising the use of solar energy

Introduction

Climate change and global warming affect the whole of the planet and any attempts to live sustainably need to be on a global scale. The role of architects, however in promoting sustainable developments is an important one. This is because buildings and activities relating to them are responsible for a major part of the energy and other resources that have an environmental impact on our planet. The challenge for architects is to create climatically-responsive architecture that is in tune with its environment and context. Such a task requires technical rigour and attention to detail when the building envelope is designed. Although the approach offered here is of a technical nature, it should not be an excuse for uninspiring design but rather a design tool that feeds the creative thinking and at times can be a design generator.

The sun is both a useful source of abundant energy that can be harnessed and used, and a source of discomfort that can be energy intensive. The discussion in this forthcoming section will focus on how to make good use of solar energy for heating during the cold season and reduce its unwanted effect during the warm season.

Design for heating

In a cold climate, buildings are primarily designed to be heated. The objectives for an environmentally conscious design approach, in these circumstances, would be:

- to maximise solar heat gains;
- to minimise heat losses.

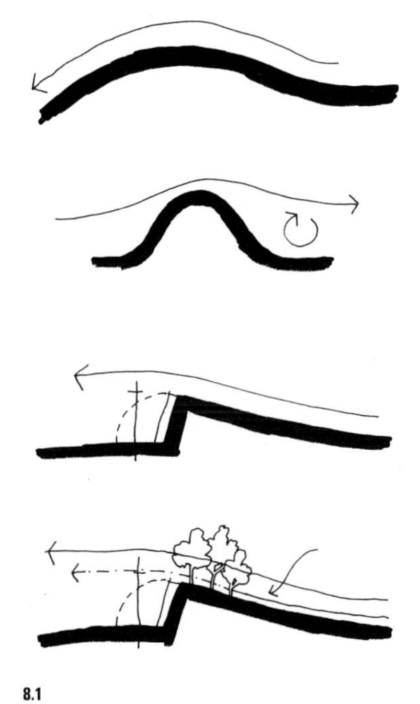

8.1

At first, these two objectives may seem as a contradiction in terms. Careful consideration of orientation, building planning, choice of materials and design features can lead to low energy design solutions that make good use of solar energy.

Maximising timely solar collection for heating purposes can be dealt with, initially by means of careful site planning. Whenever possible, the building needs to be located for maximum benefit from the microclimate. The site analysis should consider the study of solar exposure and shadows in order to establish the least overshadowed areas during the heating season. To this end the angles of the sun at certain critical times and days of the year need to be established. The analysis can make use of computer software, physical scale modelling or both. Another aspect of microclimate, which relates closely to passive solar heating, is the provision of shelter from prevailing winds during the heating season. Those winds increase heat loss by reducing the external temperature of the building fabric and increasing infiltration through cracks and openings. Both planting and local topography could be made use of. Furthermore the design of the landscape can put to good use to provide shelter. Examples of using the topography and landscape to give shelter are shown in Figure 8.1. The diagram shows that gentle slopes protect from the wind on their leeward side without the turbulence associated with steep rises above the ground. Planting the slope at the top and sides improves the situation further. Similar principles can be used to afford shelter in urban sites.

The orientation of the building is an important aspect of the design strategy when dealing with maximising the effect of solar energy during the heating season. For northern latitudes, the best orientation for capturing the sun is the south facing one. However, this does not mean that the main elevation has always to face south, provided that the surfaces collecting the solar energy (glazing, sunspaces, or walls) should do so. Heat from the sun can be collected either by direct means through translucent elements such as windows and roof lights or indirectly by means of walls and roofs. The use of this latter method, however, should be considered alongside the need to minimise heat loss by using a well-insulated building envelope. When the heat loss through the building fabric is likely to outweigh the heat gain from the summer sun, collection of solar energy by means of active devices (roof mounted solar collectors, photovoltaic arrays etc.) is preferred.

Design for cooling

In moderate climates such as that of the UK, most dwellings do not require cooling. For non-domestic buildings, however, there is a need for cooling at certain times of the year. The combination of internal heat gains from lighting, equipment and occupants can give rise to uncomfortable internal temperatures. This is particularly an issue in the presence of external solar gains such as those during the summer months. The various gains that can contribute to the risk of overheating are illustrated in Figure 8.2. The strategy for dealing with the problem of overheating varies according to the type of heat gains, and the way they reach the building. The following section describes some of the approaches that can be used.

The control of summer solar gain by means of shading devices can be an effective way of keeping the inside of the building cool without using energy intensive mechanical services. In sunny weather, opaque external surfaces will absorb a large amount of solar heat gain. This heat, if not dealt with, will find its way to the inside of the building causing overheating. Whenever possible shading should be considered, particularly for the roof. This could be done either by vegetation or other buildings. Such issues are usually considered at site planning stage. The use of light coloured external finishes combined with heavyweight construction is a long standing method of solar control in warm/hot climates. Further discussion of heavyweight construction or thermal mass will follow.

The largest component of solar gains is that through glazed surfaces such as windows. With solar radiation intensity typically reaching 0.5 kW/m^2, one can begin to form a picture of the heat gains. For instance

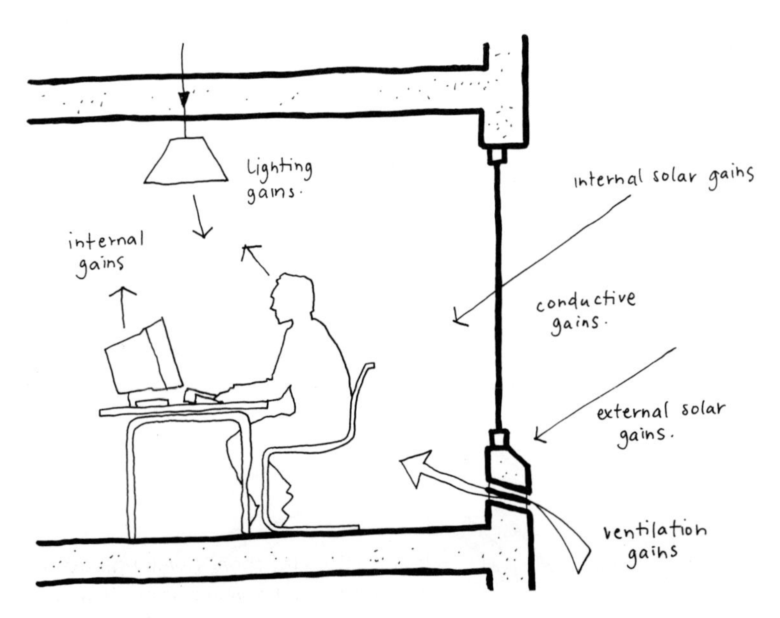

8.2

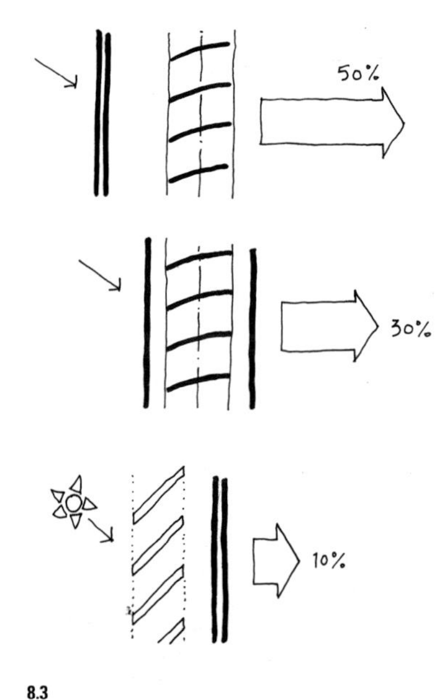

8.3

an office with $25m^2$ of floor area and $6m^2$ window area would get around 3 kW of heat gains, which is more than that received from three people and their computers occupying the space. In dealing with solar gains through glazed surfaces, the first issue that could be considered is the orientation of the building. If it is possible, glazed facades should be facing north or south. The latter orientation offers the advantage of winter gains from low sun angles but relatively little gain in summer due to high solar elevation. South west and south east facing rooms would be more vulnerable to overheating due to lower sun angles. If, for practical reasons, the use of a less than desirable orientation is to be used, shading the façade is to be considered. External shading devices are more effective than internal ones (see Figure 8.3). If the shading devices, in the form of louvers, are located between the panes of double glazing, their effectiveness is close to that of external ones with lower costs associated. Movable shading devices give a better response to changes in sky conditions than that afforded by fixed shading. Horizontal shading features are better suited to south facing windows while south east and south west façades are better served with vertical louvers. This is due to lower vertical and horizontal angles of incidence (see Figure 8.4). For effective shading devices, the designer should make use of the information on the site and the solar movement in order to investigate the most appropriate of devices. Such an investigation can be carried out using various means. These include computer modelling and physical scale.

Heat given off by electrical equipment is not necessarily a problem in dwellings. In commercial, industrial and educational buildings, the combination of this equipment with high density occupation and high

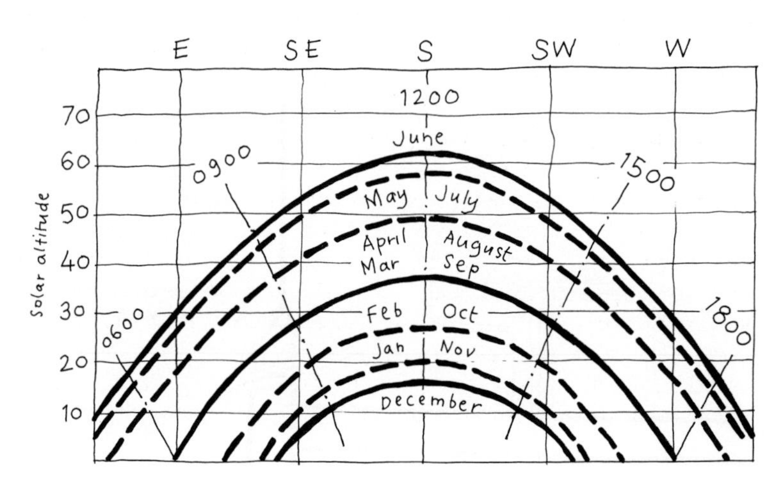

8.4

levels of artificial lighting use mean that there is a great deal of internal gain. These can be useful in winter to the point where they contribute to reducing the heating demand. In summer however such gains become a burden on the comfort balance of the building interior. The following simple steps could help reduce the need for cooling:

- The artificial lighting system should be controlled to make use of both daylight and changes in occupancy.
- Whenever possible, low energy equipment should be specified.
- Localised mechanical extract ventilation (i.e. adjacent to photocopiers) would help reduce both heat gains and air pollution.

Other approaches to minimising the need for cooling are also made use of when the environmental conditions allow. These include natural ventilation for cooling and the use of thermal mass.

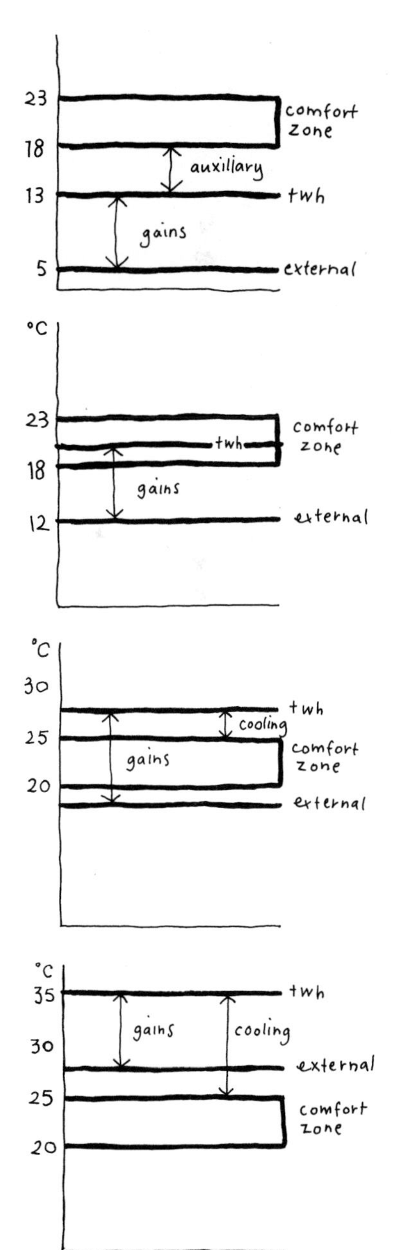

8.5

Natural ventilation

Natural ventilation is an efficient way of cooling the building. Because there are no mechanical forces driving it, it occurs when the right environmental conditions (wind, its direction, buoyancy, etc.) are present. As long as the external temperature is lower than the internal one, there will be some heat loss from the inside and a resulting cooling effect. For it to be effective for cooling, the external temperature must be lower than the comfort temperature in the room. In order to explain this statement the example illustrated in Figure 8.5 is given. Imagine conditions where the external temperature is 18°C and the temperature inside the building is reaching 28°C due to all types of gains (from occupants, equipment, lighting, solar gain through glass, etc.). Given that this temperature is above the maximum limit for comfort (20°C–25°C for a naturally ventilated building during the warm season), the outside air entering the room will cause the internal temperature to drop to a comfortable level. The temperature drop will depend on the volume of air entering the room which itself depends on the size of openings, wind direction and the presence of features that facilitate the movement of air inside the building. The conditions described in this example are typical of many commercial and industrial buildings from late spring to mid-autumn in a climate similar to that of the UK. The need for natural ventilation to provide fresh air was discussed briefly in Volume 1 of this series. The following section will describe some of the processes associated with natural ventilation. A good understanding of those principles is important, from a designer's point of view.

Wind driven ventilation

In the case of wind driven ventilation, the movement of air into, out of and across a building is determined by the wind-induced pressure around the building. When the wind blows against a building, some of the pressure builds up on the windward surfaces and some of it deflects past them. A pattern of airflow, similar to that shown in Figure 8.6 will form around the building. The airflow pattern highlights two main features that are relevant to ventilation:

- The wind pressure distribution in the horizontal plane is characterised by high-pressure areas on the windward façade and low pressure on the sides and leeward elevation.
- In the vertical direction, the windward side experiences pressure variations across the same façade (windward one) as well as across the whole elevation (including the roof).
- This pattern of pressure variation indicates the possible airflow paths that any natural ventilation system could exploit (see Figure 8.7). Further discussion of latter point will follow shortly.

Stack effect

This commonly used expression refers to ventilation caused by thermal buoyancy. A volume of hot air will rise when surrounded by cold air, in a similar way to an object released below the water line will float to the surface. When air warms up, it expands and becomes lighter than cold air surrounding it and floats. As it moves upwards, it creates a void that will be filled with cold dense air that sinks to the bottom. Once the temperature of this air rises, the process is repeated again and a current is generated. The pressure that drives the warm air upwards is dependent on the temperature difference between warm and cold air and the height of the warm air column (vertical distance travelled by warm air until outlet point). This is illustrated in Figure 8.8. The stack effect is at its utmost effectiveness in winter when the temperature difference between inside and outside air is highest. However, ventilation as a means of cooling is most needed during the summer. Under these conditions columns of air are created with temperatures higher than that for comfort in order to induce greater pressure differences and hence more ventilation. Such high temperatures can only be practical if created in unoccupied spaces such as solar chimneys and spaces well above head height. The use of such features is well known in both traditional architecture (see Figure 8.9) and contemporary buildings such as the BRE office building, the Ionica building in Cambridge, the Inland Revenue building in Nottingham and so on.

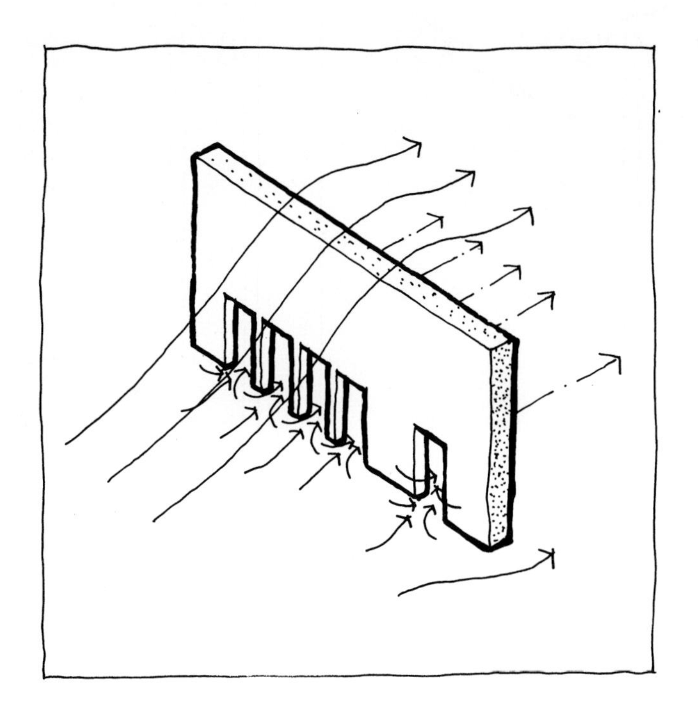

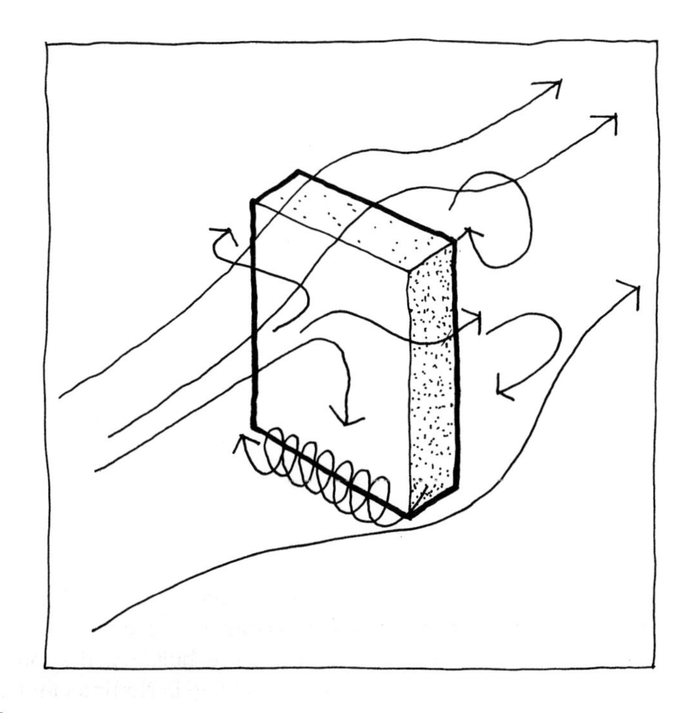

8.6

8.7

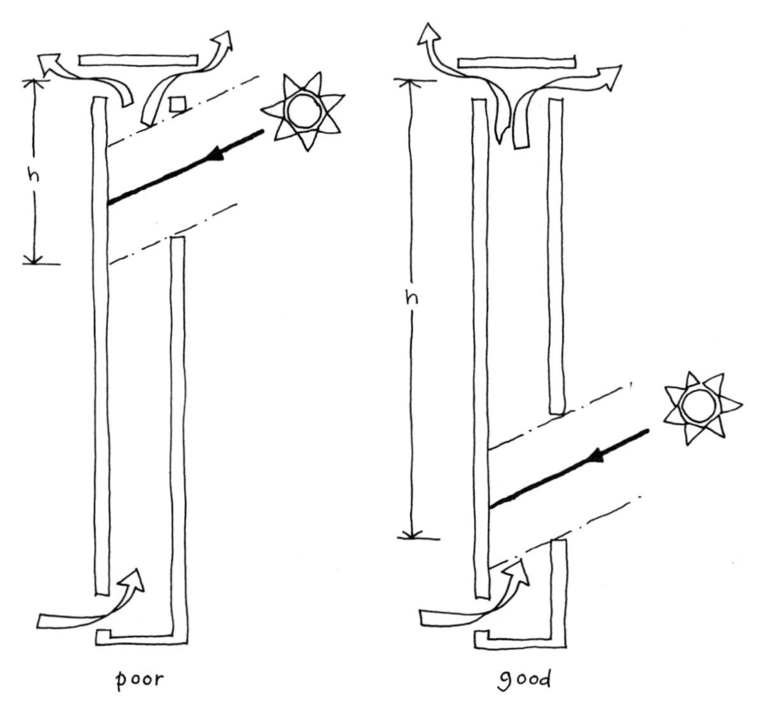

8.8

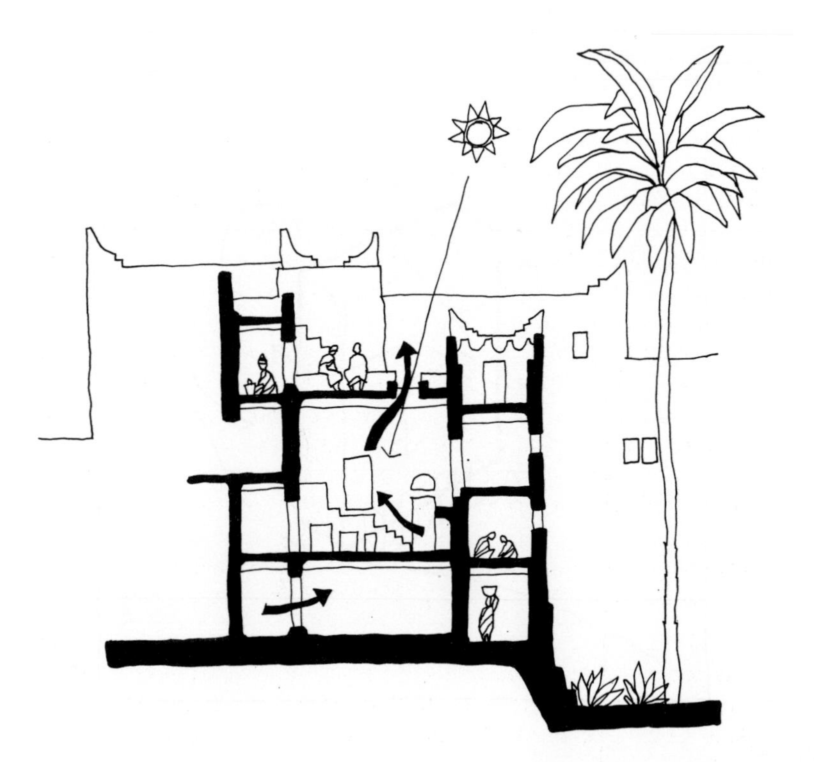

8.9

Natural ventilation and room depth

The effectiveness of natural ventilation depends on the horizontal distance that the air can travel from the point of entry in the façade. Because of this, the maximum depth to which a room can be naturally ventilated is influenced by window configuration (one side or both). For single-sided window configuration, ventilation can be provided up to 6m in depth or twice the height of the room. The movement of air, in summer, is due to wind turbulence rather than stack effect. Having high and low openings in the single-sided window will increase the effectiveness of ventilation as the difference in height between openings will behave like a stack with air drawn in at low level and exhausted at high level. This would result in an effective ventilation depth of around three times the height between the openings for summer ventilation. Wind driven ventilation can reach depths of around three times the floor to ceiling height or around 9m. Cross ventilation with double-sided window configuration can be very effective for wind driven ventilation for summer cooling. Depths up to 4 times the room height can be effective. If openings at different heights are used as described previously for the single-sided windows, the effect of stack can increase the effective depth up to 5 times the height of the room.

Thermal mass

Thermal mass is the ability of a material to absorb heat. This is not to be confused with thermal conductivity (ability to conduct heat). The physical property that describes a material's ability to store heat is its specific heat. This is the heat energy required to raise the temperature of a kilogram of material by 1°C (kJ/kg°C). Since in the case of buildings, it is customary to deal with volumes of material rather than their weight, the use of the volumetric specific heat is more relevant (kJ/m^3°C). Table 8.1 shows typical values for the specific heat of a selection of materials. For thermal mass to be effective in absorbing heat from the inside of the building, for instance, it needs to have more than just high volumetric specific heat. The material needs to be in contact with the air in the room. Furthermore, increasing the material's surface area, by means of undulations, will increase its ability for heat exchange. A practical way of comparing the thermal mass of every day's forms of construction is to use their *admittance*. Table 8.2 shows typical admittance values for a selection of some common wall constructions.

The way the thermal mass is distributed around the room has an impact on its cooling effectiveness. This is due to the fact that only a certain thickness of the material has an effect on the 24-hour temperature cycle. This is around 50mm of concrete or equivalent. The presence of any

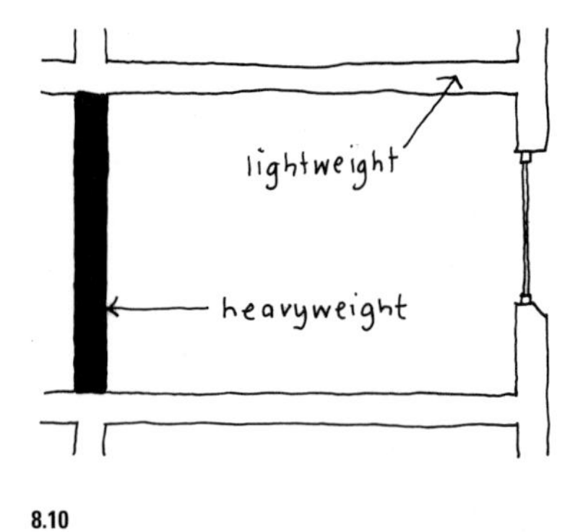

8.10

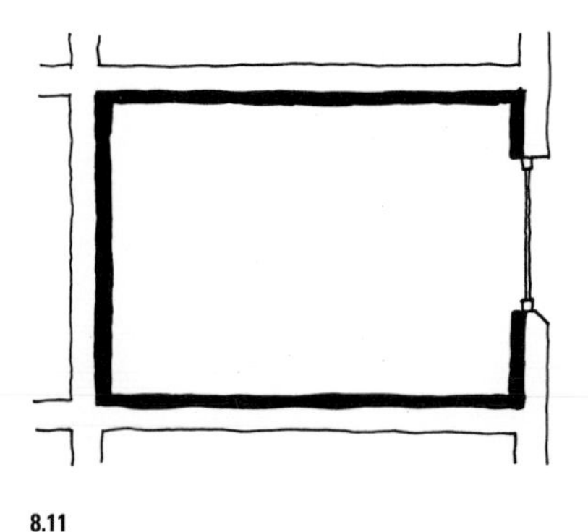

8.11

Table 8.1 Typical values of specific heat of some building materials

Material	*Heat capacity (kJ/m³oC)*	*Specific heat (kJ/kg°C)*
Concrete, dense	1,760	0.84
Concrete, lightweight	1,000	1.00
Brick	1,360	0.80
Gypsum plaster	1,050	1.10
Hardwood	900	1.23
Softwood	730	1.20
Fibreboard	300	1.00
Expanded polystyrene	25	1.00
Water	4,200	4.20

Table 8.2 Admittance values of some common wall constructions

Construction type	*Admittance (W/m²K)*
210 mm solid brickwork, with 13 mm internal plasterboard lining on battens	1.0
105 Brick/100 mm light block partial fill cavity with internal plaster	3.0
210 mm solid brick, plastered internally	4.5
150 mm cast concrete	6.0

insulation in between the mass and room air would reduce the cooling effectiveness drastically. The amount of thermal mass shown in Figure 8.10 will be far more effective when distributed around the room as shown in Figure 8.11. This is because the area through which heat is exchanged between the mass and the room air is far greater. When the mass is isolated by lightweight materials such as plasterboard lining, suspended ceiling systems and raised floors, it will have little effect on the thermal behaviour of the building. The use of thermal mass for cooling purposes can be useful even in a moderate climate such as that of the UK. On the other hand when designing for heating, the impact of thermal mass on energy use needs to be carefully considered against the building's pattern of use.

Chapter **9**

Contemporary architectural response

Introduction

This section discusses two buildings from different parts of the world. What they both have in common, is the desire of their designers to produce buildings that are responsive to their environment without recourse to excessive use of energy to produce tightly controlled environmental conditions inside them.

The BRE office

Although this office building was completed a decade ago, it still represents a high benchmark for buildings aspiring to be responsive to their environment and using minimum energy to create a comfortable working environment. According to Thomas and Stevens (Thomas 1999), this building is 'one of the first buildings to result from a holistic view of construction'. The Office of the Future, as it is known, is located at the Building Research Establishment (BRE) on the outskirts of Watford, some 15km north-west of London. Despite being only 300m away from the M1 motorway, the site does not seem to suffer a great deal from noise or air quality problems. It is fairly open and consists mainly of two and three-storey buildings. The location is fairly exposed to wind from all directions, although the south-west direction seems to be prevailing in terms of wind distribution. The design brief asked for a landmark building with the highest in architectural standards, the latest in energy efficiency innovations and the best possible rating in environmental assessment. In order to achieve such standards, very limiting energy use targets were set. Energy consumption target was set at 47kWh/m^{2}yr for delivered gas, and 36kWh/m^{2}yr for delivered electricity. These figures correspond to 34kg/m^{2}yr of carbon dioxide emission. The energy

Table 9.1 Summary information for the BRE office (based on Jones 1988)

General	
Client	BRE
Architect	Feilden Clegg Architects
Date of completion	1996
Gross floor area	2,000 m^2
Cost	£3 million
Energy:	
Orientation	Main façade South
Natural ventilation	100% gross floor area (approx.)
Night time ventilation	Natural
Thermal insulation (envelope)	Above standard
Use of thermal mass	Yes
Lighting control	Yes
Need for electric lighting	5% of floor area during daylight hours
Electricity use (mains)	28%
Photovoltaics	5%
Passive solar and daylight	22%
Natural gas	45%
Total consumption	83 kW/h/m^2/year
Heating	47 kW/h/m^2/year
General electric usage	23 kW/h/m^2/year
Artificial lighting	9 kW/h/m^2/year
Cooling	3.5 kW/h/m^2/year
Mechanical ventilation (extraction in WCs)	0.5 kW/h/m^2/year

consumption figures represented an improvement of 30 per cent over existing best practice guidelines at the time. In addition to strict limits on energy use, the brief set comfort criteria as follows:

- The internal temperature (in offices) is not to exceed 28°C for more than 1 per cent of yearly working hours (20 hours).
- The same temperature is not to exceed 25°C for more than 5 per cent of yearly working hours (100 hours).

These criteria were used to test the design proposals and help refine them. A summary of the main features of the building is given in Table 9.1.

Building form and fabric

The building caters for about 100 staff occupying 1,300m^2 of office space complemented by 800m^2 of seminar and auxiliary facilities. The offices are arranged over three storeys. The building has an L shaped floor plan (Figure 9.1) with the offices occupying the east-west wing

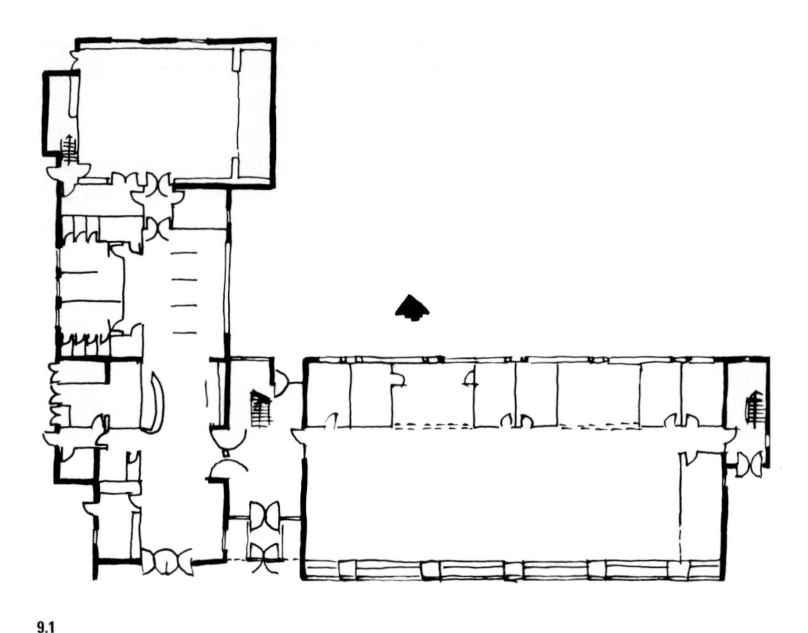

9.1

over an area 30m × 13.5m. The layout consists of a southerly open plan office zone 7.5m deep, a 1.5m corridor and a 4.5m deep northerly zone occupied by cellular offices. The floor-to-ceiling height is 3.4m on ground and first floors and varies between 2.5m and 5.0m under the sloping roof of the top floor. The location of the building on site, presented the opportunity to make use of solar radiation on the south façade without shading from adjacent buildings.

The form of the building was arrived at through consideration of the strict energy targets. The design team agreed that both solar energy and daylight should be exploited to the maximum in order to reduce both heating and lighting loads. The reduction in cooling loads was behind the strategy to use natural ventilation and shading. These, together with the site constraints, led the designers to opt for a shallow plan building with three storeys and around 50 per cent glazing on the south façade. The limit on glazing was to avoid an increase in cooling loads that would have caused overheating (comfort criteria not likely to be achieved). To bring that under control, extra energy would have been required for cooling (energy target not likely to be achieved).

Given the strict energy targets, the building fabric has to be highly insulated. External walls are of brick, cavity block with 100mm Rock wool insulation. This gave the wall a U-value of 0.32 W/m^2K. To provide added thermal mass, the 150mm internal leaf of dense block work has a dense plaster coating. The partially insulated concrete slab gave the floor a U-value of 0.33 W/m²K. The roof construction consists of 75mm timber deck with 200mm Rock wool insulation and aluminium cladding has a U-value of 0.16 W/m²K. Double glazed windows with low-emissivity glass achieved a U-value of 2.0 W/m²K. The combination of a highly insulated envelope with thermal mass and natural ventilation has helped reduce both heating and cooling loads and achieve the energy and comfort targets.

Ventilation strategy

Given that a typical air conditioned office would produce around 170kg of carbon dioxide for every metre squared of floor space per year, and having set the target for the building to be 34kg/m² per year, it was quite clear to the design team that a sealed and air-conditioned building was out of the question and that a natural ventilation strategy was required. The strategy had as its basis the following considerations:

- Minimise the energy use associated with ventilation and make use of both cross ventilation and the stack effect.
- Maximise the effect of night cooling by linking ventilation paths to the thermal mass.
- Extend the effect of stack to the cellular offices on the north side. This required an air flow path through open plan offices to be maintained.

The solution that the design team came up with consisted of a sinusoidal concrete slab providing thermal mass, air paths connected to the solar chimneys and space for service ducting (Figure 9.2). The slab's wavy form provided extra surface area for the thermal mass.

In summer, the single sided ventilation for each of the northern and southern zones merge to become a cross ventilation operation. This is helped by, the ducts in the wavy slab and the windows at both ends (Figure 9.3). On days of low wind, the solar chimneys on the south side allow stack ventilation to take place and draw the air from the office. Whether or not having the external surface of the stacks glazed helps in promoting air movement upwards is still open to debate. Under low wind speed conditions or during night-time cooling, low load propeller fans are used to provide mechanical assistance. The building management system ensures that the fans are only used when it is absolutely necessary.

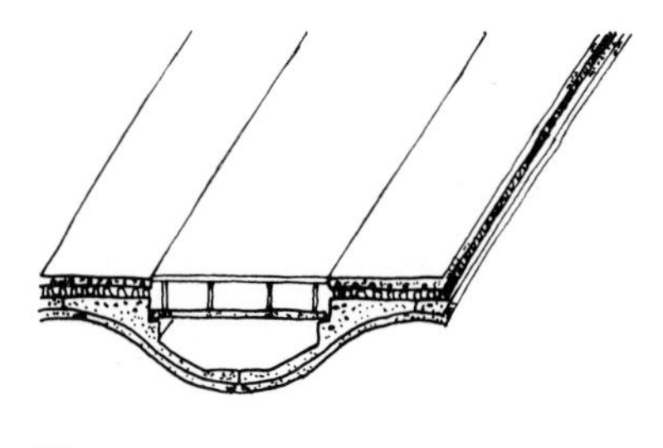

9.2

During the heating season, the operation of the ventilation system is reduced to providing fresh air for health and air quality reasons only as there is no need for cooling. This is done by means of automatic control of the high level windows. The automatic control can be supplemented by user control if and when desired.

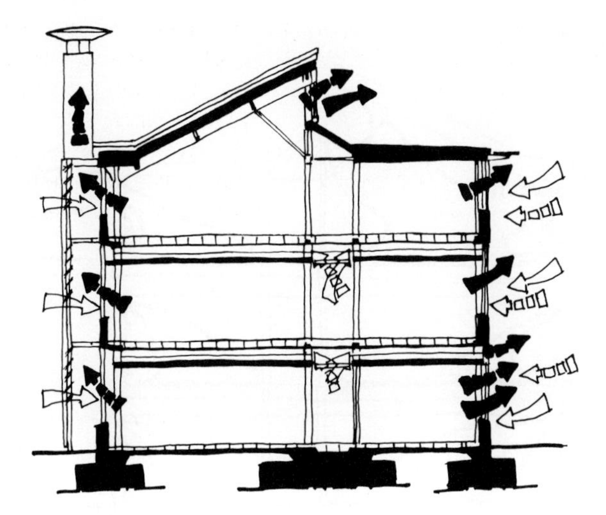

9.3

Solar radiation and daylight

For the natural ventilation and thermal mass strategy to work, it needed to be considered alongside the reduction in both cooling loads, which are mainly from the sun, and lighting loads, by using daylight. The south façade with its glazed area had to have some form of solar control. Computer modelling of various glazing ratios was used to simulate various scenarios of heat gains, heat losses, daylight factors and internal gains due to lighting. With the level of control proposed, the glazing ratio was limited at 50 per cent. The solar control is provided by external motorised glass louvers. Although they are primarily under the control of the building management system, there is the option of manual override by the users. The louvers are made of 10mm toughened clear float glass. The presence of a white ceramic coating on the underside allows the glass to transmit 40 per cent of light and reflect 50 per cent of the solar radiation falling on it. Given that daylight levels in summer are high and the louvers can be left almost horizontal, the daylight levels inside the office are not compromised (Figure 9.4). At the same time they exclude half of the solar gain. This delicate balance is achieved through the careful control of the louvers by solar position and external light level. If the sun does not reach the windows, the louvers are tilted towards the building acting as light shelves reflecting light into the inside of the building. If the sun can get to the windows and the external light level is above its set point, the position of the louvers is automatically set by the control system to block out direct solar radiation. If the external light level is below the set point, the sun is allowed in.

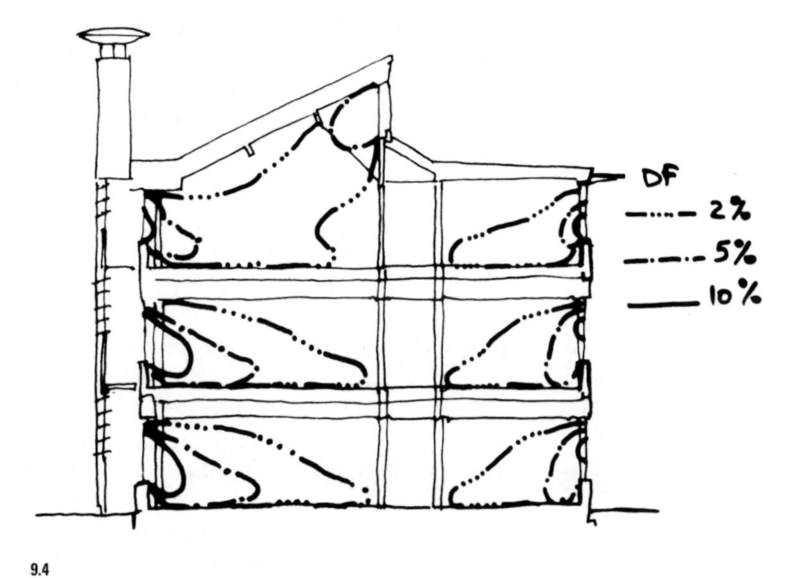

9.4

Heating and cooling

Although the design of the various services is a specialist area, the discussion regarding the Environmental Office is restricted to those issues that relate to the building design (planning, fabric, orientation and so on). The designers opted for a highly insulated building fabric. Even by today's standards, the U-values achieved in the BRE office are low. This meant that the heat losses are kept to a minimum. In order to minimise the need for cooling in summer, the following measures were introduced:

- The orientation of the building made use of solar exposure in both maximising solar gains and minimising heat losses.
- The building form took into account the orientation and the need to design for low energy.
- The use of external shading by means of automatically controlled motorised glass louvers.
- Thermal mass in the floor slabs was extensively used in conjunction with night time assisted cooling. This has helped to reduce cooling loads during the day.
- The ventilation strategy made use of both cross ventilation and stack effect.
- The provision of daylight and control of artificial lighting meant that gains due to lighting are reduced in summer.

These various passive design strategies were complemented by some low energy heating and cooling services. These only operate on a need to do basis and include a highly efficient condensing boiler and geothermal heat pumps that provide both heating and cooling if and when needed.

Sustainable construction

Whenever possible, the choice of materials and their procurement has taken into account sustainability issues. The following are some of the measures taken during the construction of the Environmental Office:

- The materials from the building that previously stood on the site were recovered at the tune of 96 per cent by volume. Some of the material (brickwork and concrete) were crushed and used as hard-core. The timber was used to make furniture and the steel was cut up and sent for recycling. Electrical accessories and mechanical plant were given to charity to be used for community projects.
- Recycled aggregate resourced locally was used, instead of coarse aggregate, in 1500m^3 of concrete in various parts of the structure.
- Blast furnace slag, which is an industrial waste, was used in concrete alongside cement. Instead of 100 per cent cement, a mixture of 40 per cent cement and 60 per cent blast furnace slag was used. This means less embodied energy in the concrete.
- When virgin materials were used, the choice took into account the energy issue. The timber used for the ceiling in the top floor, which in itself was a compromise between structural loading and thermal mass, was sourced from a renewable source. Aluminium sheets were used for the roof. Despite its high-embodied energy, aluminium was used due to its ease of recycling.
- By designing out the use of air conditioning, no HCFCs and HFCs associated with air conditioning were used.

The BRE Environmental Office had a highly demanding brief with very strict energy targets and very environmental credentials. The design team has put the environmental issues at the heart of the design approach. The result is a building that crossed the boundaries in terms of what could be achieved without the excessive use of energy intensive electrical and mechanical services. It has set a benchmark, in terms of low energy design, for others to follow. Not only did it demonstrate that even the highest of environmental criteria can be achieved but it also opened the door for more improvement in low energy sustainable design.

Apicorp headquarters

This building carries more significance than the average office block or major company headquarters in Europe or North America. Anyone who has seen the Dubai skyline lately would not fail to notice how out of touch and out of place the skyscrapers and tall concrete and glass buildings are. This practice, which has intensified in the last few years, has lasting negative effects on both the cultural identity of the Middle East and the development of design and construction skills that are in tune with the regional climate and environment.

Apicorp is a financial institution based in Khobar, Saudi Arabia. In 1995 they held a competition to design their new headquarters. The winning entry, which was designed by DEGW was completed in 2000. The building is located on the Gulf coast with climatic conditions that would be a monumental challenge to any designer. The daytime air temperature can reach 40°C and above for up to six months of the year. For the remainder of the year it falls to a mean of 20–30°C. Night time temperatures can fall as low as 10°C. The coastal air is characterised by high levels of relative humidity. This can reach 70 per cent, and sometimes even higher (90 per cent). The lack of vegetation in this hot arid climate renders the potential for shading impossible.

Building form and fabric

The main element of the building is the shallow barrel-vaulted concrete roof used both as an environmental buffer as well as an all-embracing form for the courtyards around which the office space is arranged according to the concept of office-as-village. The offices are arranged in two three-storey bays on either side of a central elliptical courtyard (Figure 9.5). This top-lit space acts as the formal and social nucleus of the building with its front part used as a reception area and the rear part providing access to the auditorium, prayer room and canteen. The central courtyard is surrounded by four smaller courtyards that emphasise the concept of the office-as-village. On each of the first and second floors the two main office wings are connected by means of a bridge crossing over the main courtyard.

The structural grid is 6m by 9m, with the latter being on the east–west axis and represents the width of the ribbed concrete vaults. These are supported by in situ concrete beams. The vaults support a built up roof consisting of in situ concrete over profiled steel deck with insulation and ceramic tiles. The floor construction consists of a waffle in situ concrete slab with a raised floor over a plenum some 800mm high. The floor to ceiling height is 3m. This height extends to 4.40m on the top floor (to the peak of the vault).

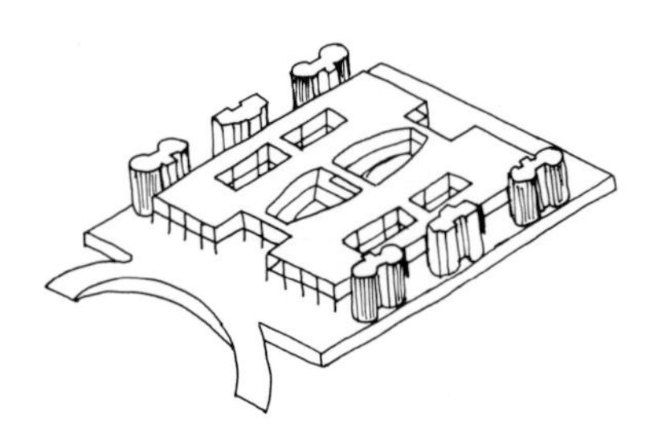

9.5

Environmental conditions

The building benefits from a huge thermal mass, but according to most reviews, the extreme conditions of air temperature, and the heavily saline atmosphere makes the use of such a traditional strategy very limited. This is because the high air resistance would require large fan loads to draw cool night air through the building.

Solar shading is at the heart of the environmental strategy given the very high solar gains. The thermally heavy concrete roof provides shading and a heat sink for the interior. Given the high summer solar angles (up to 81°) the roof overhang acts as a shading device for the façades as well (Figure 9.6). The east and west façades benefit from supplementary shading by screens.

9.6

The deep plan building is controlled as two separate zones. The perimeter area is subjected to modified daily temperatures. Room fan coil units, located in the raised floor, deal with any fluctuations in loads. The more stable deeper zone, beyond the secondary courtyards, requires less intervention from a mechanical system. A conventional displacement ventilation system is used.

Even without the benefit of free cooling associated with thermal mass, the environmental control strategy demonstrated a 60 per cent reduction in annual energy consumption compared with a typical North American office (Slessor 1999).

Part **2**

Bibliography

Baker, N.V. and Sanderson, M. Thermal comfort for free-running buildings, *Energy and Buildings*, 23(3) (1996), 175–82.

BRE, Part L explained, The BRE Guide, Report BR 489, BRE (2006).

de Dear, R. Adaptive, thermal comfort in natural and hybrid ventilation, Proceedings of HybVent Forum'99, Sydney, Australia (1999).

de Dear, R.J. and Brager, G.S. Developing an adaptive model of thermal comfort and performance, Report No. SF-98-7-3 (4106) (RP-884) (1998).

Energy Saving Trust, Improving air tightness in dwellings, Report No. GPG 224. (2005)

Jones, D.L., *Architecture and the Environment, Bioclimatic Building Design*, Laurence King (1998).

Slessor, C. Sheltering sky, *The Architectural Review*, Vol. CCII, no. 1213 (1998).

Thomas, R. (ed.) *Environmental Design, An introduction for architects and designers*, 2nd edn. E & FN Spon (1999).

TSO, Limiting thermal bridging and air leakage: Robust construction details for dwellings and similar buildings, TSO (2002).

Webliogaphy

http://www.cmdl.noaa.gov/ccgg/trends/, accessed on 15 /01/ 2007.

Part 3
Energy systems and services in buildings

Introduction

Energy use in buildings has been shown to make a large proportion of the total energy use (see Chapter 6). The design of building services systems, such as heating and mechanical ventilation, is a separate specialist area outside the remit of the architect. The discussion that follows in the forthcoming chapters is not about how to design these services. Its focus is rather on the energy issues associated with building services, as part of the bigger sustainability equation.

The pattern of energy use relating to the provision of comfort and functionality is different from one type of building to another. In domestic buildings, the bulk of the energy is used to provide space and water heating. Non-domestic buildings, on the other hand have a different pattern of energy use, with cooling and lighting energy use being important. Furthermore, commercial and industrial buildings require other energy intensive services such as equipment, machinery, communication and mechanical transportation (conveyors, lifts, etc.).

The discussion will deal with each of the two main building types separately, highlighting the main components responsible for energy use, with a view to exploring some low energy options that designers can be aware of and take into account when making design decisions.

Chapter **10**

Energy systems in domestic buildings

Introduction

Energy use in domestic buildings in 2001 amounted to around a third of the overall primary energy. This is equivalent to 71 million tonnes of oil. Hot water and space heating combined make up 80 per cent of the total energy used in the domestic sector. This chapter will discuss the main features of the various environmental services that are responsible for the use of energy in domestic buildings. Water based space and hot water heating systems consist, generally, of a number of components. The heat is generated using an appliance (in most cases a boiler) that runs on a particular type of fuel. The heat is distributed around the building using a system of pipe work and delivered at destination using heat emitters.

Heat generating systems

The type of fuel used is a decision that is taken by different parties according to the method by which the dwelling is procured. Only in self-build projects will the owner or end-user have a say in such a matter. Otherwise, it is left to the developer and their designers to decide. Such decisions are usually taken based on some economic and legal considerations. These include: capital costs (system), fuel costs, maintenance costs and emission legislation. This is hardly sustainable, since environmental considerations beyond what the statutory requirements called for, are not taken into account.

Traditionally solid fuels have been used to provide a source of heat. These consisted of coal products and logs of timber burnt in open fires and stoves. The need for storage space and removal of ash and dust, lack of automatic control and the constraint imposed with smoke emission legislation make them less attractive compared to gas and oil. A typical gravity fed, solid fuel boiler is shown in Figure 10.1 Recent technical advances in the design of solid fuel burners have made them into good alternatives to gas and oil burning appliances. This is particularly important when the fuels used are derived from renewable biomass sources. A typical solid fuel system is shown in Figure 10.2. They burn bituminous fuels and can be used even in smokeless zones. The system is self-cleaning with automatic feed operation. Another advantage of this system is that it can be used in buildings with heating loads as low as those required for a two bedroom, semi-detached dwelling.

Although it is rare to see oil boilers being specified for newly built dwellings, they are still in use in existing buildings particularly in rural areas where gas is not piped. When considering fuel cost, oil is very competitive (see Figure 10.3). However, oil requires space for storage in a tank outside the building and some fire-resistant barrier between the two. The oil is pumped to fan assisted oil burners similar to the one

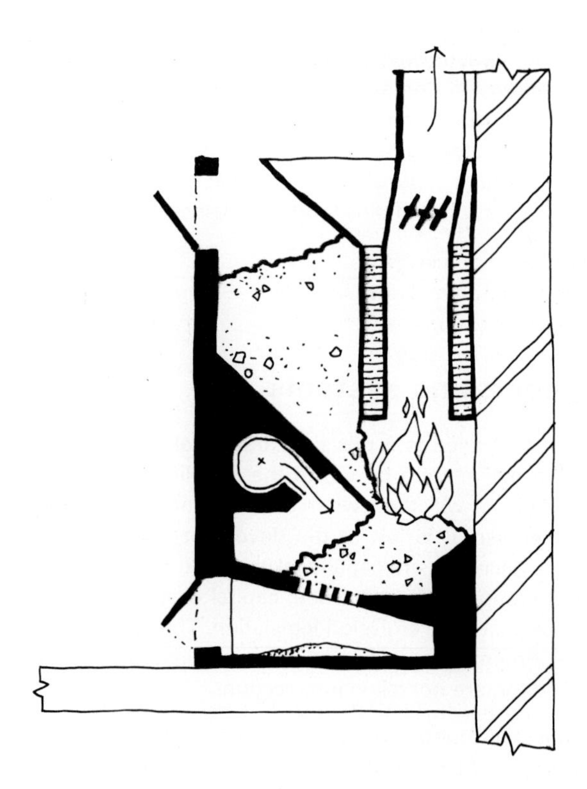

10.1

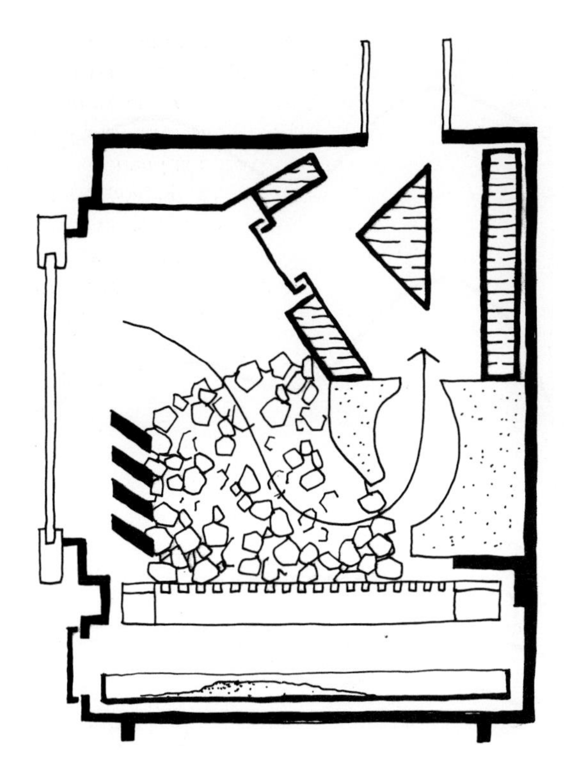

10.2

shown in Figure 10.4. Among their advantages, oil fired boilers have less complicated flue systems, compared to traditional solid fuel ones. Maintenance is minimal and annual service is usually adequate. They lend themselves to automatic control whether it be thermostatic or time based control of heat output.

Over the years, different types of gas have been used as fuel. The two main ones that are found in use nowadays are natural gas and liquefied petroleum gas (LPG). North Sea gas provides the main bulk of natural gas mains distribution in the UK. It is cleaner and has a higher calorific value than the town gas that it supersedes (Figure 10.5). Part of the heat generated in conventional gas fired boilers is discharged to the atmosphere with the combustion gases (carbon dioxide and water vapour). Modern condensing boilers make use of some of that otherwise wasted heat by condensing the water vapour and the flue gases. Such boilers have a higher efficiency than conventional ones. Figure 10.6 illustrates, diagrammatically, a typical domestic scale condensing boiler. These boilers are already a requirement for new dwellings in many European countries. In the UK, although they currently cost more than conventional boilers (in terms of capital), they present a

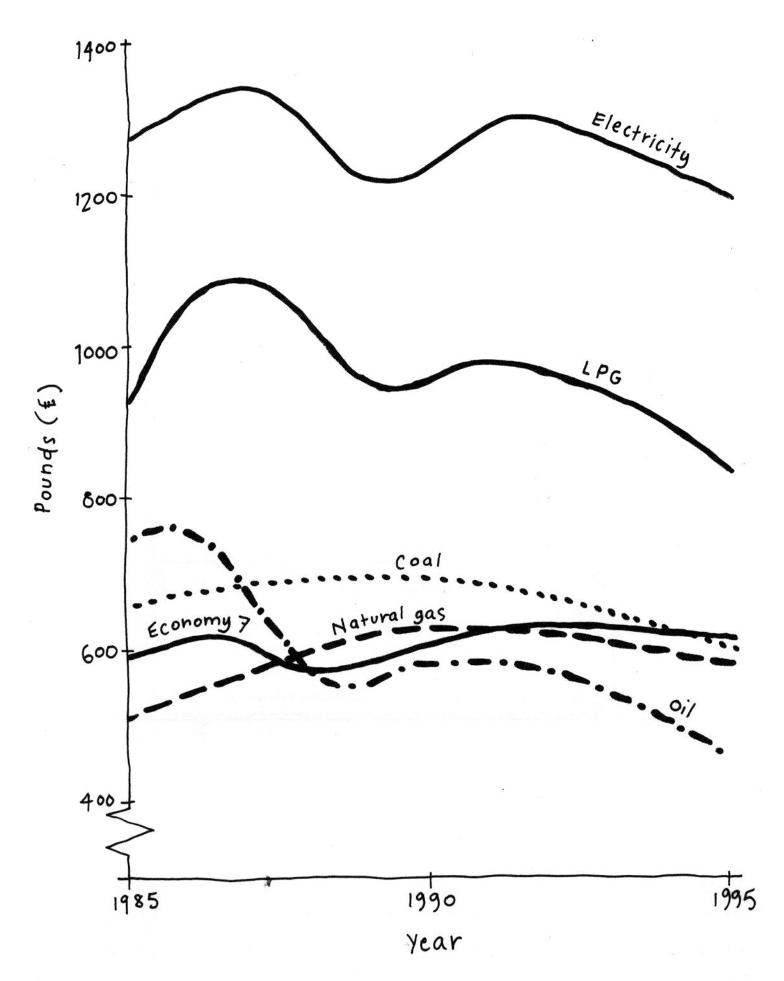

10.3

more cost effective future alternative as they already have low running costs (less fuel and high efficiency) and their capital costs are likely to fall as the manufacturing economies of scale will improve with compulsory uptake.

Distribution systems

From an architect's/designer's point of view, being aware of the various components of a heating system is useful when deciding on certain aspects of the building fabric such as the amount of insulation and its position with regard to any thermal mass in the building envelope. The heat generated by any appliance is distributed throughout the building

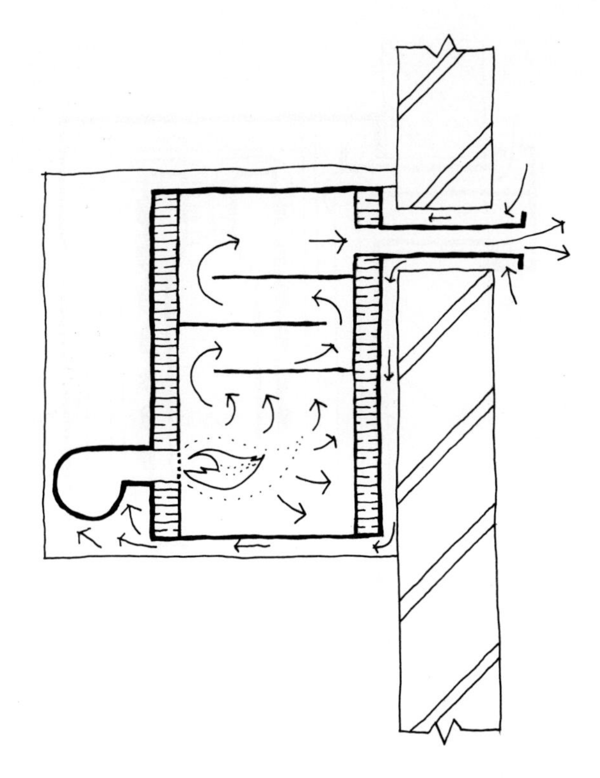

10.4

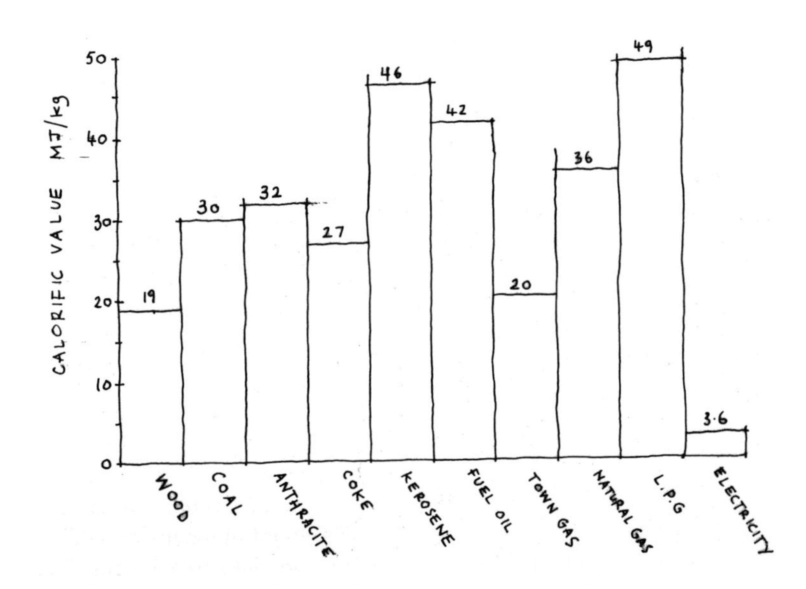
CALORIFIC VALUE MJ/kg
50
40
30
20
10
0
19
30
32
27
46
42
20
36
49
3·6
WOOD
COAL
ANTHRACITE
COKE
KEROSENE
FUEL OIL
TOWN GAS
NATURAL GAS
L.P.G
ELECTRICITY

10.5

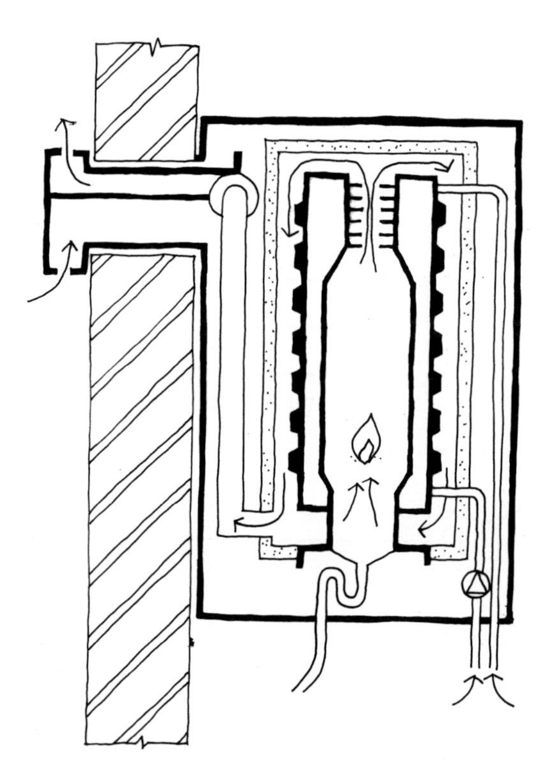

10.6

using a medium being carried in a system of pipes (for water) or ducts (for air). When reaching its destination, the heat is delivered by means of emitters while the heating medium returns to the boiler/plant. A pump or a fan provides the motive power required to move the medium around.

Low-pressure hot water heating systems usually found in domestic and small scale commercial applications use either a one or two-pipe distribution system. The second type is typical of contemporary systems as they offer effective distribution of heat/hot water and flexible control of heat emitters. Figure 10.7 shows different pipe arrangements for both one and two-pipe systems. In practice, a combination of a number of the configurations can be used in the same building, depending on building form and floor layouts. For instance if the building consists of similar floor layouts and a north-south aspect, the use of a ladder system would offer better options to control the heating loads according to the façade orientation.

High-pressure hot water and heating systems are commonly used in both large-scale commercial and domestic buildings. The pressure in the system is maintained by means of steam trapped at the top of the

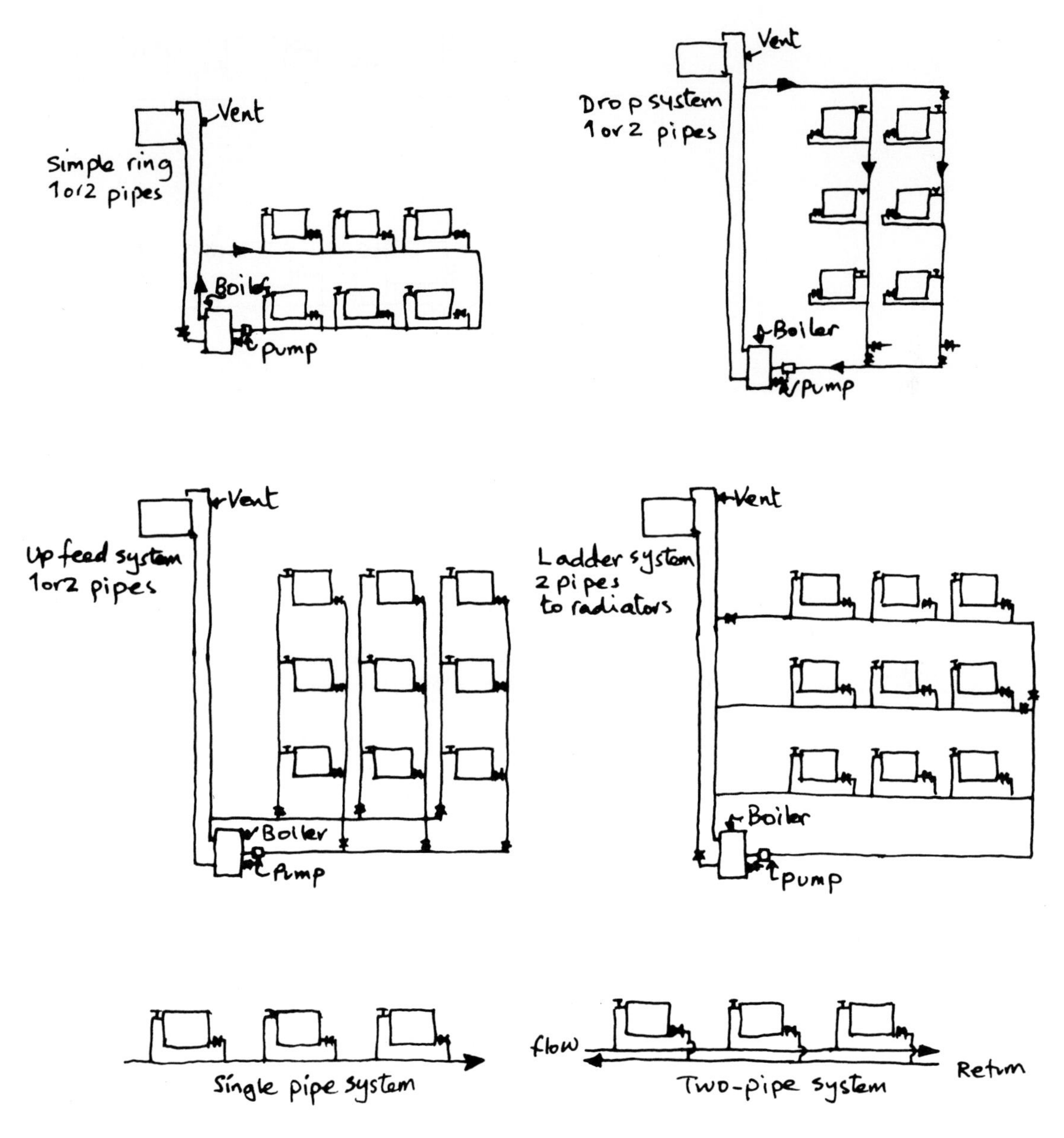

Vent
Simple ring
1 or 2 pipes
Boiler
pump
Vent
Drop system
1 or 2 pipes
Boiler
pump
Vent
Up feed system
1 or 2 pipes
Boiler
Pump
Vent
Ladder system
2 pipes
to radiators
Boiler
pump
Single pipe system
flow
Return
Two-pipe system

10.7

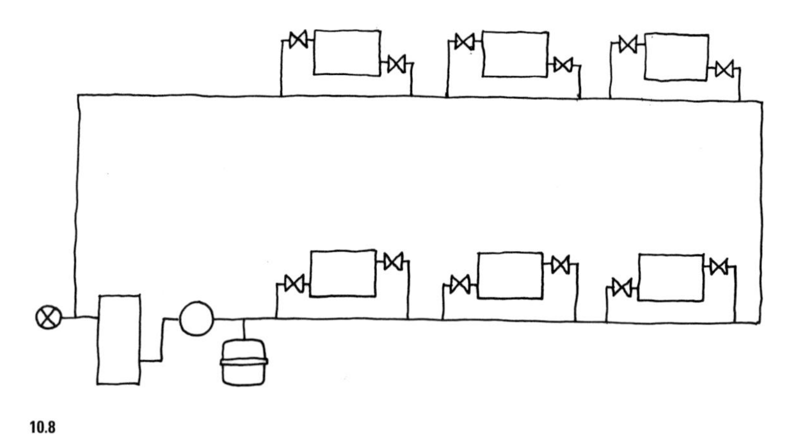

10.8

boiler. A more common form of pressurisation in small domestic installation is the use of a small pressure vessels filled with nitrogen. These do not require any power or maintenance. Such a system is shown in Figure 10.8. The use of pressurization does away with the feed and expansion cistern and vent pipes.

This can be advantageous from a designer's point of view as there is considerable freedom in locating the boiler, particularly if it is gas fired. The pipe arrangements described earlier for the low-pressure systems apply to this type of heating and hot water installations.

Warm air heating systems using a central plant are not common in the UK. However, the use of mechanical ventilation is sometimes required for a variety of reasons. From a designer's perspective, knowing what the space requirements are for such installations, is useful if not necessary. Ventilation systems for internal lavatories would consist of extraction grilles and fans to drive the air. These are self contained units serving one bathroom at the time. For larger systems, where several bathrooms are served by the same installation, the air ducts need to be separated and the system would use two fans, with one of them on stand-by. The separation of air streams, to avoid contamination of exhaust and inlet, is achieved by serving the various rooms using branches from the main trunkings called shunts. These should be at least 1m long and incorporate two bends (see Figure 10.9).

Panel heating systems

In certain cases, space heating is provided by means of panel heaters consisting of annealed copper pipes or as currently unjointed plastic ones. The pipes have 15mm to 20mm diameters and can be embedded

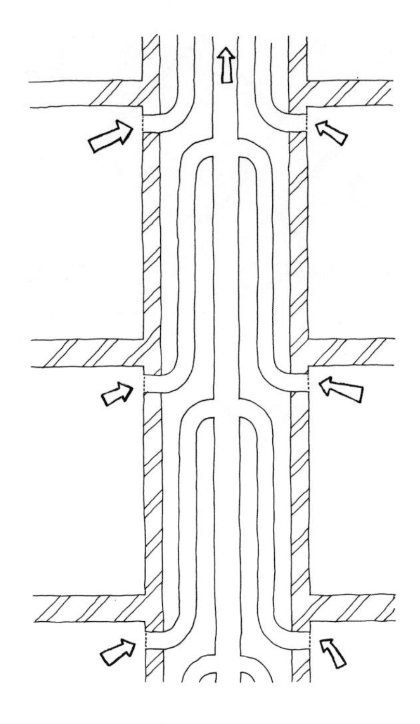

10.9

in the floor, ceiling or wall. Although all three applications provide uniform distribution of heat, under-floor heating is more cost effective (it runs at lower temperatures) and more efficient from a thermal comfort point of view. This is the case because the combination of radiant heat from the floor and convective heat upwards would contribute to reduce temperature fluctuations between head and toe for the human body. Such conditions are perceived to enhance the body's thermal comfort. Although electric under-floor heating systems have been used, their use is steadily being phased out to water ones as the latter are more energy efficient and have lower running costs. Whichever system is be used, the layouts are similar. However, manufacturers' data and advice should be made use of and heeded. A typical layout is shown in Figure 10.10. Both systems require the coverage of pipes and insulation on the underside. The pipes are usually embedded in a cement-sand screen some 70mm thick with 50mm being the minimum thickness. A typical detail of the construction and insulation of an under-floor water heating system is shown in Figure 10.11. The effectiveness of such heating systems can only be realised if the way they are controlled takes into account the effect of the thermal mass (slow to warm up and

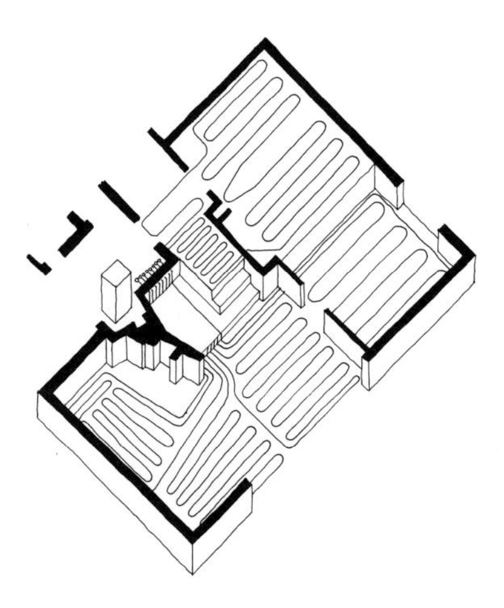

10.10

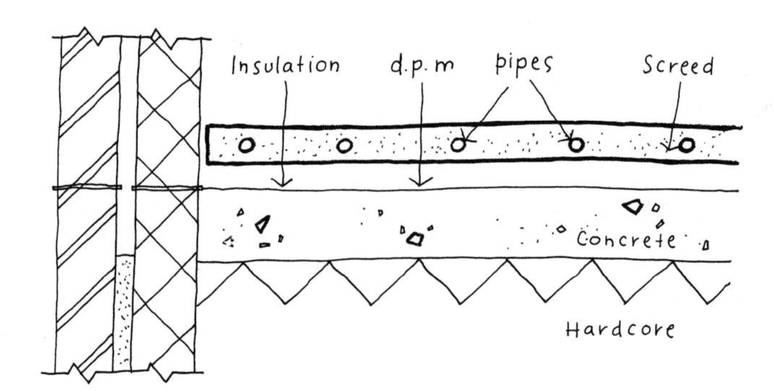

10.11

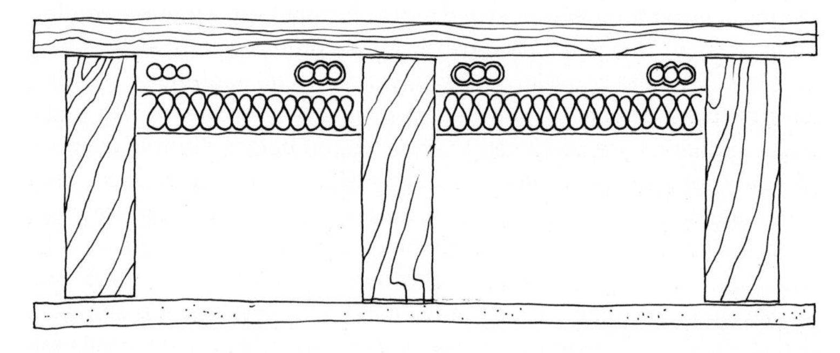

10.12

cool down). An alternative system, which is relatively new to the UK, seems to offer better control and lower installation cost. It uses triple flexible thermoplastic rubber tubing with a 7mm diameter for each tube. The system can be used with concrete floor or timber ones as illustrated in Figure 10.12.

Chapter **11**

Large scale energy systems

District heating

Large scale heating plants that serve several buildings from a single central plant is referred to as a district heating system. Such a plant can be part of a CHP system or fired using a conventional boiler. In principle, it is similar to the installation serving a single building (such as the heating system for a dwelling), but large enough in size and scale to be able to heat an estate, a whole community or even a small town.

Having a centralised plant for a large number of buildings will save space in individual buildings. There are different variations of this type of heating installations depending on their size. A block system is when a large building has a single central boiler delivering space heating and hot water to individual self-contained units. The energy delivered to users is metered and the user would pay for what they use. They also have access to control the energy output in their own space. Typical applications include blocks of flats and shopping malls. When several buildings share a centralised boiler plant, the system is known as a group system. Such a system is typical of housing estates, prisons, hospitals and holiday camps. Distribution pipe work is often underground in well insulated ducts. When a group heating system is enlarged to serve a district or small town, it is referred to as district heating. The operational principle is the same as the two previous types except that the water is pressurised to ensure efficient delivery. Strategically located heat exchangers process the pressurised water and lower its temperature from 120 °C to 80 °C at atmospheric pressure to make it safe for domestic use.

All variants of district heating described here lend themselves to be fired by renewable low impact fuels such as biomass, waste incineration and bio fuels. They can also be combined with CHP plants. Apart from conventional combustion processes, district heating systems can use alternative sources of heat such as geothermal heat, surplus or waste heat from industrial processes and solar power.

Air conditioning

Air conditioning is about creating and maintaining an internal environment at a predetermined level of air temperature and relative humidity regardless of the environmental conditions outside. Apart from the health implication of using air conditioning, which will be discussed later, it is absurd to design a building without due consideration of the external conditions simply because air conditioning can maintain the environment inside it under control. Generally, the plant includes equipment to heat, cool, reheat, humidify, dehumidify, clean and propel the air to be distributed to its destination. There are two main types of installation to be found in use: centrally located systems and packaged units.

Central systems consist of an air-handling unit strategically located around the building and providing treated air to individual rooms around the building using a series of ducts. In some instances, further local treatment of air is required at room level. These systems can use either air on its own to carry the heating/cooling or a combination of air and water. Under these circumstances, a water pipe circuit will run alongside the air duct. The air-handling unit performs a number of functions that include:

- Drawing fresh air from outside and mixing it with re-circulated air.
- Filtration of mixed air.
- Preheating the air, in winter.
- Humidifying the air, using steam or spray washing (this latter process is no longer popular as it is believed to increase the risk of bacteria).
- Eliminating excess moisture from the air.
- Chilling the air in summer, using chilled water cooled by a refrigeration unit (heat pump).
- Reheating the air, in winter, to achieve the desired temperature.
- Propelling the air using a fan with a sufficient velocity to deliver it through a system of ducts.

The diagram in Figure 11.1 illustrates the main components of an air–water system. It offers more flexibility in controlling temperature and air volume delivered to different zones of the building. The system delivers ducted air to the rooms where it is mixed with induced room air. The system requires more space for ducting and pipe work and more energy as both heating and chilling plant is required to provide energy in water to both the air-handling central plant and individual induction units for each of the rooms (or zones).

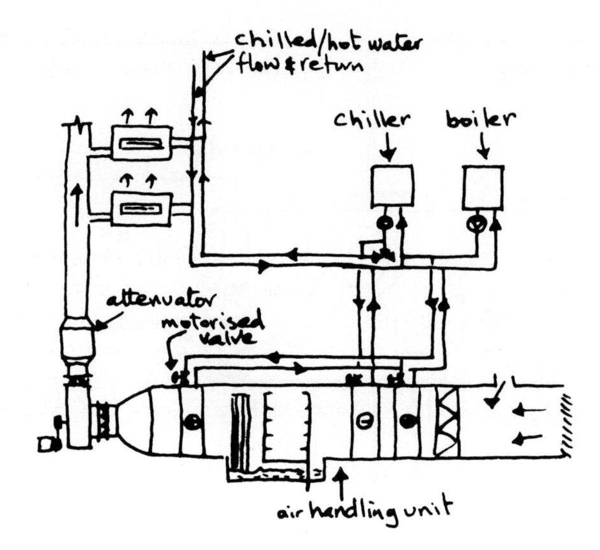

11.1

The second main type of air conditioning systems is packaged units. These are self-contained units for small to medium size applications. They offer the flexibility and low capital costs compared to central units. However, in the long term their running costs are likely to be higher. Furthermore, if they are just an add-on to an already designed building fabric, they can become an eyesore that changes the appearance of the building. An example of a packaged window unit is shown in Figure 11.2.

Air conditioning and associated services account for a large share of energy use in buildings. Given that the energy used is not renewable and the energy use is not efficient, there is huge scope for reconsidering the use of air conditioning as an absolute solution to environmental comfort. According to research into energy costs in offices, the office with highest energy cost has an energy bill 15 times that of a low energy building. Needless to say, the high cost office was an air conditioned, deep plan, over glazed office.

Apart from the energy and emission implications of using air conditioning in buildings, these systems have some health issues that the designer needs to be aware of. The first of these is sick building syndrome, which remains a mystery in terms of what actually causes it. It is recognised in terms of symptoms experienced by people who work in modern air-conditioned buildings. These symptoms include one or more of a number of ailments including headaches, skin irritations, dry throat or eyes, lethargy and loss of concentration. Although it is not fatal, it is recognised as a contributor to absenteeism and loss of efficiency.

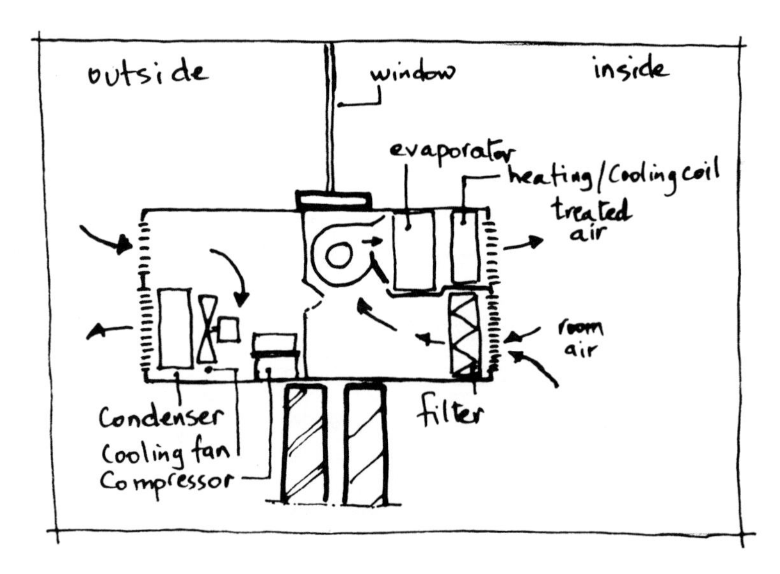

11.2

The second health-related problem associated with air-conditioned buildings is humidifier fever. According to the London Hazards Centre humidifier fever is a non-infectious building related illness. It is caused by inhaling water droplets from humidifiers contaminated by micro-organisms. The illness has been reported more in industrial buildings than offices. It was found that some micro-organisms breed during the air conditioning plant shut down at weekends and holidays. The dead husks, which dry into a fine dust, get into the air which building occupants inhale. Treating spray water in the humidifier with a biocide can be a solution. An even better one is to replace water humidifiers with steam injection humidifiers.

Legionnaires' disease is another air-conditioned buildings related illness. Unlike the previous two, this one can result, and has resulted in fatalities. The first known outbreak was in 1976, when, during an American legionnaires' convention, 29 people died, out of 182 who reported symptoms. Since then there have been many outbreaks around the world. One of the latest cases was in July 2006 in Paris, when an outbreak from a suspected cooling tower caused the death of two people. The first recorded outbreak in the UK was in Kingston Hospital in 1980, when two people were killed and nine other were infected. The bacteria that causes the illness thrives in the warm humid environment around air conditioning systems. The solution to this problem lies in abolishing wet coolers and replacing them with air-cooled condenser units. An alternative solution is to introduce a strict maintenance regime and to keep records of maintenance treatments. This has been effected through the Health and Safety Commission.

Chapter **12**

Low energy systems

Heat pumps

A heat pump is mainly a refrigeration system similar to that used in a domestic refrigerator, but produces a heating effect rather than a cooling one. The cycle consists of a condenser that gives off heat, an evaporator that takes in heat, a compressor and an expansion valve. The components are connected by tubes in which a refrigerant circulates. The compressor is the only component that uses power. The attraction of heat pumps is that first they are efficient in terms of energy generation (typically for 1 kW of electricity consumed a pump gives off/ removes some 2.5 kW of heat, and second they can be used for both heating and cooling. They can take low-grade heat from any source (air, water, earth) and can be used to produce either heating or cooling effects.

Geothermal heat pumps use the ground, which is at a near constant temperature, as a source of heat to warm up the air inside buildings when they operate in the heating mode. When they operate in the cooling mode, the ground becomes a heat sink. A geothermal heat pump has two main parts: a circuit of underground piping outside the building and a heat pump unit inside. The underground loop can be either an open or a closed system. In the case of an open system, underground water is pumped up to the heat exchanger for heat extraction and discharged either above ground (stream/pond, etc.) or back to the ground through a separate borehole. The closed loop system, which has a pipe, buried either horizontally or vertically, collects heat from the ground by means of an antifreeze solution circulating in the pipe. The solution is chilled by the heat pump's refrigeration cycle to several degrees colder than the ground temperature. The larger the temperature difference is between the ground and the solution in the pipe, the more heat is extracted. While the open system involves pumping water out of the ground and back into it, the closed system relies on continuous circulation of the liquid in a closed loop. From an ecological point of view, the latter seems to create less disruption to the ground water.

In a heating mode, heat extracted underground is carried by the antifreeze solution in the ground loop back to the heat exchanger. The heat is then passed onto the refrigerant, of the heat pump unit, which causes it to boil and become a low-temperature vapour. The antifreeze solution is pumped back to the ground to start a new cycle. The refrigerant vapour is passed onto the compressor, which causes it to reduce in volume and heat up (hot pressurised gas). The hot gas moves onto the condenser coil, where it condenses back into a liquid and gives off its heat. The heat is passed onto a suitable medium (air for warm air heating, water for space heating or a hot water system) using a heat exchanger.

The cooling cycle operates in the same way but reversing the direction of flow of the refrigerant in the heat pump unit by turning the reversing valve at 180 degrees. Under these circumstances, the two heat exchangers of the pump swap around their roles. The heat-rejecting condenser becomes an evaporator and the heat-absorbing evaporator coil becomes a condenser. Warm air from the building passes on its heat to the refrigerant via the evaporator. In addition, the refrigerant condensing in the condenser gives off the heat to the ground loop, which carries it to the ground where it is deposited. The diagram shown in Figure 12.1 illustrates the main components of a ground source heat pump.

Closed-loop ground source heat pumps have a coefficient of performance (COP) ranging from 2.5 to 4 depending on the type and efficiency of the equipment responsible for the motive power (motor, compressor, etc.). The design of heat pumps is constantly evolving and their efficiency is improving. The coefficient of performance is the ratio of energy output from the system to its energy input. For instance, a heat pump with a COP 4 would produce 4kW of heat energy for every 1kW of electric energy that the compressor consumes. It is understood, that the higher the temperature of the ground (or the source used, air or water), the more energy the pump can extract for heating or cooling, the higher its efficiency is.

The plastic pipes that make up the ground loop are placed in one of two layouts horizontal or vertical. A horizontal layout is typically found in rural areas where buildings stand in large plots of land. The pipes are buried in trenches 1.0 to 1.8 m deep. Usually the length of pipes depends on the amount of energy to be extracted and the temperature of the ground. An estimated 30m length of pipe would be needed for every 1kW of energy to be extracted. For the latest information on the sizing of the ground loop, data from installation contractors would need to be consulted.

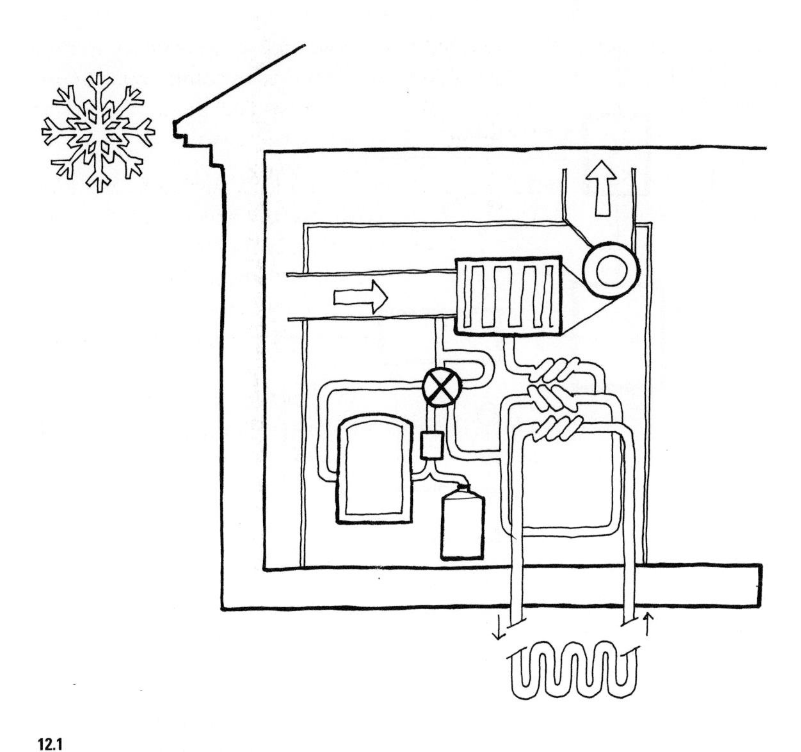

12.1

In densely built urban and suburban areas where a horizontal loop would run into the adjoining properties, a vertical layout is more appropriate. Boreholes 150mm diameter and 18 to 50m deep are drilled to house the vertical pipes. A pipe length of around 22m would be required for every 1kW of energy extracted.

Combined heat and power

Electricity generation is notoriously inefficient as large amounts of heat are released into the atmosphere in the form of hot flue gases, or as in some processes in the form of hot water from the cooling towers. Conventional power stations using generators connected to engines are only around 35 per cent efficient. Combined heat and power (CHP) is a relatively new process by which power generation and useful heat are produced in the same plant, thus increasing its efficiency. Typical applications are found in large commercial or public buildings such as factories, hospitals and hotels. These can use either gas or oil fired electricity generators.

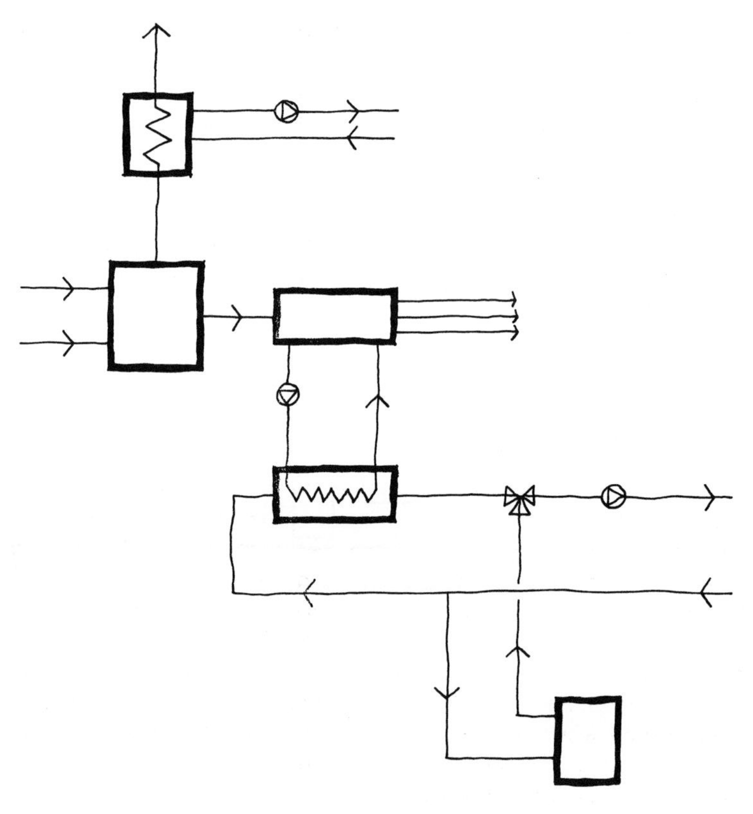

12.2

Most of the energy wastage in conventional power stations is in the generator cooling water. In CHP plants heat from either flue gases or the hot water from the cooling system, is reprocessed for heating buildings. Figure 12.2 shows a diagrammatic representation of an industrial CHP plant. Until recently, CHP plants were not viable for smaller buildings such as individual dwellings. Lately gas powered micro-CHP units have been developed, to provide domestic heating and hot water as well as some electrical power up to 3kW. Apart from scale, the main difference between industrial CHP plants and their small-scale counterparts is the type of power upon which the emphasis is placed. Industrial CHP plants are designed, primarily, to generate electricity and heat is a useful by-product. In the case of micro-CHP systems, the demand for heat is the main driver for such plants and the delivery of electricity becomes the by-product. Such systems would have even higher efficiencies than large industrial CHP plants as the transmission losses (from plant to consumer) are inexistent. Although the use of alternative green fuel types to fire micro-CHP plants is currently not viable due to transport costs to individual homes, these difficulties are likely to be surmounted, as more economic and environmental pressures would produce an increase in market take up and reduce costs. Furthermore, the use of such fuels to fire these systems would go a long way towards achieving lower carbon footprints. It is estimated that the UK has about 1,000 micro-CHP systems in operation as of 2002. These are mainly Sterling and reciprocating engine types. The support of the UK government through both legislative and financial measures is likely to create growth in this market. Some estimates put the number of UK households that can be suitable for this type of technology at 14 to 18 million.

Heat recovery

With the increased emphasis on air tightness in buildings, the need for ventilation is even greater and with it comes the penalty of heat loss by convection. The use of heat recovery ventilation would help reduce heating loads by recovering heat from outgoing warm air and channelling it back into the incoming cool fresh air using a heat exchanger of the recuperative type. Such a heat exchanger is one in which the two streams of air, for instance, are separated at all times by a solid barrier. In others words the two air streams do not mix, which is an advantage in ventilation systems as the warm exhaust air usually contains a high concentration of pollutants. A large variety of heat exchangers are found in various applications.

The one used particularly in domestic ventilation heat recovery is the plate-fin type usually found in kitchens or bathrooms. The unit is self-contained and has two sets of ducting and two fans that make a balanced ventilation system with air to air heat recovery (see Figure 12.3). The efficiency of the heat exchanger to recover thermal energy from exhaust air depends on the rate at which exhaust air is extracted from the room. The higher the rate, the quicker the air passes through the exchanger, the less time for it to extract heat. Data according to Nicholls (2002) suggest the type of relationship between extract rate and efficiency for an air to air heat recovery unit as illustrated in Figure 12.4. In mechanically ventilated dwellings (as is the case in apartments in high rise sealed towers in urban areas), instead of using separate heat recovery units for each of the rooms, a whole apartment mechanical ventilation with heat recovery is installed. The unit is small enough to be located in a typical kitchen cupboard. The system uses the same principle as the air to air heat exchanger described above. It is worth mentioning that for the heat recovery system described in this section the only components that require energy input are the fans.

The heat recovery system described above can also be found in commercial buildings, where thermal energy from exhaust air in air

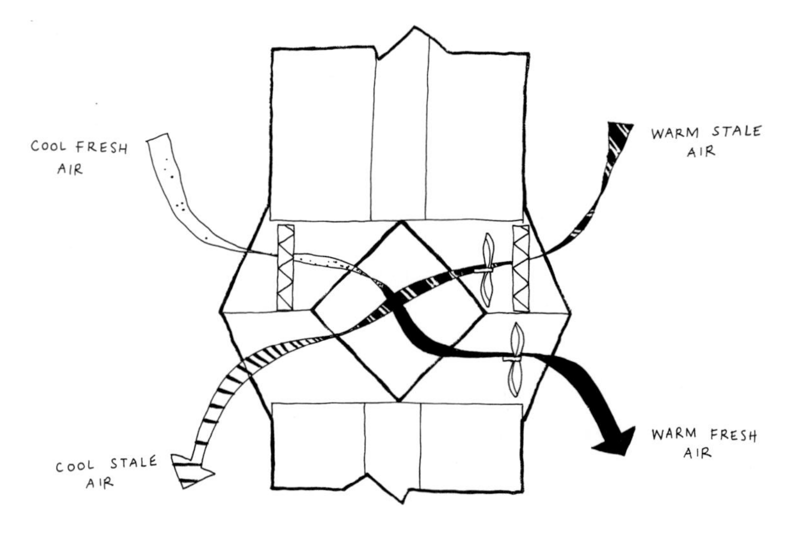

12.3

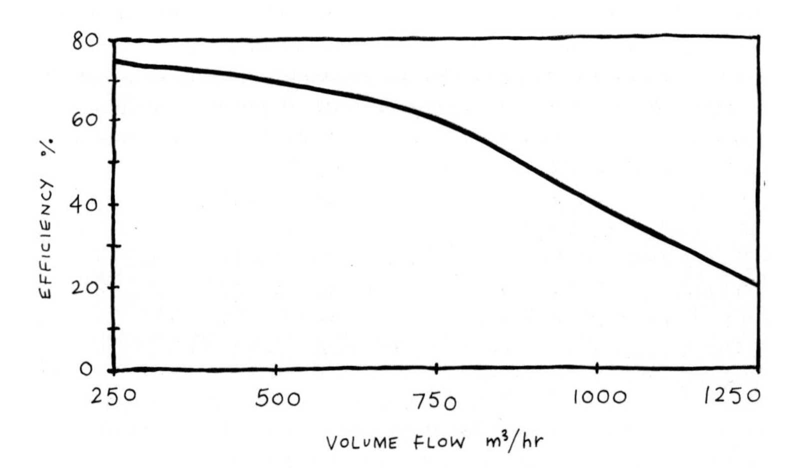

12.4

conditioning systems can be recovered. This method of heat recovery is more favourable compared to recirculation of warm exhaust air and mixing it with fresh air. Another heat recovery system used in commercial buildings makes use of thermal wheels. A thermal wheel is made up of a slow rotating wheel, on which a matrix of tubes is mounted. While the wheel rotates through the exhaust hot air and inlet cold air streams, air flows through the tubes causing heat to be exchanged

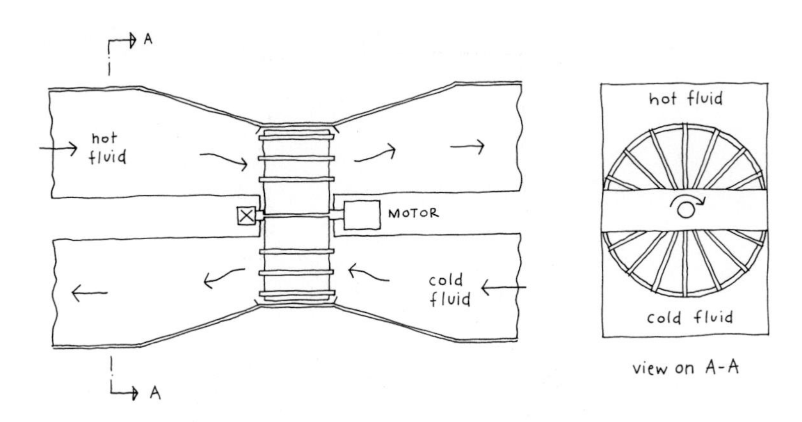

12.5

between the two streams without any mixing of fresh and used air. The diagram in Figure 12.5 illustrates the principle of such a regenerative heat recovery system. When the exhaust air passes through the upper half of the wheel the matrix of tubes is warmed up. As the wheel rotates slowly, the warm half of the matrix moves into the path of the incoming cool intake air and causes it to warm up before it is delivered into the building. A thermal wheel can have an efficiency as high as 85 per cent. This can mean a large reduction in heating loads and subsequently less energy is consumed and fewer emissions are produced. The thermal wheel has a number of advantages; including the high efficiency, low cost low energy use (in the motor) and ease of maintenance. It has the disadvantage of possible cross contamination between the two streams of air. This may not be an issue for standard commercial interiors such as shops and offices. On the other hand, it would not be wise to use such a system in a clean environment such as a hospital operating theatre, for instance.

Chapter 13

Green options

Biomass

Biomass is a term used to refer to material derived from plants and animals. Concerns about the sustainability of using conventional solid fuels have led to the development of boilers that run on biomass, which is carbon neutral, or at least, with a lower carbon footprint. Other biomass related technologies include biologically produced gases and oils. Unlike fossil fuels, fuels derived from biomass are renewable and biodegradable resulting in little harm to the environment. The use of biomass to derive usable fuels, not only helps with the energy and greenhouse gases (methane), but also contributes to solving the problem of waste management and storage. Around four-tenths of the total waste produced in the UK is agricultural or farm related (crop, animal, wood). The technology of deriving fuels and extracting energy from biomass is well known throughout the world. The discussion here is limited to some UK examples.

One of the methods of using biomass to generate energy is the burning of waste to produce either heat or electricity. This includes timber, farming and packaging waste. The burning process takes place in large-scale incinerators. Examples of such plants include the Sheffield municipal refuse incinerator that burns 120,000 tonnes of waste a year and produces 28MW of heat used in a district heating system. A second example is that of the Eye power station in Suffolk that runs on a mixture of chicken droppings, straw and wood shavings. It burns some 125,000 of chicken litter and produces 12.5MW of electricity. A secondary by-product of the plant is the reduction of nitrates leaking out of the droppings into the groundwater system if a conventional waste disposal method were used.

An alternative method to burning waste is to process it and produce pellets or briquettes of combustible material. The solid fuel produced in this way can be used either on its own or alongside other conventional fuels to fire large-scale plants generating power or electricity. Unlike the previous method of direct incineration, in this waste derived fuel production, the waste material needs to be processed, separated and carefully prepared. Although this makes it more expensive compared to waste combustion with heat recovery, it is a worthwhile process, as it meets the usual criteria: first, it generates energy from a renewable source, second, it reduces waste and third, it reduces harmful emissions (methane) which would result if the waste were disposed of in landfill sites. Several local authorities in the UK have invested in refuse derived fuel plants. According to Eastop *et al.* (1995) it is estimated that the pay-back period on a £400,000 installation would be less than two years.

Waste derived fuels can be used to fire domestic heating systems. Two such systems are wood pellets and wood chip boilers. Wood pellets are manufactured from waste timber (shavings, sawdust, etc.) from sustainably-managed forests. They have a higher density and lower moisture content than wood chips. Although they are more expensive in comparison, they require less storage space and produce less ash. Boilers running on wood pellets lend themselves to automatic feed and control of heat output in the same way as conventional boilers. Wood chips are processed from waste timber products and purpose grown forests in the same way as wood pellets. The method of processing, however, is less rigorous resulting in irregular shapes and sizes and higher moisture content. This makes them cheaper than pellets but on the other hand, they require more storage space. They do not lend themselves to the automation of boiler operation and they produce more ash.

The exploitation of waste from landfill sites for methane gas represents one of the promising potentials for biomass. Burying municipal and industrial waste in landfill sites is a common practice in the UK. When organic matter from the waste decomposes in the absence of air (oxygen), methane gas is produced. Not only is this gas one of the greenhouse gases, but it also represents a hazard as it can cause explosions. Although exploitation of methane gas from landfill sites in the UK began back in 1970s, its application has been slow despite the obvious advantages it presents. Other methods of producing biogas include the processing of energy crops or sewage waste in anaerobic digesters. The gas obtained this way has a higher energy content than that obtained from landfill sites. The gas obtained from the various processes described above is usually used in CHP plants.

Apart from waste based solid and gas fuels, the production of biomass related fuels extends to the use of 'virgin' biodegradable material such as crops grown specifically to extract fuels. Such crops include flax seed and rape seed (Europe), corn and soyabean (USA) and sugar cane (Brazil). These crops can be processed to produce biogas as described for methane derived from waste products. They can also be used to produce oils that fire diesel engines.

Solar water heating systems

Making use of the available solar energy to reduce the building energy loads takes the form of passive and active measures. Passive design strategies have already been discussed elsewhere in this volume and in Volume1. The purpose of this section is to discuss some of the active approaches to solar heating.

The effectiveness of any device capturing solar energy depends primarily on the availability of solar radiation. This varies according to the geographical location, time of year and orientation. Furthermore, one has to consider the daily variations in solar radiation. For detailed solar data the reader is referred to specialist climatic data sources. In the UK, the Chartered Institute of Building Services Engineers is the body behind the publication of such data. For the purpose of this discussion, the data shown in Figure 13.1, reproduced from Nicholls (2002), is used to explain the general trend for solar radiation intensities. The following comments would be useful to the reader:

- From March to September, a horizontal surface would receive more radiation than any of the vertical surfaces. This is explained by the high solar angles during the warm season, as the sun tends to be high in the sky (58° at noon on 21 June). The low solar altitude (12° at noon on 21 December) in winter means that the vertical surface receives less solar radiation.
- The south facing surface receives solar radiation continuously throughout the year. However, in the height of the summer (June),

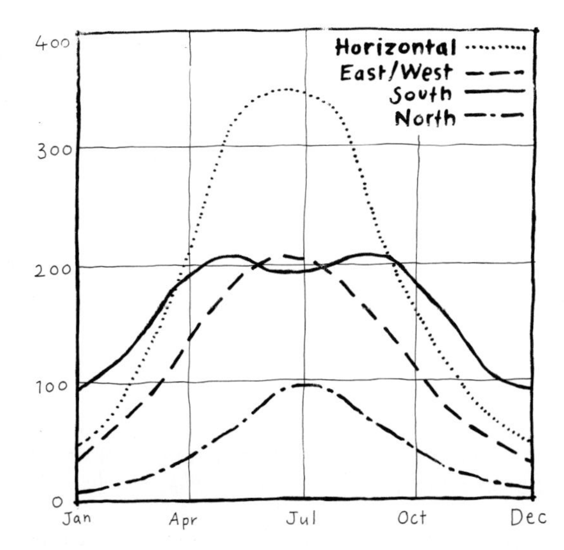

13.1

the east and west facing surfaces receive higher intensity of solar radiation as their daily exposure time is longer.

- East and west facing surfaces have the same pattern of average daily solar intensities. However, it is worth bearing in mind that when one of them is exposed to solar radiation, the other one would be in the shade. On these surfaces, the intensity peaks during June only to drop off quickly to below those levels for the south facing and vertical surfaces.
- The north facing façade is characterised by a low intensity curve. It receives the least amount of solar radiation at all times of the year. This is so as direct solar radiation can only reach this surface at low intensity times during the early morning and late evening during the summer. For a large part of the year the north facing side of a building is in the shade.

When deciding on the orientation of any solar energy collection devices, the patterns of solar intensities described above ought to be taken into account. Usually a solar collector is orientated within 30° to the east and west of south for it to benefit from the majority of the available solar radiation.

The uptake of solar water heating in the UK has always been hindered by economic arguments such as capital costs and payback periods – if only the damage to the planet had a 'penalty' attached to it. That would change the equation of the payback formula. Although by today's prices, a solar hot water system would have around a 15 year payback period, the last few years have seen a change in attitudes and water heating using solar collectors is becoming popular among domestic users in the UK.

Solar water heating is more practical and achievable than solar space heating. This is because space heating is required when solar radiation is at its lowest intensity, while the need for water heating is an issue even in summer. A typical solar water heating system can provide enough hot water for a family of four, during the summer period. In winter, however, such a system can only be used to supplement a conventional hot water system and help it reduce energy use. Although such a system can be sized large enough to produce enough hot water in winter, it would not be economical in summer. This is the case because the heat output from such a collector would be greater than that required for the hot water in the building. Two types of collectors are found in practice: the flat plate and the evacuated tube collectors. Flat plate collectors are rectangular modules with a typical size of 0.6m by 1.5m. They can be combined in any number to suit the application and connected in series. The main components of the collector consist of a black painted or coated metal plate (steel or aluminium), tubes for fluid circulation, an insulation board and glass cover on top. The components are held in place by a metal frame that allows the collector to be mounted on the rooftop. Figure 13.2 shows a typical section through a flat plate collector. The glass cover allows solar radiation to pass through and traps the heat creating a greenhouse effect. The collector plate absorbs both direct radiation and heat trapped in the cavity above it. The pipes behind the plate heat up by conduction and transmit heat onto the fluid. This can be either water in the case of direct systems or an antifreeze mixture in the case of indirect systems. Direct systems circulate the water directly from the hot water cylinder as illustrated in Figure 13.3. These collectors are easy to install which makes them attractive to the DIY enthusiast.

Evacuated tube collectors, though they work on the same principles of absorbing solar radiation, use a different technology. They are more efficient and cost more than the flat plate collectors. The collector consists of a glass tube housing an absorbing long narrow plate with a fluid tube running down its centre. Instead of using thermal insulation to keep the heat in, the glass tube has some of its air removed. This helps reduce convective heat loss. The effect of this, combined with the low emmissivity coating on the plate, makes this type of collector the most efficient. This type of collector is ideal for climatic regions with diffuse solar radiation (i.e. overcast sky conditions prevail). The collectors can be connected to a header tube to form an array of tube collectors. Figure 13.4 shows the basic component of an evacuated tube collector. The heat distribution system is the same as that for the flat plate collector. For both types of collectors, a pump is generally required to ensure the correct flow of water. The pump can be powered by a photovoltaic array mounted on the roof.

Photovoltaic cells

Photovoltaic cells or PV for short, work on the principle of converting light energy into electric current. Two types of cells are found in practice. Crystalline systems, the more efficient and expensive ones, use the electronic properties of crystals to generate direct electric current from the

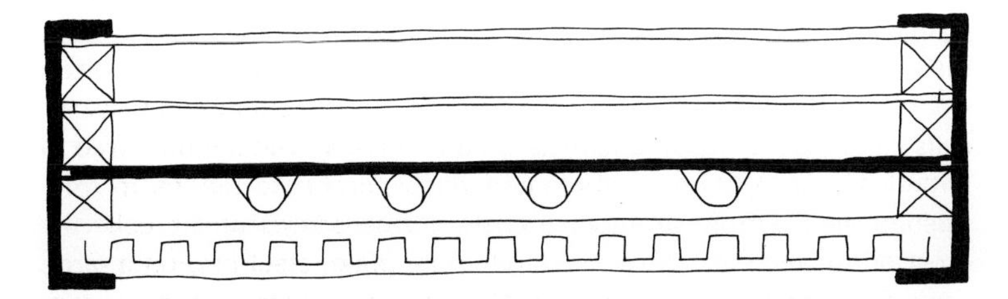

13.2

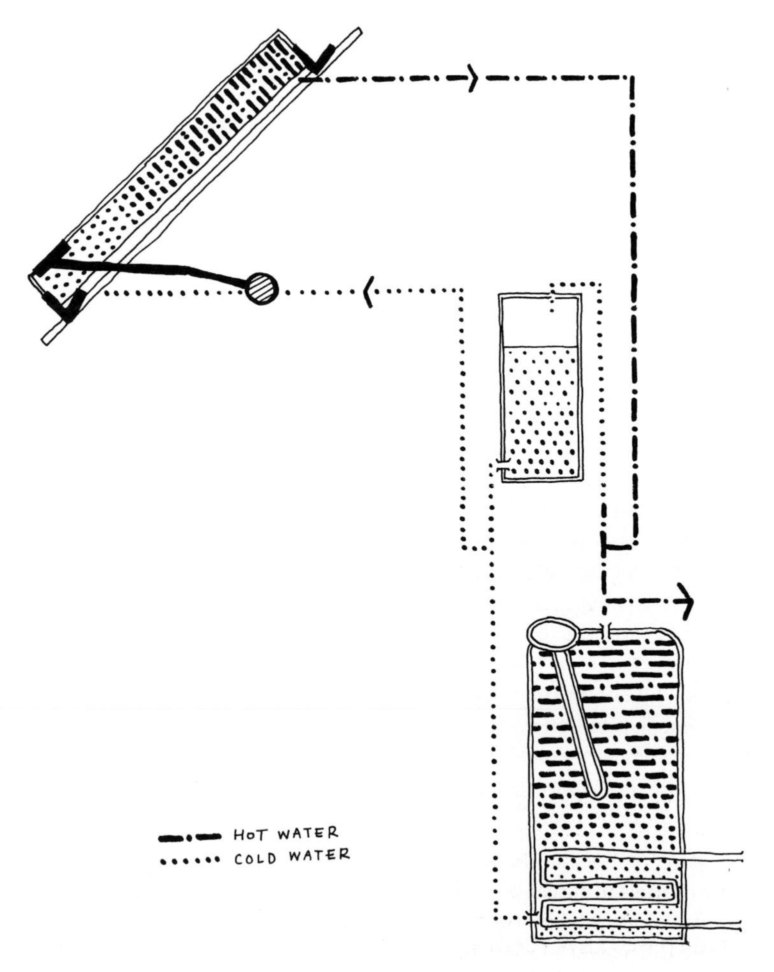

13.3

light energy falling on the cells. Thin film systems make use of the technology of semi-conductors to generate the direct current from the light energy. In comparison, these are less efficient but incur less capital cost. For both systems, if they are to be connected to the electricity grid, the current needs to be converted from DC to AC using an inverter. Apart from exporting electricity to the grid the power generated by PV cells can be used instantaneously on a low voltage circuit or stored in batteries if the location is remote and there is no connection to the grid. Despite their current prohibitive costs, PV cells represent one of the most promising ways forward to generate green electricity on a large scale. They have no environmental impact (noise, emissions, etc) nor any moving parts, and can be integrated into the building fabric in an

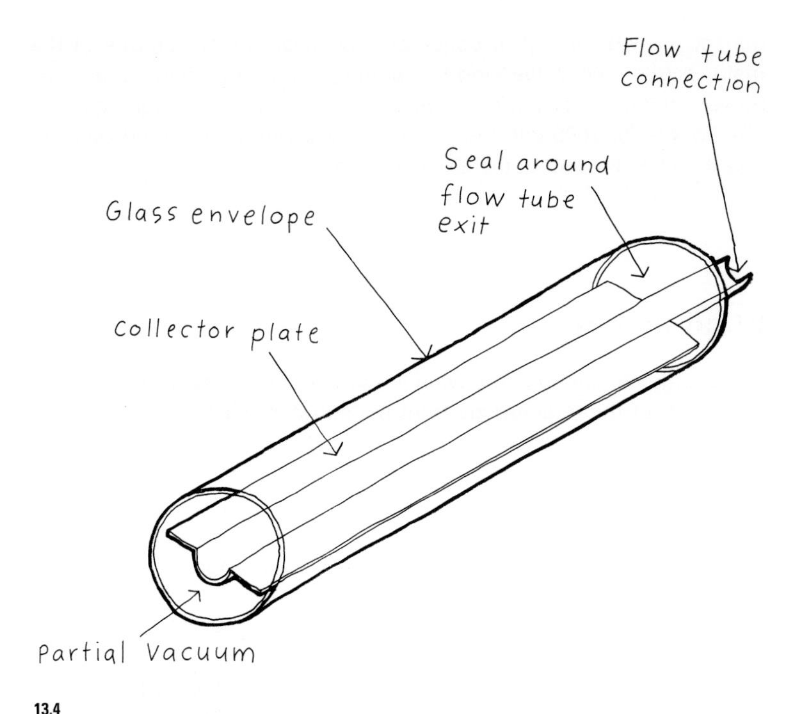

13.4

aesthetically pleasing way. This latter method of using them would improve their economic viability as they can be used as a cladding system for the building. Photovoltaic cells are arranged in arrays to form panels to suit applications of almost any size. They can be mounted on flat roofs, pitched roofs and even on vertical surfaces (as in the case of the CIS Tower in Manchester, UK). In the case of new build or major upgrading of the building fabric, the PV arrays can be used as roof coverings instead of conventional tiles/slates or to replace cladding panels. The harnessing of solar energy by means of PV throughout the world is on the increase year by year. The three major producers of PV power are Germany, Japan and the US. Between them they have 90 per cent of the world's solar electric capacity. Germany was the fastest growing PV market in 2005, but since then new initiatives in Portugal and Australia are likely to change the market trends. According to 2005 statistics, the world's output from PV installations was around 703MW. However, this is only a drop in the ocean as it represented 0.04 per cent of the global demand at the time. Although the picture has changed somehow, since then, the proportion of PV based electricity to the global demand is still minute. The German market, with over 1,000MW of installed capacity in 2006, owes its success to some deregulation legislation introduced in 2004. The other big market, Japan, which led the table in 2004 and second only to Germany in 2006, encouraged market growth through a policy of subsidies. The UK as one of the major economies in the world is lagging behind the major economic powers and other countries whose economies are of a lower standing. The figures for 2006 put it in eleventh place with an installed capacity less than 0.5 per cent of the German capacity.

Wind power

The energy contained in the wind is estimated between 1 per cent and 3 per cent of the total energy from the sun that reaches earth. At first glance, this may not sound a great deal. Comparing it to the energy converted into biomass through photosynthesis, it is between 50 and 100 times more. The energy crisis of the 1970s triggered a wave of interest in converting wind power into electricity using rotating turbines. Some countries have made considerable progress on the road to replacing fossil fuels. According to 2006 statistics, 20 per cent of Denmark's electricity use is from wind power, while those for Spain and Germany stand at 9 per cent and 7 per cent respectively. In terms of installed capacity at a global level, wind generated electricity accounts for 1 per cent. However this is likely to change as the installed capacity is growing at a steady rate.

The UK wind power installed capacity is still lagging behind that of comparable economies. While Germany tops the global league with 20.6 giga watts (GW) in 2006, the UK came in at eighth place with a capacity of just under 2GW. One of the obstacles to wind energy proliferation is believed to be the attitudes towards wind turbines particularly when large-scale wind farms are located onshore.

13.5

A wind turbine consists of rotating propeller that turns an electricity generator using a gearbox. These are mounted on top of a mast some 25–30m high. The high position of the turbine gives ground clearance and puts the propeller in the path of high wind velocity. The diagram in Figure 13.5 shows a typical wind turbine. A number of turbines grouped together form a wind farm. The distance between turbines is around 10 blade diameters. A typical wind turbine would have an output that ranges from 0.5MW to 1.5MW. Depending on the number of turbines in a wind farm and their individual output, a total output is likely to be upward of 10MW. The most challenging of issues facing wind generated electricity, is the lack of consistency and continuity of airflow, hence the intermittency of power generation. Although a wind turbine deals with changes in wind direction, for it to be able to cope with variation in its output, the power generated needs to be either stored in batteries or fed back to a mains grid. Given the extra costs involved in the installation of offshore wind farms, these need to be of a larger scale than onshore ones for them to be competitive. On the other hand, offshore wind farms have a much greater exposure to wind and do not cause annoyance to the general public. Given that the UK is surrounded by sea, offshore wind farms could make a serious and considerable contribution to the green energy basket.

For small-scale wind derived electricity generation, other planning and safety issues come into play. In densely populated areas where buildings are close to each other, having wind turbines with long rotating blades is not a practical idea. In rural areas where there is sufficient distance between buildings wind turbines could be an option. Newer smaller wind turbines can now be purchased from local DIY stores. They can simply be plugged in to the mains and as long as they are running they offset electricity consumption. An alternative way of using small-scale wind turbines is to connect them to a hot water system with a backup from a conventional boiler. When enough electricity is generated to heat up the water, the boiler automatically shuts off. At times when the energy generated is not enough to keep the water at the required temperature, the generator's output is used to preheat the water in the storage cylinder and the boiler would provide the rest of the heating load. Even under these conditions, there may be times when the generator's output would exceed the load of the hot water system. Having the turbine plugged in to the mains would enable it to export the surplus to the grid and offset it against the electricity consumption when the turbine's output is low or absent.

Water power

When water is on the move, its kinetic energy can be converted into other forms of energy. Traditionally, water wheels were used to convert water energy into mechanical energy to turn flour mills. The generation of electricity is a well known and used method of energy production. Although different methods can be used to harness water power and convert it into electricity, the most widely used method is hydroelectric power from dams. In this process, water held in a reservoir behind a dam is allowed to flow from high to low level through ducts containing turbines. The kinetic power of the gushing water causes the turbines to turn and drive a series of generators. The energy extracted from the water depends on the volume of water behind the dam, the height from which the water flows (until reaching the turbine) and the water's outflow. Sometimes the topography of the site would create the right conditions for hydroelectric generation. Such an example is the highlands of Scotland where plenty of rainfall combined with height differences provides an ideal location for hydroelectric generation. Hydroelectric plants contribute 2 per cent of the UKelectricity supply.

This is quite a small proportion for a country that is considered the birthplace of commercial hydroelectric generation. Cragside in Rothbury, England was completed back in 1870. Compare the UK position to the global one and a difference is shown. Electricity generated from hydropower accounts for 19 per cent of world electricity and leads the renewable energy table.

Hydroelectric plants have economic and environmental advantages. The operating cost of these plants is immune to fuel cost increases, as it does not use any. Furthermore, the labour costs are minimal given that plants are fully automated and require few personnel during operating hours. Even the capital costs involved in the construction of these plants are reduced when the dam is used for other purposes (irrigation, flood control, water supply, leisure, etc.). The fact that hydroelectric generation does not involve the burning of fossil fuels, they make no contribution to carbon emission. On the other hand, if these plants are on a large scale, they can cause environmental damage to surrounding aquatic ecosystems and can create problems to fauna and flora both upstream and downstream as well as population displacement. Despite all these challenges, hydroelectric generation provides an opportunity to generate renewable energy particularly if some of those technical and environmental challenges are being considered. It has predictable outputs, little or no greenhouse emissions and no waste.

Generating electricity using the kinetic energy of seawater when moving due to tides and currents is another way of exploiting the power of water. Two methods are used for power generation, tidal stream systems and barrages. The first method involves the use of kinetic energy from water currents to power turbines immersed in the sea. Underwater turbines work on the same principle as wind turbines. However, with the density of water many hundred times that of air, they generate significant amounts of energy. When using this method of generation, the choice of location is important, as the turbines need to be placed in the way of fast currents. On the other hand, their output is easier to manage, as the movement of currents tends to be predictable. This technology is still in its infancy and commercial prototypes of various designs are being tested. In 2003, a 300 kW rotor was tested off the coast of Devon, UK. The system has an 11m diameter rotor that works with the tide in one direction. A larger capacity twin rotor turbine has been scheduled for testing in September 2007 in Northern Ireland. It has a capacity of 1.2MW and will be connected to the grid. Further development of the technology is under way with a view to testing a small 'farm' of tidal turbines. Unlike hydroelectric generation, the use of underwater turbines does not cause any disruption to the ecosystem.

The second method of tidal power generation involves the use of barrages just as in hydroelectric generation, but this time the location of the 'dam' is on an estuary. The barrage traps the water in a basin. As the water level on the other side of the basin drops at low tide, a height difference is created and used to get the flowing water to turn turbines and generate electricity. Just like dams on rivers, tidal barrage systems can disturb the estuarine ecosystem if they are on a large scale. The largest installation of this type is on the river Rance, in France, which has been in operation since 1967. It has an installed peak power of 240MW and an annual average of 68MW, which is equivalent to a total annual output of 600GWh. The UK has a huge potential for tidal power. The river Severn on its own has an estimated maximum capacity of 8,600MW.

Converting the power of surface waves into either mechanical or electrical energy is another way of exploiting the kinetic energy of water. The technology of wave power is still at an early stage of its development, but it certainly offers the potential for another clean energy option for the future. There are numerous systems of extracting wave power being developed throughout the world. Two of these, that seem to show more promise, are the Pelamis system and the AquaBuoy device. The Pelamis wave energy converter is a floating device made up of articulated sections that move with the wave motion. The resistance to motion between the sections creates pressure that drives a hydraulic motor via a ram. A commercial installation with a capacity of 2.25MW is being tested off the Portuguese coast. The first UK based wave farm projected has secured funding from the Scottish Executive in 2007 and will be built at the European Marine Energy Centre in Orkney. Its capacity is estimated at 3MW. Future plans for Scottish wave energy is to have 30MW farms that can provide electricity for 20,000 homes from each farm. The AquaBuoy device converts the vertical kinetic energy of the wave into electricity using a turbine driving a generator. The first experimental installation of this kind is being constructed in Portugal. The demonstration plant has a 2MW capacity and the project, which is supported by industry and the European Commission, has plans for a large scale commercial installation with a capacity of 100MW.

Generation of electricity from the kinetic energy of water represents a feasible alternative to fossil fuel derived energy. It is clean, efficient and its ecological impact can be minimised if the size of installations and their locations (submerged rotors, dam based turbines etc.) are properly managed.

Fuel cells

A fuel cell can be thought of as battery. However, unlike a battery, a fuel cell does not run down or require recharging as it will produce energy in the form of electricity and heat as long as there is a fuel supply. The basic construction of a fuel cell consists of two electrodes surrounding an electrolyte. Oxygen from the air passes over one electrode (cathode) and hydrogen (from any hydrocarbon fuel) over the second electrode (anode), generating electricity, water and heat (see Figure 13.6). Unlike the internal combustion engine, despite using fossil and biomass derived fuels to extract hydrogen, the fuel cell does not carry the penalty of harmful emissions and generates heat and water as well as electricity. Although the science behind fuel cells has been well known for over 150 years, building efficient and inexpensive fuel cells is far from resolved. The technology is still at its developmental stage albeit there are small scale experimental applications. In the UK, the use of this technology started appearing at the beginning of this decade. There are currently around a dozen projects using fuel cell technology with more planned for the future. The trials that began in 2004, for a fuel cell powered house, are considered to be the world's first of their kind for a domestic application. The cells were used to supply dwellings, owned by the Black Country Housing Group in Telford, UK, with both electricity and hot water. Each unit delivers 4.4KW of power. Research is continuing to improve the efficiency of cells and the methods of extracting hydrogen. Despite it being at an early stage of its development, the fuel cell technology offers a huge potential to generate green energy.

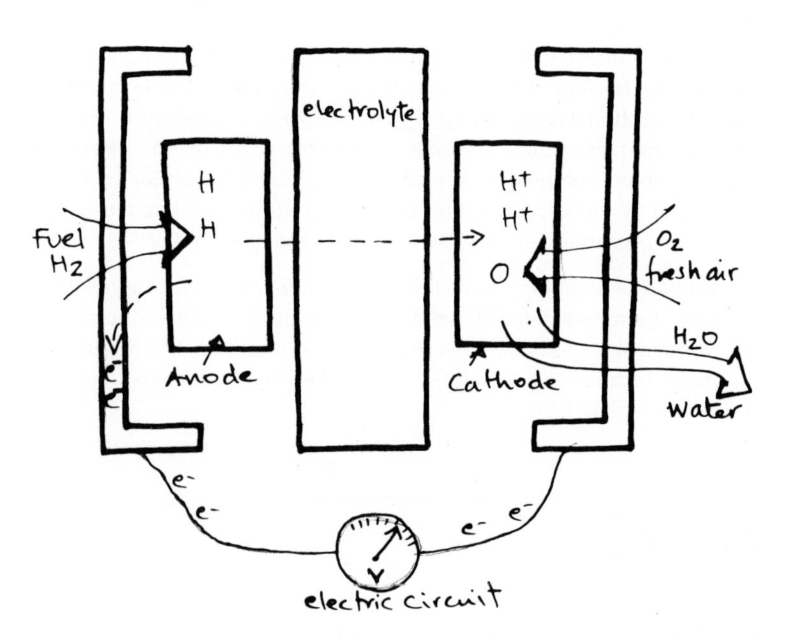

13.6

The future

After the publication of the IPCC report in 2007, even the most cynical of doubters would set aside their doubt about the effect of greenhouse gases on climate change. While a decade ago the merits of sustainability were more of a wish to strive to accomplish, the weight of both argument and public opinion makes it a necessity for the preservation of the planet for future generations that sustainability is becoming a way of life. It is no longer tenable that this issue is merely the concern of designers but rather a way of life that shapes policies and informs individual behaviour. That said, designers and scientists have a social and moral responsibility to lead the way.

The various chapters in this section have described, briefly, some of the systems by which, energy is generated, used and distributed in buildings. Although there is recognition, even among the most hardened of environmental campaigners, that fossil fuel will still be used while there are resources; there is now the realisation that those resources are running out fast. The need to find alternative sources of energy has never been greater. We are fortunate as science and technology are on our side. One has only to look at what has been achieved in the field of low waste low carbon, and even no carbon energy generation during the last two decades, to appreciate that technological change is possible. However, technological advances on their own are not going to give the answers, if decision makers, designers and clients are not onboard. Looking at examples where green technology energy generation has been a success (Germany, Japan, etc.), the role of decision makers is crucial, whether be it through market regulation, legislation, investment or a combination of these. As designers, we need to be imaginative and bold in our thinking in order to present clients with design solutions that are ecologically sensitive, affordable and inspiring. It is our responsibility to act today in order for our grandchildren to have a future.

Part **3**

Bibliography

Baker, N. and Steemers, K. *Energy and Environment in Architecture, A Technical Design Guide*, E & FN Spon (2000).

Building Research Energy Conservation Support Unit (BRECSU), Energy Consumption Guide No 10, DOE (1990).

Burberry, P. *Environment and Services*, 8th edn, Longman (1997).

Eastop, T.D. and Croft, D.R. *Energy Efficiency for Engineers and Technologists*, Longman (1995).

Frazer, D.W., Tsai, T.R., Orenstein, W., Parkin, W.E., Beecham, S.J., Sharrar, R.G., Harris, J., Mallinson, G.F., Martin, S.M., McDale, J.E., Shepard, C.C., Bracham, P.S. Legionnaires' disease: description of an epidemic of pneumonia. *New England Journal of Medicine*, 297: 1189–97 (1977).

Greeno, R. *Building Services, Technology and Design*, Longman (1997).

Hall, F. and Greeno, R. *Building services Handbook*, 3rd edn, Elsevier (2005).

IPCC, Summary for policymakers, in *Climate Change 2007: The Physical Science Basis*, contribution of Working Group I to the Fourth Assessment Report of the Intergovernmental Panel on Climate Change, (Solomon, S., Qin, D., Manning, M., Chen, Z., Marquis, M., Averyt, K.B., Tignor M. and Miller H.L. (eds), Cambridge University Press, Cambridge, United Kingdom and New York) USA, (2007).

Nicholls, R. *Low Energy Design*, Interface Publishing (2002).

Smith, P. and Pitt, A. *Concepts in Practice: Energy, Building for the Third Millennium*, Batsford (1997).

Webliography

www.emc.org.uk (accessed on 25 July 2007).

www.lhc.org.uk (accessed on 25 July 2007).

Part 4
Buildings and lighting design

Chapter **14**

Light, vision and colour

Introduction

Architecture and light are inextricably linked. The form of a building is first perceived by the light from the sun and the sky that is reflected from the building's external surfaces. The aesthetic appearance and emotional sensation of an internal space are influenced by and interpreted through the interplay of light, colour and texture. Le Corbusier said that 'architecture is the masterly, correct and magnificent play of masses brought together in light' and many great architects, such as Louis Kahn and Tadao Ando, have used light as a fundamental design element in their buildings. Architectural lighting is both an art and a science, requiring an understanding of not only the physical properties of natural and artifical light sources but also the visual effects the lighting will create when introduced into a space. In this chapter the basic principles of light, vision, and colour are described.

Visible light

Visible light is part of a much broader span of radiation called the electromagnetic spectrum. This spectrum ranges from very short wavelength gamma rays (~10^{-12}m) to very long radio waves (~1000m). Visible light is in the wavelength range 380 (violet) to 770 (red) nanometres or nm (where a nanometre is 10^{-9}m). This range of wavelengths is recognised and interpreted by the eye-brain system to produce the sensation of vision. The choice of this spectral range for vision is evolutionary – the sun's spectrum at sea level is most intense at these wavelengths, and so the eye–brain system has adapted to work most efficiently in this wavelength range (see Figure 14.1).

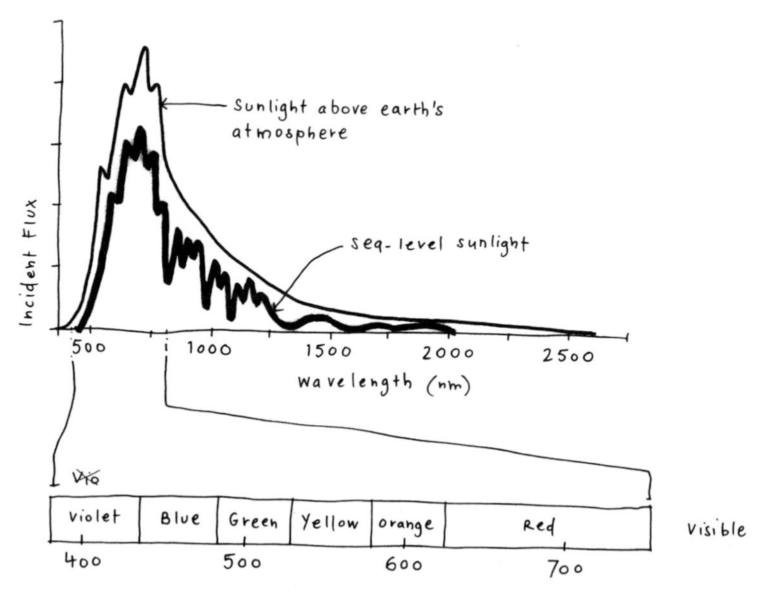

14.1

Beyond the violet end of the visible spectrum is ultraviolet (UV) light in the wavelength ranges from 100 to 400nm. Although it is invisible to the human eye UV can do damage to skin (sunburn) and to organic materials (fading carpets, curtains and artwork). It is particularly important to control UV exposure in museums and art galleries in order to protect exhibits, which can create a conflict with a design aim to light these spaces naturally. Beyond the red end of the visible spectrum lies infrared radiation (IR). This is also invisible to the eye and is experienced as heat. Many light sources will produce UV and IR in addition to visible light. Since it is only the visible light that is actually wanted then these other radiations, particularly the IR, only serve to reduce the efficiency of an artificial light source when it converts electricity to light.

A basic lighting system illuminating a surface, as shown in Figure 14.2, will contain four elements: the light that is emitted from a source, the direction that the light travels in, the light that strikes the surface and the appearance of that surface arising from the light that is reflected from it. Each of these components is quantified by specific lighting units.

Luminous flux: this is the total amount of light emitted in all directions by a source and has the unit of lumen (lm). A 100W incandescent light bulb will typically have a luminous flux of approximately 1,500 lumens,

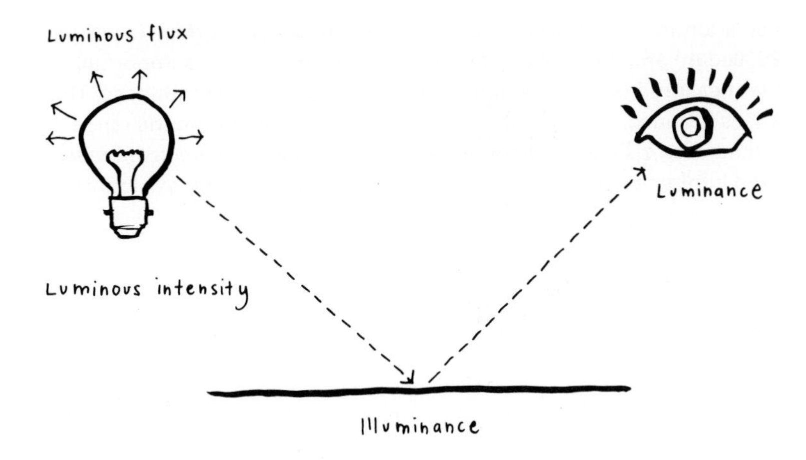

14.2

a 100W fluorescent tube might emit around 8,000 lumens and a 400W metal halide lamp's output will be over 40,000 lumens.

Luminous intensity: this is the amount of luminous flux flowing in a particular direction and has the unit of candela (cd). In terms of a lighting scheme it is obviously important to know how much light will reach different surfaces in a space. For example, a bulb in a spotlight reflector might have the same luminous flux as a bulb in a diffusing lamp shade. They will emit the same number of lumens but the spotlight will produce a very bright light in a narrow beam whilst the other bulb will shine less brightly but in all directions.

Illuminance: this is the amount of luminous flux shining on a surface area and has the unit of lux (lx). One lux represents one lumen of light shining evenly over 1m^2 of surface. Illuminance is one of the easiest and most relevant lighting terms to measure and it is widely used when specifying the task lighting requirements for a space. The external illuminance on the ground from an overcast sky is around 5,000 lux and from a bright sunny sky around 100,000 lux. The internal illuminances for a building will typically be: 50 lux (bedroom), 100 lux (general room lighting), 500 lux (general office) and 1000 lux (detailed visual tasks).

Luminance: this is the measured brightness of a surface and has the unit of candela per m^2 (cd/m^2). It indicates the amount of light that is reflected by the surface or emitted by a light source. The luminance is not a fixed entity but is dependent upon the amount of light illuminating the surface, the angle at which the surface is viewed and the reflective properties of the surface. White paper under office lighting may have a luminance of approximately 100cd/m^2 whilst grey paper under the same conditions may have a luminance of 50cd/m^2. An overcast sky has a luminance of 3000cd/m^2; a fluorescent lamp's surface is around 8000cd/m^2 and the sun's surface is 1,650 million cd/m^2. As important as the measured brightness (luminance) is the *perceived* brightness. This arises because, as will be discussed later, the eye adapts to the range of luminances visible in a field of view. A car headlight has a fixed measured luminance but will be *perceived* to be much brighter at night than in the day due to the contrast with the dark surroundings.

Vision

The physical world is captured by the eye as light enters through the pupil, is focused by a lens onto a surface at the back of the eye called the retina, which converts the light into signals that are transmitted to and interpreted by the brain. An analogy is sometimes (incorrectly) drawn between the human eye and a camera in that both have apertures, lenses and photosensitive receivers. However, whereas a camera will record what it sees the eye–brain system is driven to try and interpret whatever it observes in terms of context, experience and expectation. This need for the eye–brain system to try and make sense of whatever it sees is the basis of many optical illusions. In the Kanizsa triangle, shown in Figure 14.3, a white triangle appears to overlay the other shapes but it does not actually exist – cover the three spherical shapes and the triangle disappears.

For the shapes shown in Figure 14.4 the eye-brain system cannot decide which is the foreground and background and so switches between seeing the silhouettes of two heads and an ornate vase.

The retina consists of light receptors called cones and rods. There are approximately 6 million cone receptors in the retina and they are clustered around the centre of the retina and operate during good lighting conditions (photopic vision), such as in the day. They are colour sensitive, being most responsive to yellow-green wavelengths of light (the most abundant in the solar spectrum). Rod receptors operate during low light conditions (scotopic vision), such as at night. There are approximately 100 million rods located around the periphery of the retina. Although rods are more sensitive than cones they are not colour sensitive – their main function from an evolutionary point of view was to see potential danger rather than appreciate an object.

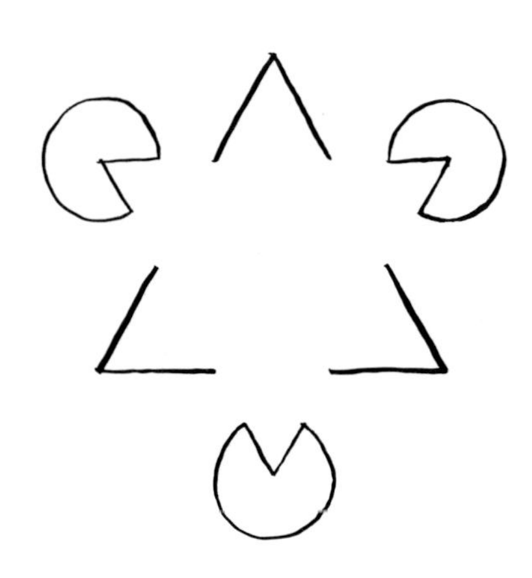

14.3

When the eye views a scene it may see a large variety of luminances or brightnesses, for example a bright sunlit window in a dark coloured wall. The eye can cope with a certain range of brightness but if the contrast between the bright and dark areas is too large then the sensation of glare will occur. There are two types of glare – disability glare and discomfort glare. Disability glare affects the ability to see objects in detail and often arises from reflections off surfaces. Common examples of disability glare include reflections from glass cabinets housing exhibits in museums and images of surroundings reflected off a computer screen. Discomfort glare causes visual discomfort and may be the result of a very bright object in the field of view, such as an unshielded light bulb or the sun seen through a window. Minor levels of glare can be irritating but at high levels glare can impede performance or even endanger people as they move around unfamiliar spaces. Therefore, one very important aim in a lighting design is to try and control the range of brightness likely to be experienced by a building user.

14.4

Another major lighting design consideration is adaptation. This is the process by which the eye adjusts to varying lighting levels as a person moves around a space. In bright light the eye's pupil will contract to reduce the amount of light entering the eye (a minor adaptation mechanism) and receptors on the retina chemically reduce their sensitivity (the major adaptation mechanism). Conversely, under dark lighting conditions the pupil will dilate and the retina's receptors will alter to become more sensitive. All adaptation processes take a finite time – when a light is switched off and a room goes dark then it will take a few minutes before rod vision is established and shapes can be perceived. However, when a light is switched on in a dark room then cone vision activates quickly, normally within a few seconds, and good vision is restored. During both dark and light adaptation the eye's ability to see is impaired, and this is obviously a potentially dangerous situation for a building user. Consequently, one of the key lighting design aims is to provide space and time for people to adapt to changing lighting levels. For example, in cinemas or art galleries lighting levels should gradually decrease between external entrances and the viewing spaces accompanied, preferably, by ramped rather than stepped walkways. The architect Louis Kahn, who was a master of using light in his architecture, planted trees with high canopies in front of the entrance to the Kimbell Art Museum in Fort Worth, Texas to provide shade as the first stage of the adaptation process when moving from the bright Texas exterior to the much darker museum galleries.

Colour

Colour is an important consideration in lighting design, both in terms of the colours used on the surfaces of a space and the colour properties of the natural and artificial light sources used to illuminate that space. Colour can have a psychological influence on space perception - for example, dull reds create a warm and relaxing sensation whilst blue-whites appear cool and hygienic. Colour can also be used to create visual interest or to highlight specific features. Classification systems for colour need to deal with two conditions – the colour of surfaces and the colour of light sources.

Surface colour classification systems often rely upon three components to describe the colour. The Munsell System, which was fully discussed in Chapter 12 of Volume 1 of the *Technologies of Architecture* series, uses the parameters *hue*, *value* and *chroma*. Hue is the subjectively dominant spectral colour of the surface. There are ten Hue bands - five main groups (red R, yellow Y, green G, blue B and purple P) and five subgroups (RY, YG, GB, BP and PR). Value V represents the degree of lightness of the surface on a ten point scale, where V=0 is totally black and V=10 is perfectly white. In practice, V varies from 1 to 9. A useful relationship is that the light reflectance of a surface with value V is given approximately by V × (V–1) per cent. For example, a very bright surface with a Value of 8 would have a light reflectance of 8 x 7 or 56 per cent. Chroma represents the degree of saturation or intensity of the colour and is based on an 18 point scale from 0 (completely neutral) to 18 (completely saturated). A Munsell colour is written as HUE VALUE/CHROMA. A red paint might have the Munsell classification 5R 4/10, where the 5R shows the red is a pure red colour, the 4 shows the value to be fairly dark and the 10 shows that the colour is fairly saturated. In British Standard BS 5252 *Framework for colour co-ordination for building purposes*, the three variables for coloured surfaces are hue, greyness and weight. Hue is the same concept as for Munsell, but 12 hues are specified as even number pairs i.e. 02 = red-purple, 10 = yellow, 18 = blue. Greyness represents the amount of grey in the colour on a five point letter scale where A = maximum greyness and E = clear, vivid colour. Weight refers to the lightness of the colour and is similar to the Munsell Value. Weight is specified as odd number pairs from 01 (light) to 55 (dark). A BS 5252 colour is written as HUE GREYNESS WEIGHT. A BS 5252 colour might be 08 B 15, with 08 being a yellow-red, B being very grey and 15 being a light tone.

Light source colour classification systems need to describe the spectral content of the light emitted by the source. Although different light sources may appear to produce 'white' light, the proportion of each of the spectral colours in the light may vary greatly. The proportions of the colours are called the spectral power distribution. Sunlight has a fairly even distribution of colours across the spectrum whilst an incandescent filament light bulb has much more red than blue and a fluorescent lamp can have an uneven distribution of colours, with peaks in some colours and gaps in others. Figure 14.5 shows the spectral distributions of some light sources (sunlight, incandescent, fluorescent and metal halide).

The spectral distribution of a light source is important because it impacts upon the perceived colour of a surface – this effect being called colour rendering. A red surface will be strikingly red under a red rich light source such as an incandescent light. Under a red deficient source,

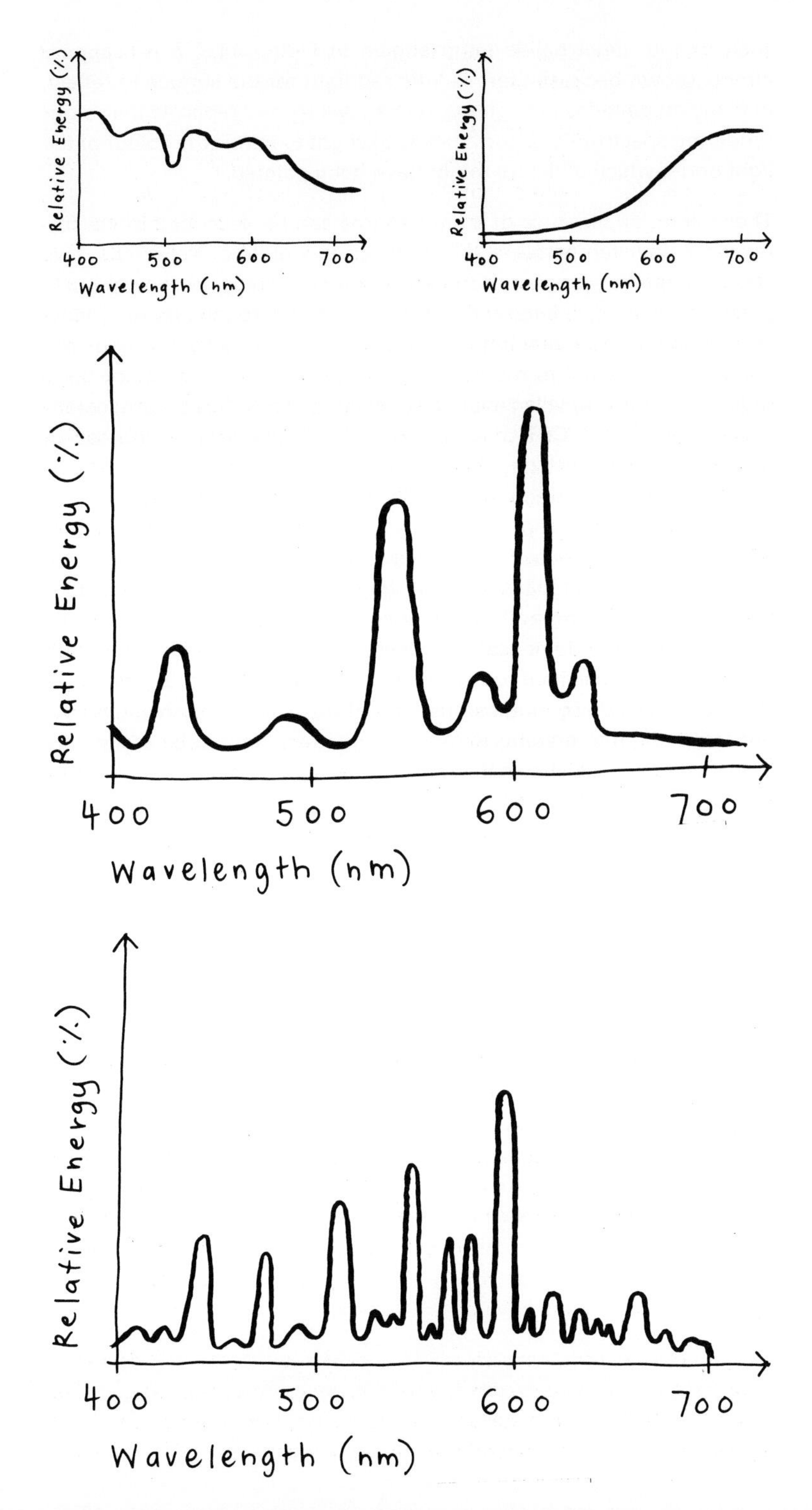
Relative Energy (%)
400
500
600
700
Wavelength (nm)
Relative Energy (%)
400
500
600
700
Wavelength (nm)
Relative Energy (%)
400
500
600
700
Wavelength (nm)
Relative Energy (%)
400
500
600
700
Wavelength (nm)

14.5

such as the metal halide lamp shown in Figure 14.5, it will appear almost brown because there is little red light for the surface to reflect. In many art galleries the lighting system will try and replicate the colour rendering spectrum of a north facing skylight to mimic the colour of the light under which a picture might have been painted.

The 'colour' appearance of a light source can be described by its correlated colour temperature (CCT), which has units of Kelvin (K). This classification is based upon the way many materials, as they are progressively heated, change colour from dark red, through orange, yellow and white to, when very hot, light blue. The colour output from a light source is compared to the output of an idealised heated 'black body radiator'. For example, an incandescent lamp, which has a warm colour appearance, has a CCT of around 2,800K. Conversely, a fluorescent lamp with a cool bluish daylight appearance might have a CCT of around 5,000K. Note that, paradoxically, a 'warm' appearance lamp has a low temperature and a 'cool' appearance lamp has a high temperature. The design importance of knowing a lamp's CCT is that the colour will influence the way a space looks. A way of describing a lamp's colour rendering quality is the CIE general colour rendering index R_a. This is based upon a 100 point scale in which a reference incandescent lamp (because of its excellent full spectral colour distribution) is given a R_a value of 100. Side by side comparison of test colours illuminated by a test lamp and the reference lamp allow the test lamp to be assigned a R_a value. Table 14.1 shows the rating scale.

Table 14.1 CIE general colour rendering index

Colour rendering group	*CIE colour rendering index R_a*	*Typical application*
1A	$R_a \geq 90$	Accurate colour matching is needed, such as colour print inspection
1B	$90 > R_a \geq 80$	Accurate colour judgement and/or good colour rendering appearance, such as for show displays
2	$80 > R_a \geq 60$	Moderate colour rendering is required
3	$60 > R_a \geq 40$	Colour rendering is of little importance, but colour distortion is unacceptable
4	$40 > R_a \geq 20$	Colour rendering is of no importance and colour distortion is acceptable

Chapter 15

Daylight principles

Introduction

Historically, sunlight and daylight were the primary sources of illumination and building designers understood how to bring natural light into spaces at the appropriate time. The Great Temple of Ammon in ancient Egypt and the Pantheon in ancient Rome are examples of the planned and controlled use of daylight. The development of artificial lighting in the twentieth century meant that designing with natural light became a lost art. However, the environmental and financial costs associated with electric lighting have led to a renewed interest in the use of daylight in sustainable buildings. In this chapter some basic principles of daylight are discussed.

Daylight

Electricity generation is a very inefficient process, and since virtually all buildings in developed countries are lit by electricity then artificial lighting has a large energy impact. For example, in the UK the total annual electricity consumption for lighting is around 230,500GWh, producing around 9 per cent of the UK's total CO_2 emissions. In offices 10 per cent to 30 per cent of primary energy consumption is used by lighting. Also, each year 8 million fluorescent lamps are disposed of, many in landfill sites, and such lamps contain environmentally hazardous materials such as mercury. Finally, people prefer spaces that are lit by natural daylight and sunlight rather than predominantly by electric lighting. Therefore, there are many good reasons for trying to develop a lighting design in a building that is energy efficient and environmentally friendly. Such a design will make extensive use of daylight, integrate the use of

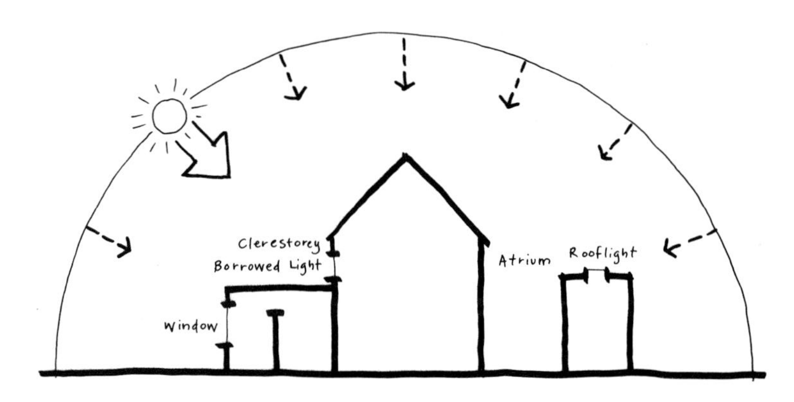

15.1

electric lighting with daylight availability, use high efficiency lighting equipment and avoid high levels of electric lighting.

The sources of natural lighting in a building are the sun, the sky, and the building's glazing system (see Figure 15.1).

For daylight design purposes a 'worst case' situation is often taken as a grey overcast sky with no visible sun. There is a standard type of overcast sky for calculation purposes called the CIE Standard Overcast Sky. With this sky the luminance distribution is such that the sky overhead is three times as bright as the sky at the horizon. Traditionally, under these sky conditions daylight in buildings has been quantified in terms of a parameter called the Daylight Factor DF and its components. The daylight factor is the ratio of the horizontal daylight illuminance at a point in a building, E_i, to the horizontal daylight illuminance outdoors under an unobstructed CIE Standard Overcast Sky, E_o, expressed as a percentage:

$$DF = \frac{E_i \times 100\ \%}{E_O}$$

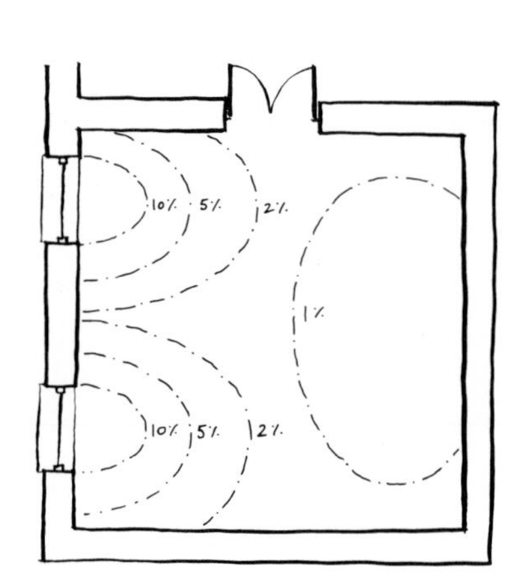

15.2

In the UK the design value of external illuminance is often taken as 5000 lux. If the horizontal illuminance at a point in a room was 200 lux and the external horizontal illuminance was 5,000 lux then the DF at that point would be (200 x 100 per cent)/5000 or 4 per cent. Typical recommended minimum DF values are: corridors 0.5 per cent; dwellings 1 per cent; offices and classrooms 2 per cent; factories 3 per cent to 5 per cent; art studios and galleries 4 per cent to 6 per cent. The complex point to point variations of DF across a room are often simplified by showing contour lines of equal DF in plan, as shown in Figure 15.2. Notice how small the DF value is (1 per cent) for a large part of the rear of the room.

It is possible to use a relative measure like the Daylight Factor to estimate daylight because of the way the eye adapts to slow changes in brightness. If the eye can view both the outside world and inside of a room then, as the outside gets brighter and the room gets brighter, then the relative brightness will appear to stay fairly constant.

The components of the daylight factor relate to the illuminance from the sky (sky component SC), daylight reflected from external surfaces (externally reflected component ERC) and daylight reflected from within the room (internally reflected component IRC), as shown in Figure 15.3(a), (b) and (c). Each component is defined as a ratio to the external illuminance and so

$$DF = SC + ERC + IRC$$

The sky component tends to dominate the daylight factor for rooms with a good view of the sky except at the back of a room, where ERC and IRC may be of similar magnitudes to SC.

Average daylight factor

The Daylight Factor is not easy to use in design as it relates to specific points in a space and does not give an indication of how daylit a room might appear. To overcome this restriction the concept of the Average Daylight Factor or ADF was developed. The ADF represents the mean daylight factor across a room, normally based on the horizontal working plane (often taken as a height of 0.7m above floor level for offices and 0.85m for industrial and all other building types) and the areas of the wall surfaces below the centre of the window height. ADF is given by the equation:

$$ADF = \frac{W\theta\, T}{A\,(1 - R^2)}$$

where W is glazed area, θ the angle of visible sky (see Figure 15.4) from the centre of glazing, T the transmittance of glazing, A the total area of enclosing room surfaces and R the average reflectance of the enclosing room surfaces. Typical values of T are 0.80 and 0.65 for clean single and double glazing respectively, while for light coloured rooms R will be approximately 0.5.

The likely appearance of a daylit room for a given ADF value is shown in Table 15.1. A room will usually look daylit if it has an ADF of at least 2 per cent.

A useful aspect of the ADF concept is that by rearranging its equation it is possible to estimate the area of glazing W required to produce a desired ADF i.e.

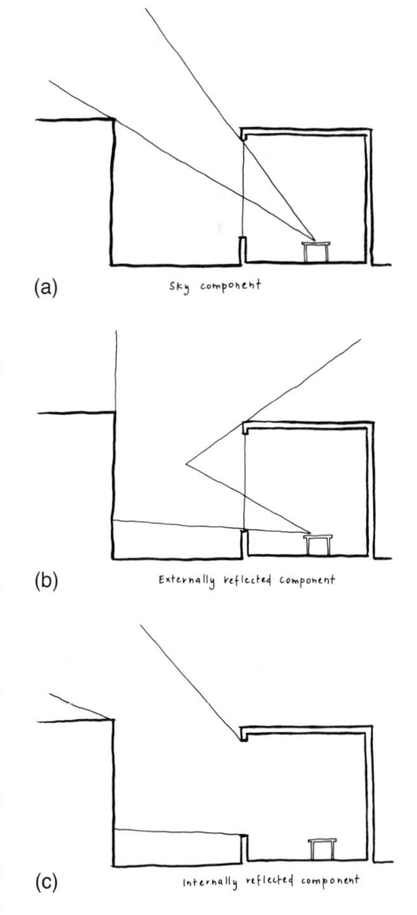

15.3

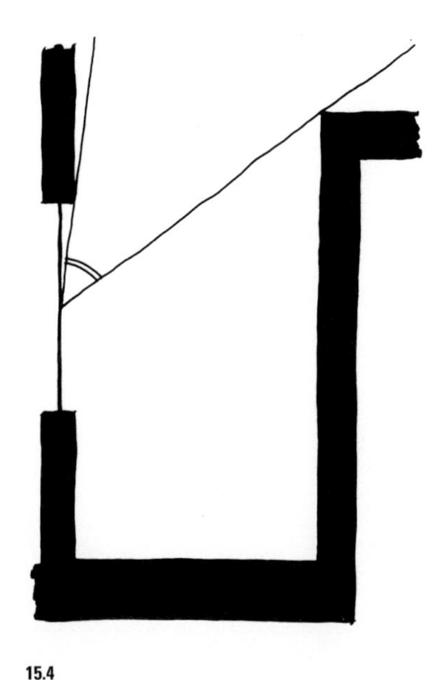

15.4

Table 15.1 ADF and the subjective appearance of a room

ADF is less than 2%	*ADF is from 2% to 5%*	*ADF is greater than 5%*
• Room looks gloomy • Electric lighting on most of the time • Room looks artificially lit	• Room looks daylit • Supplementary electric lighting sometimes needed • Optimum daylight range for overall energy use	• Room is strongly daylit • Daytime electric lighting rarely needed • Major thermal problems from large windows

$$W = \frac{ADF \times A\,(1 - R^2)}{\theta T}$$

For example, in a room with a total surface area A of 100 m², R of 0.5, T of 0.65 and an unobstructed window ($\theta = 90°$) the area of glazing W to produce an ADF of 5 per cent would be

$$W = \frac{5 \times 100\,(1 - 0.25)}{90 \times 0.65} = 6.4\,\text{m}^2$$

However, ADF is only an approximate measure of how well a room may be lit naturally and makes no allowance for the shape of the room or the distribution of the glazing. For example, if the room in the ADF example above was a very narrow and very deep rectangular room with all 6.4 m² of glazing placed in an end wall, then the room would generally appear gloomy. The key to a well lit space is that some sky is visible. The point in a room at which the sky is hidden is called the no-sky line, as shown in Figure 15.5. Anywhere in a room which is beyond the no-sky line will not appear to be well lit.

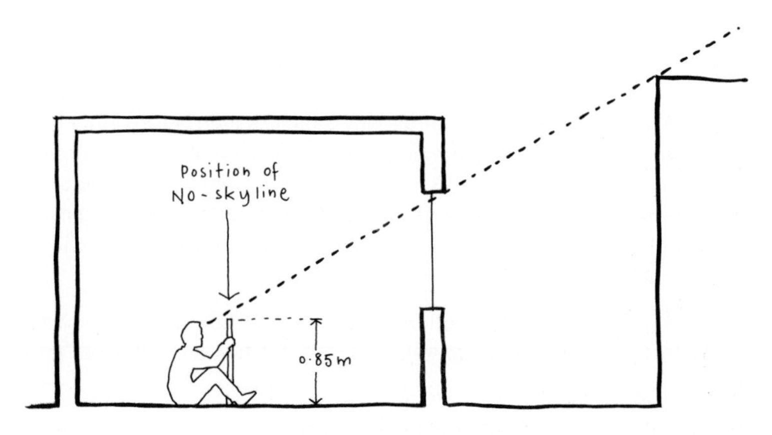

15.5

Room depth for daylight

One of the most difficult aspects of using natural light to illuminate a room is that daylight levels drop very rapidly with distance from the window wall. Typically, beyond around 6m from a window wall a room will start to look subjectively gloomy. Even if a room has the minimum suggested ADF value of 2 per cent it may be too deep in plan to be daylit successfully. A room with depth L from the window wall will be adequately daylit if the following inequality is met:

$$\frac{L}{w} + \frac{L}{h} \leq \frac{2}{(1 - R_b)}$$

where L is the depth of the room, w the width of the room measured across the window wall, h the height of the top of the window above the floor and R_b the area weighted reflectance in the rear half of the room (typically 0.5). For example, is a room 8m deep, 4m wide and with a window head height of 2m too deep to be satisfactorily daylit? The left hand side of the equation gives (8/4) + (8/2) or 6 whilst the right hand side is 2/(1–0.5) or 4. As 6 is obviously not ≤ 4 then the room is too deep to be well daylit by the window. The limiting depth of a room for daylight can be enhanced if:

- the room's depth is similar to the room's width;
- the room's depth is no more than twice the height of the top of the window;
- light coloured surfaces are used at the rear of the room.

Daylight and glare

A design that is trying to utilise daylight may incorporate large glazing areas which can create other environmental problems, including glare. Therefore, one very important aim in daylighting design is to try and prevent glare by controlling the range of brightness and contrast likely to be experienced by a building user. Some control measures include

- sizing the windows correctly to provide view, daylight and some solar gain;
- using controllable and moveable shading devices, such as Venetian blinds;
- reducing the contrast between the window and its wall by using light walls and deep, splayed reveals;
- positioning computer work spaces perpendicular to windows;
- partitioning large, open plan spaces;
- orientating the building so that its major axis runs east-west.

It is not a good idea to try and control glare with the use of tinted solar control glazing. Such glazing can drastically reduce daylight levels and disturb the view out when some windows are open. Innovative daylighting systems, such as prismatic glazing, reflective louvers and light shelves (to be discussed in Chapter 16), can be effective in controlling glare, particularly that arising from bright reflections from computer screens.

Chapter 16

Daylight design

Introduction

Designing a building that will utilise daylight in a controlled, energy efficient and aesthetically pleasing manner is not simply a question of using large areas of glazing. Such an approach will only create a new set of problems. Instead, daylight design has to be an integral part of the overall design process. A design strategy to ensure good daylight conditions in a building should consider

- daylight availability and sky conditions;
- the site and any obstructions;
- the form of the building;
- interior planning and design;
- window and façade design;
- innovative daylighting techniques;
- testing of the design strategy.

Daylight availability and sky conditions

The design sky for many parts of the world is the 'worst case' situation of a grey overcast sky with no visible sun (the CIE Standard Overcast Sky mentioned in Chapter 15). Such a sky will produce low levels of diffuse light and window openings (both in walls and roofs) will need to be quite large to bring adequate amounts of daylight to interior spaces. These openings are potential weak spots in the façade for solar overheating and winter overcooling, and so shading systems and energy efficient glazing systems are integral components of a daylighting strategy. For areas of the world where clear sky conditions prevail then both the sky and the sun will represent sources of very bright light. Openings can be much smaller but the ingress of direct sunlight must always be controlled. For all sky types it is desirable to make most use of south and north facing glazing for daylight. Southerly glazing is relatively easy to shade using horizontal devices that will not interfere with the view out and north glazing will require no shading (in the northern hemisphere) and admit skylight. East and west facing openings are the most difficult to shade as the lower sun means vertical shading devices must be used, which have a very negative impact on the view through a window.

The site and any obstructions

Most new developments on a site will have some sky obstructed by existing buildings, topography or vegetation. Any obstructed sky, particularly for cloudy climates, represents a potentially significant loss of daylight available to a building. It is, therefore, important to have a good awareness of the obstructions on the site and the sky blockage they will create at locations on the façades of the new buildings. To check if good daylighting on an obstructed site is possible, a simple assessment can be made by drawing a section of the new building and an existing obstruction. Draw a line from a point 2m above ground level on the new building to the top of the obstruction and measure the angle between the line and the horizontal, as shown in Figure 16.1. If this angle is less than the critical obstruction angle h given in Table 16.1 for various latitudes then there is potential for adequate daylighting of the new building.

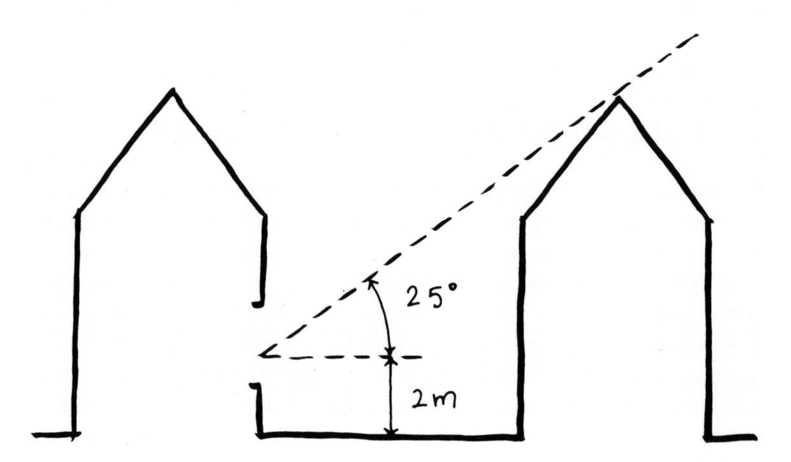

16.1

Table 16.1 Critical obstruction angles for different latitudes

Latitude	*Critical obstruction angle h less than*
Up to 40°	40°
40° to 45°	35°
45° to 50°	30°
50° to 55°	25°
55° to 60°	22°
Over 60°	20°

The form of the building

The greater the surface area to volume ratio of the building then, normally, the better the daylighting levels will be in the building. Consequently, a long and narrow building (measuring, say, 60m wide by 15m deep in plan) is generally preferable to a square building (measuring 30m by 30m in plan) even though both buildings have the same floor area. If an atrium is formed in the core of the building then the daylight levels will be even higher. Before artificial lighting was available building designers were aware of the need to keep buildings shallow for good natural lighting, and a variety of such building forms were developed (Figure 16.2).

Interior planning and design

Open plan spaces are advantageous for daylighting and any partitions, for example, for acoustic privacy, should be made from light-transmitting materials such as such glass blocks. Non light-transmitting partitions should be positioned perpendicular to the window wall, be light coloured and as low as possible. Work and activity areas should be positioned in locations appropriate to the level of lighting task – for example, photocopiers, toilets and kitchens can be located in non-perimeter areas, allowing people to sit and enjoy working in good daylight conditions close to windows. Large areas of dark colour should be avoided, and surface finishes should have high reflectances in the range: ceilings > 80 per cent; walls 50 per cent to 70 per cent; floors 20 per cent to 40 per cent and furniture 25 per cent to 45 per cent. Surfaces should have matt rather then gloss finishes to ensure good daylight distribution and avoid reflected glare.

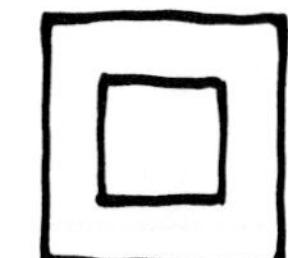
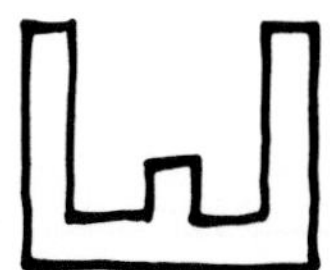
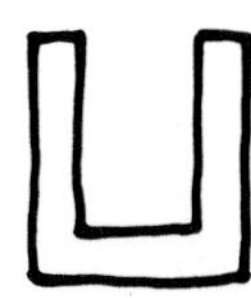

16.2

Colours should be chosen under daylight conditions and checked against the proposed artificial lighting to ensure good colour rendering.

Window and façade design

The area of a room that can be usefully daylit by a window is frequently overestimated. Daylight levels fall rapidly with distance from the window wall, as shown in Figure 16.3.

Adequate daylight penetration for typical ceiling heights will only be approximately equal to 1.5 times the distance from the floor to the top of the window for north facing glazing or overcast skies (Figure 16.4). A window head of 3m will only illuminate satisfactorily to a distance of around 4.5m from the window wall. If the window is south facing and sunlit, or contains a reflective element such as a light shelf (to be discussed later) the daylight penetration may increase by up to 2.5 times the window head height (i.e. 7.5m depth for a 3m window head height) – see Figure 16.5. In general, window area should be around 20 per cent of room floor area to avoid excessive overheating in summer and excessive overcooling in winter.

The position and shape of openings in a building's envelope are as important for good daylighting as the size of the glazing elements. Windows should be placed high on a wall and, if feasible, ceiling heights should be raised to accommodate this. It may be desirable to provide smaller lower level glazing for view purposes. Windows should be positioned in more than one wall as this enhances daylight distribution and penetration and creates a much more pleasing visual environment.

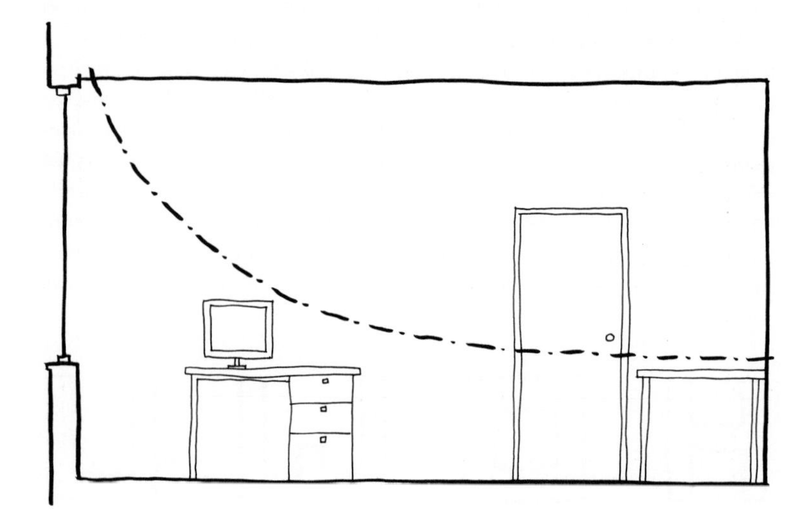

16.3

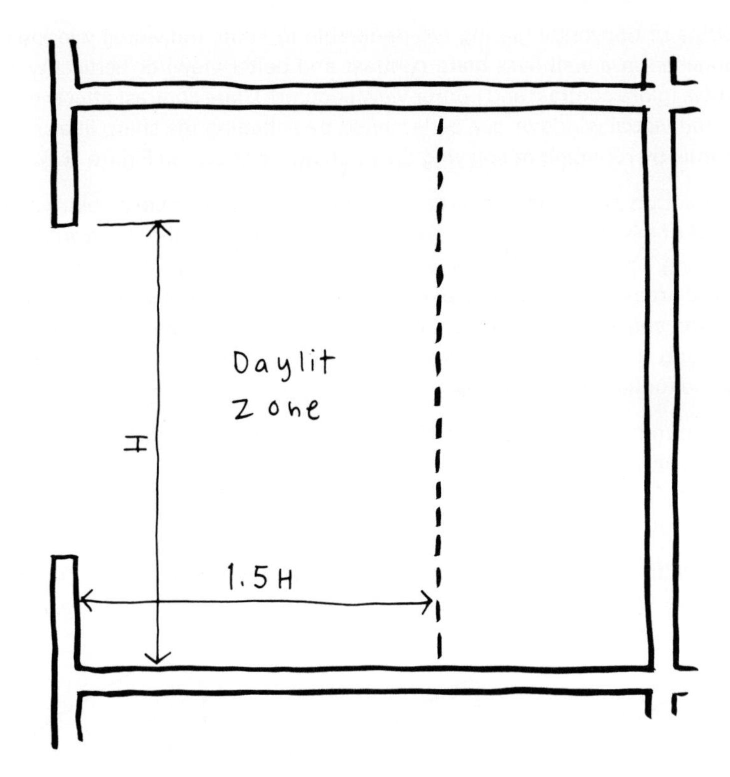

16.4

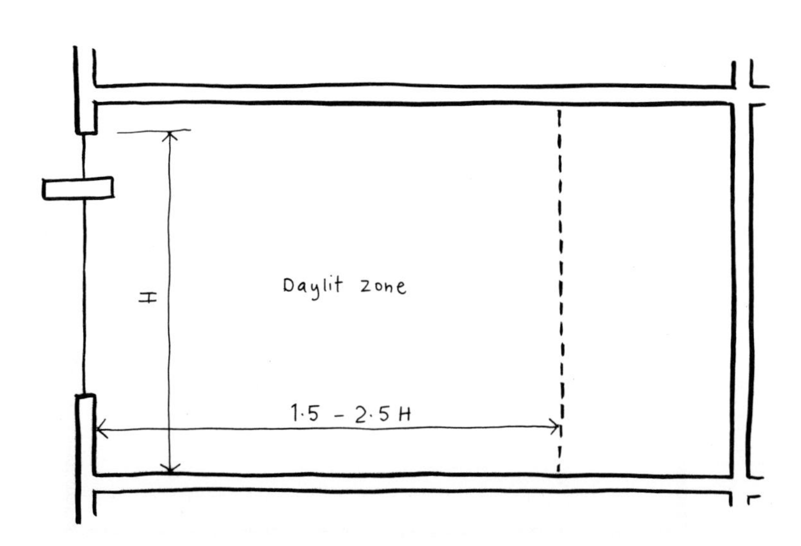

16.5

Strips of horizontal glazing are preferable to either individual windows punched in a wall (less glare contrast and better view) or vertical windows (glare contrast and poorer view content). Glare contrast effects due to individual windows can be lessened by softening the sharp lines of a frame; by rounding or splaying the opening, as shown in Figure 16.6.

In built up areas, where vertical windows may have a very obstructed view of the sky, positioning glazing at high levels in either horizontal or sloping positions is a means of producing high daylight levels over large areas with the potential of creating a more even illuminace distribution compared to a vertical window. The main disadvantages of toplighting are the glare risk and the lack of a view. Figure 16.7 shows some toplighting examples.

The number and separation of skylights needed to provide good light levels in a space can be expressed as a multiple of the height of the space. Any side windows will reduce the number of skylights required (see Figure 16.8).

A similar approach is adopted for clerestory and sawtooth windows (Figure 16.9).

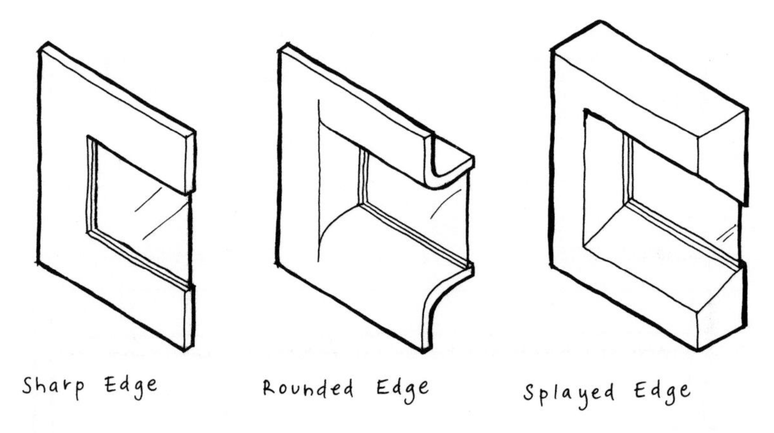

16.6

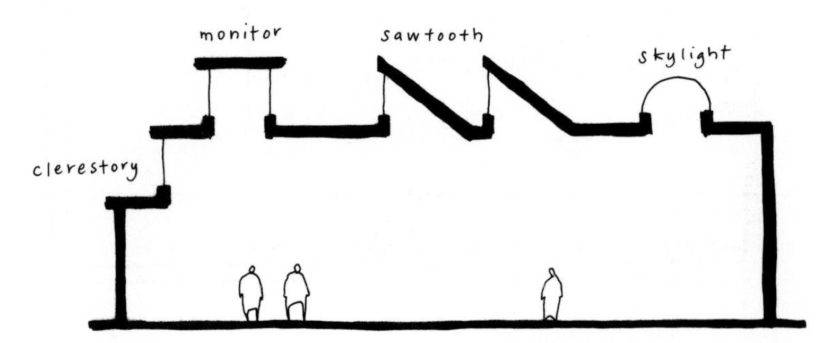

16.7

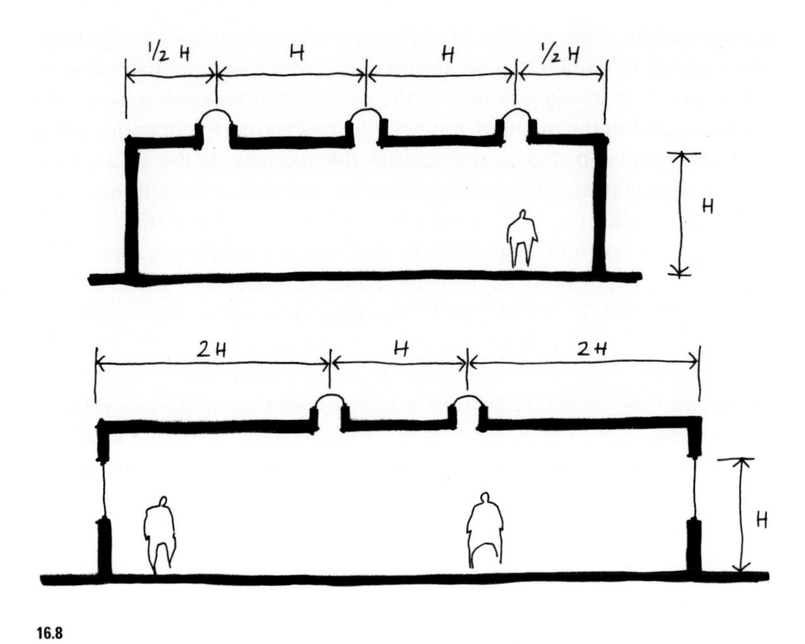

16.8

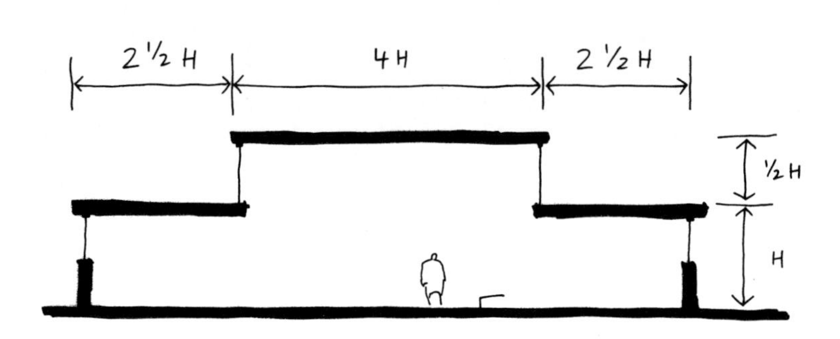

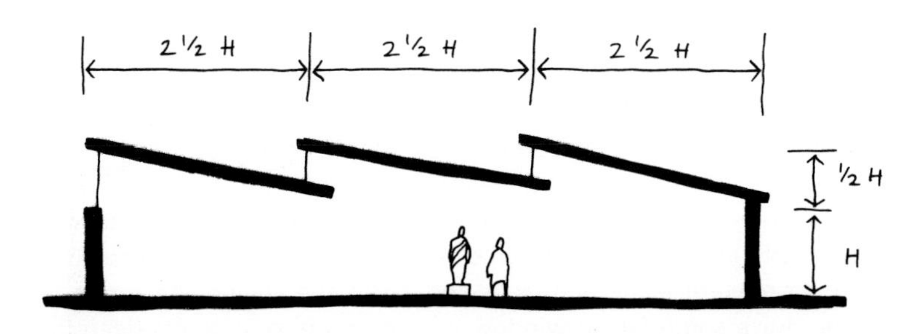

16.9

Atrium buildings are another, and very popular, example of toplighting. The success of daylighting an atrium well and the spaces that adjoin it will depend upon the size and shape of the atrium opening, the light transmittance of the opening, the obstructions across the opening (such as glazing bars and structural supports), the geometry of the atrium well and the reflectances of the surface forming the well. The light transmittance of an atrium opening can be severely reduced by glazing losses, dirt accumulation and obstruction in the plane of the opening. Typically, half the incident external light will be lost as it passes through the atrium roof. A low atrium is much better for daylighting than a tall one – doubling the height of an atrium from three to six storeys can reduce the daylight factor on the atrium floor by around 50 per cent. Similarly, changing the atrium surface reflectances from a high reflectance of 75 per cent to medium reflectance of 50 per cent will roughly halve the daylight levels on the atrium floor. Daylight levels can be improved by splaying out the walls of the atrium (so that more sky is visible) and by increasing the size of windows at lower levels in the atrium well.

Innovative daylighting techniques

A major design problem with using daylight is the rapid decrease in daylight levels with distance from a window, leading to the parts of the room not close to the window appearing gloomy. To try and overcome this basic problem a number of innovative daylighting techniques have been developed that attempt to redirect more daylight to the back of a room. These techniques include the light shelf, mirrored systems, prismatic glazing and light pipe.

Light shelf

A light shelf is a light coloured horizontal or nearly horizontal baffle that is positioned inside and/or outside a window and which reflects light via the ceiling to the back of a room, as shown in Figure 16.10. It can also serve as a solar control device. Light shelves must be carefully positioned and sized if they are not to act as obstructions to light. They need to be placed above eye-level, both to preserve the view and to prevent reflected glare, and so room heights must be greater than 3m to accommodate light shelves. Generally, a horizontal light shelf is best for year-round performance. For predominantly overcast sky conditions best results are obtained with an external light shelf tilted towards the room to maximise the light reflected on to the ceiling. As a rule of thumb, for a south facing window in a room up to 8 metres deep the optimum shelf tilt would be given by:

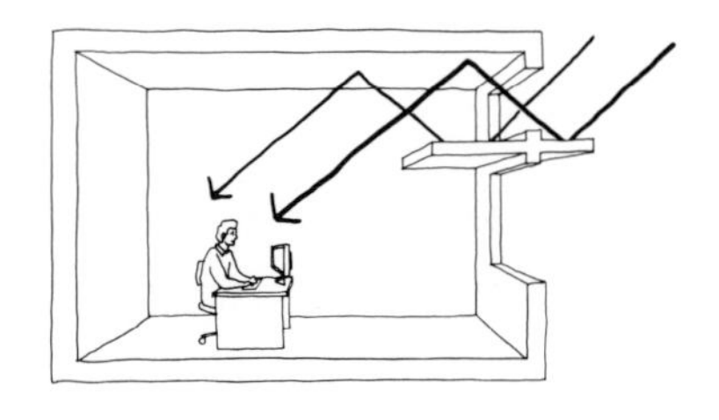

16.10

$$\text{Light shelf tilt} = 40° - (0.5 \times \text{latitude of site})$$

Mirror systems

Mirror systems are normally a series of mirrored louvers positioned above a window or set within a double glazed unit. They are usually placed in the upper section of a window to avoid glare and view obstruction problems. Mirror systems can be effective for reflecting the daylight from a low altitude sun into rooms via ceiling reflection and for solar control by reflecting solar gain from a high summer sun away from a room (see Figure 16.11). Mirrored systems can be difficult to maintain and may obstruct skylight on cloudy days.

Prismatic glazing

Prismatic glazing systems use optical principles to redirect light either into a room (low sun) or away from a room (high sun). The prismatic elements are applied to the upper part of a window either as part of the glazing or as a film that is attached to the glass surface (Figure 16.12 and 16.13). They do obscure or distort views but are easier to maintain than mirrored systems and can have a useful glare control role.

Light pipes

A light pipe system can redirect light deep into a building or even underground. It consists of a light collection aperture, the light pipe itself and a diffusing cover to emit the light. The pipe can be either a shiny metal tube that reflects light directly or solid components, such as acrylic and fibre optic bundles, which use total internal reflection to guide the light into a space. In an active light pipe system a heliostat (a mirror to track the sun) directs the sunlight down the pipe and through an emitter (Figure 16.14). Such a system is critically dependent

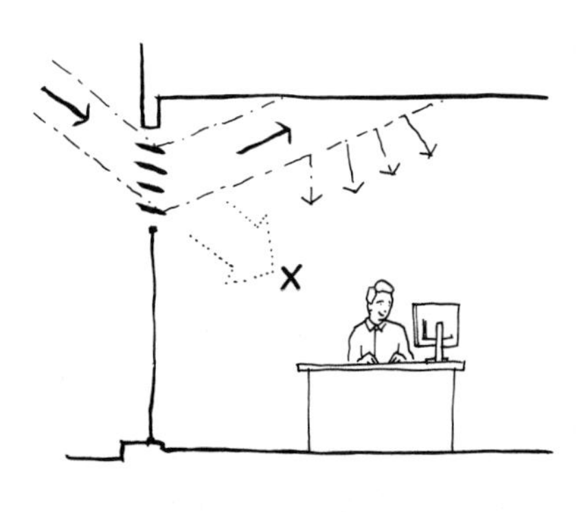

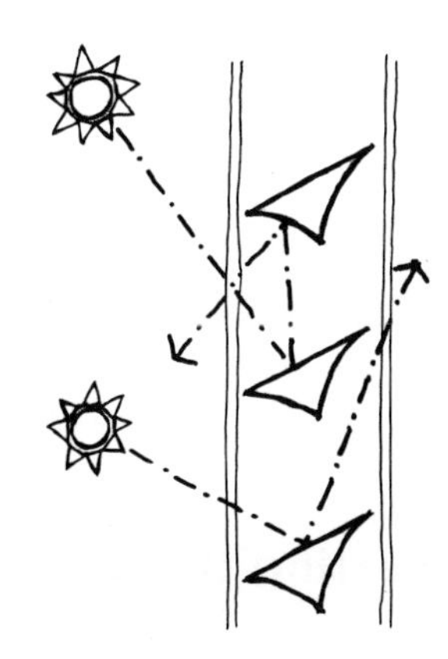

16.11

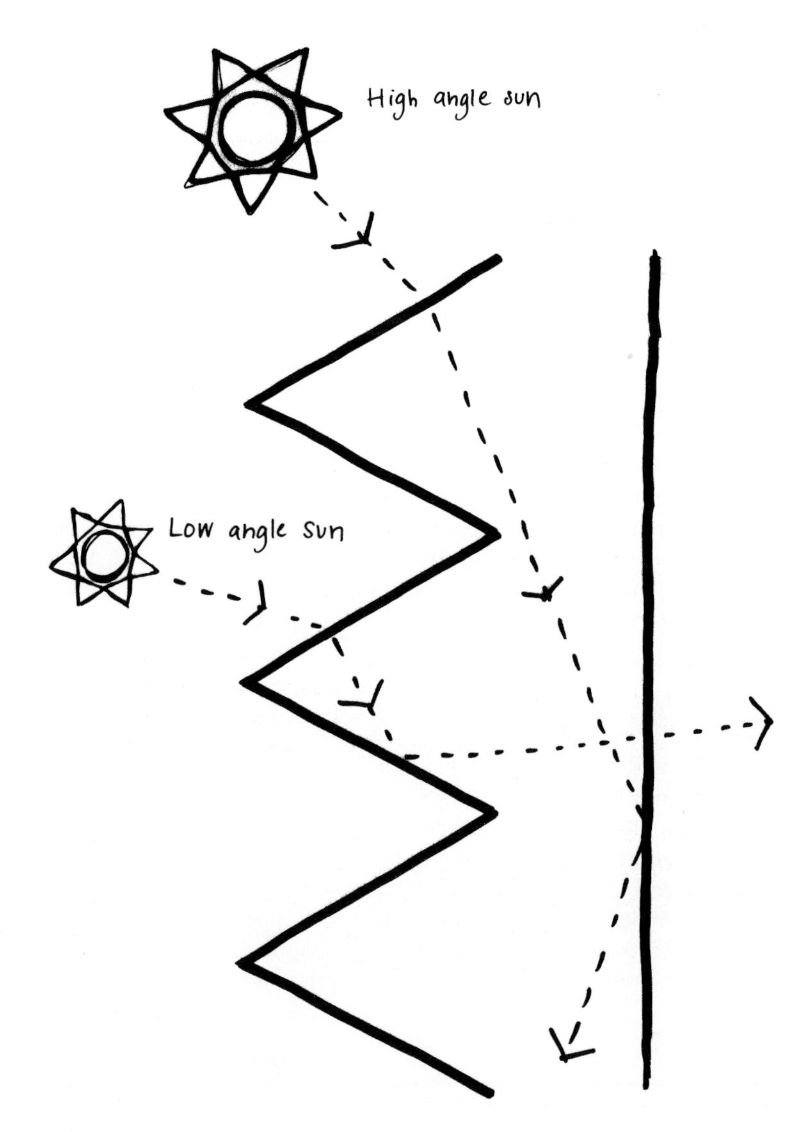

16.12

on the sun shining and can be expensive and difficult to maintain. In a passive system skylight and sunlight are collected by a transparent dome and reflected downwards via a metal tube into a room.

Testing the daylight design strategy

In daylight model testing there are no scale effects (because of the speed of light) and so physical models can be readily used to assess

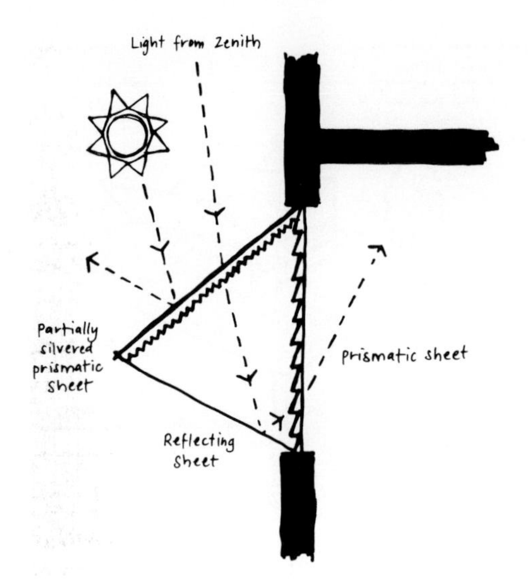

16.13

either lighting levels or visual appearance. The easiest way is to put a model outside and take measurements or photos. Provided that details such as surface colour, reflectance and texture in the model are similar to the real space then reasonably accurate results can be obtained. Figure 16.15 shows a typical arrangement.

For a more controlled luminous environment it is possible to place models inside artificial skies. These consist of either a mirror lined box with a lit diffusing ceiling or a white hemisphere onto which is shown

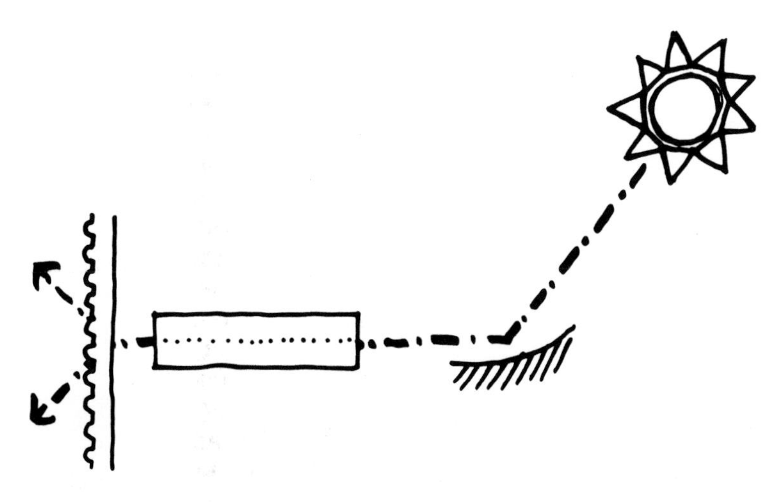

16.14

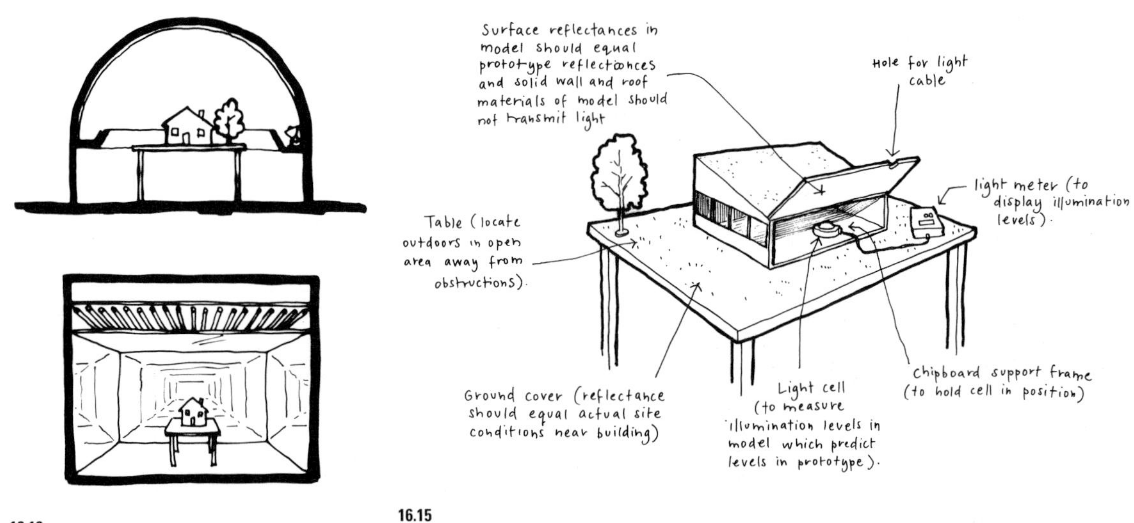

16.16

16.15

light from lamps (Figure 16.16). Both types can create CIE Overcast Sky luminance distribution. More advanced artificial skies are available which consist of arcs of lamps which can be computer controlled individually to create many different types of sky luminance distribution (for example, a clear sky).

In recent years advances in lighting computer software mean that it is now possible not only to predict lighting levels but also to generate photorealistic images of interiors which convey a real sense of how a space might look

Chapter **17**

Artificial lighting principles

Introduction

Although daylight and sunlight are excellent and desirable sources of illumination for buildings there are occasions when they are not sufficient. The most obvious time is at night, but there will be situations where a room is too big to be naturally lit, where controlled levels of illumination are required or where tasks require a specific minimum and consistent level of lighting. In these circumstances artificial lighting must be used to supplement or replace natural light. However, artificial lighting is expensive to use, requires electricity generated by fossil fuels and lamps can contain environmentally harmful materials such as mercury. Therefore, a sustainable building design will attempt to limit the use of artificial lighting through the right choice of lamp and integration with natural lighting. In this chapter the basic principles and properties of various lamps are described.

Artificial light sources

The first artificial light source was fire, which enabled intricate tasks like cave paintings to be performed in dark spaces over 15,000 years ago. The direct burning of solids, liquids and gases remained the only source of artificial light until the invention of the light bulb in 1879 by Edison. Technological advances since then mean that there are now a very large number of artificial light sources. These include

- tungsten and tungsten halogen filament lamps;
- low and high pressure mercury lamps;
- low and high pressure sodium lamps;
- metal halide lamps;
- light emitting diodes (LED).

There are basically two ways in which electric lamps produce light – by either passing a current through a solid filament to make it glow (incandescent light source) or by passing a current through a gas to ionise it (discharge light source). LEDs pass a current through a semiconductor material to produce light by electroluminescence.

Tungsten and tungsten halogen filament lamps

The tungsten filament lamp, or General Lighting Service (GLS) lamp, has historically been the lamp used to light many environments including homes, restaurants, theatres and display lighting. It is an incandescent lamp consisting of a coiled tungsten filament that is housed within a glass bulb which is filled to slightly below atmospheric pressure with inert gases (argon, krypton and nitrogen). Tungsten is a good choice of metal as it has a very high melting point (3600K) and a low evaporation rate (so the filament lasts for a reasonable time before snapping). The filler gases help reduce the rate of evaporation and mean the GLS lamp can be run at a high temperature – and the higher the filament temperature the more visible light is emitted.

GLS lamps are compact, very cheap to buy, easy to use and replace and have very good colour rendering properties, displaying a broad spectrum with a pleasing red bias (see Figure 14.5 in Chapter 14) that highlights skin tones. Unfortunately, GLS lamps have a short life of around 1,000 hours (there are 8,760 hours in a year), are susceptible to breakage and, most significantly, are very poor at converting electricity (watts) into light (lumens). The ratio of light output to electricity input is called *luminous efficacy* and has the unit lumens per watt (lm/W). GLS lamps have a very low luminous efficacy of around 12 lm/W (compared to other lamp types which can have efficacies ranging from 50 to 100 lm/W). Consequently, the energy running costs for GLS lamps are very high, which is leading to their replacement by low energy light sources such as compact fluorescent lamps. Some building regulations specify the use of non GLS lamps and there is a debate underway about whether GLS lamps should be banned completely on environmental grounds. Tungsten halogen (TH) lamps have a halogen vapour added to the filler gas that allows the lamp to be run at a higher temperature than the GLS lamp (and thus emit more light) whilst significantly reducing the evaporation rate of the tungsten filament (making the lamp last longer). The halogen vapour can only do this if the lamp's glass wall temperature stays above 250°C, and this is achieved by making the lamp small and the glass out of quartz. Colour rendering properties for TH lamps are similar to GLS but they have a much longer life (2,000–4,000 hours) and a better luminous efficacy (18–24 lm/W). Typical applications for TH lamps are display lighting, car headlights and floodlighting.

Discharge lamps

Discharge lamps contain gases (either mercury or sodium) within a glass. If a high voltage transient pulse (~600 to 1,500 volts) is passed through the gases then ionisation takes place, particle collisions or gas warming occurs and electrons can be destabilised in their orbits around the mercury or sodium atoms. As the electrons return to their stable orbit position they emit the collision energy as radiation that interacts with special coatings (phosphors) on the glass to produce visible light.

Low pressure mercury (MCF) lamp (fluorescent tube)

The most common discharge lamp is the fluorescent tube, which contains mercury vapour at low pressure (around 1.3 Pascal, compared to atmospheric pressure of 101,325 Pascal). Electrodes are located at both ends of the fluorescent tube to produce the voltage pulse which ionises the gas and frees electrons to collide with mercury atoms and temporarily raise their energy – a process called *excitation*. This excitation energy is immediately released in the form of invisible UV radiation. The phosphor lining of the fluorescent tube absorbs the UV and some of it is transformed into visible light. The general process is shown in Figure 17.1.

Different fluorescent tubes can typically have luminous efficacies in the range 50 to 100 lm\W and a lamp life of 5,000 to 10,000 hours. By using different types of phosphor linings it is possible to produce fluorescent

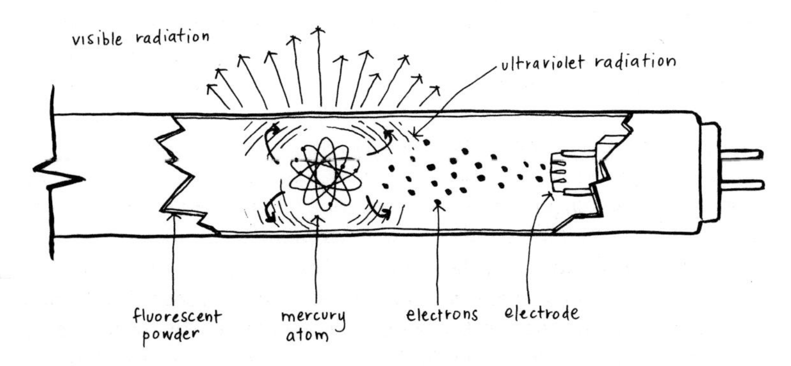

17.1

tubes with a very broad choice of colour rendering properties. This flexibility enables these lamps to have a very wide range of applications – from offices and shops to hospitals and art galleries. One disadvantage of fluorescents tubes is their physical size, but the development of compact fluorescent lamps (CFL) has extended their use into the domestic market, where they are labelled as low energy bulbs.

High pressure mercury (MBF) lamp

If the mercury vapour pressure is increased in the lamp then more excitations occur, the temperature in the lamp increases and a different range of spectral emissions occurs giving an improved colour appearance to light from the lamp. To achieve the high pressure the lamp is made much smaller, with the quartz tube that contains the mercury vapour now a few centimetres long rather than the tens of centimetres of the glass fluorescent tube. Because of their good colour rendering properties high pressure mercury lamps have been used extensively in outdoor lighting, high bay industrial areas and street lighting. However, they are tending to be replaced by high pressure sodium and metal halide lamp installations. High pressure mercury lights have typical luminous efficacy values of 30 to 50 lm/W and a life of 5,000 to 10,000 hours.

Low pressure sodium (SOX) lamp

These lamps use sodium vapour at low pressure and run at a very high tube temperature. They have impressive luminous efficacies (up to 180 lm/W), a long life (up to 16,000 hours) and reduced running costs. Unfortunately, the light they emit is in a very narrow spectral band around the colour yellow. They have been used extensively in the past for road lighting, parking areas and other external spaces where good light level rather than good light quality was required. However, the trend is to replace yellow SOX lamps with white light lamps for aesthetic, safety and security reasons.

High pressure sodium (SON) lamp

Sodium vapour is contained in a small tube and run at a high temperature to create a high pressure. Hot sodium vapour is very corrosive and the tube holding the high pressure vapour is a translucent ceramic tube made from specially processed aluminium oxide (alumina). The high pressure broadens the spectral output beyond just yellow light to give reasonable colour rendering, and by using very high pressures it has been possible to produce white SON lamps which have a similar excellent colour appearance to tungsten lamps. Efficacies for SON lamps range from 50 to 120 lm/W and they have a life of 12,000 to 24,000 hours. They have a broad variety of applications (reflecting their range of colour performance) and can be used in both industrial and office environments (for example, in uplighting). The basic form of the SON lamp, with the short central alumina tube, is shown in Figure 17.2.

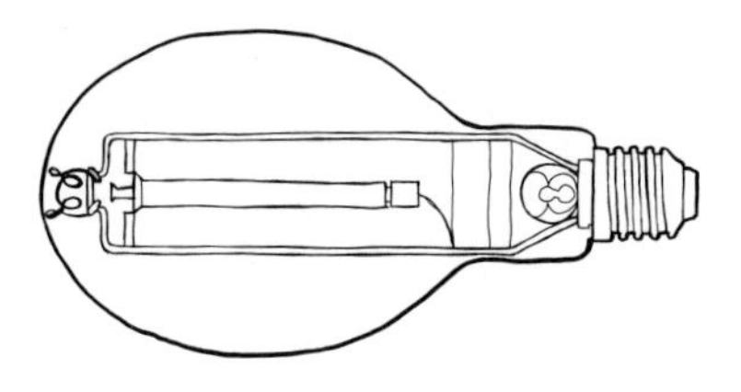

17.2

Metal halide (MBI) lamp

This is a development of the high pressure mercury lamp in which the halides of metals such as sodium, thorium, indium and thallium are added to mercury and run at a high tube temperature. These additives greatly broaden the colour spectrum of the emitted light and metal halide lamps have the best colour rendering properties of any discharge lamp. They are often used in sports stadium floodlighting where TV coverage will take place. Compact MBI lamps are also available, which allows them to be used for display and accent lighting. Lamp efficacies vary from 60 to 120 lm/W and a typical life is around 10,000 to 15,000 hours.

Light emitting diodes (LED)

The light emitting diode is an electroluminescent semiconductor which has promised to be the future of electric lighting due to its long life (~100,000 hours), low operating voltage (2 volts), efficacies of up to 40 lm/W, robustness, compact size and reasonable colour rendering. LEDs are widely used in devices such as traffic lights and emergency exit way marking but their development into significant light sources for buildings is still some way off.

Control gear for discharge lamps

Incandescent lamps can be lit simply by directly connecting them to a voltage and using a switch or dimmer to control the current flowing through them (and hence their light output). However, to ignite any form of discharge lamp it is necessary to create a high voltage pulse to initiate the ionisation process and then a means of controlling the current that is created by the ionisation. This control circuitry can take several forms and may be located external to the lamp (so that only the lamp needs to be replaced at the end of its life) or be an integral part of the lamp (as with most compact fluorescent bulbs). The choice of control gear can have a significant impact upon the performance of a lamp,

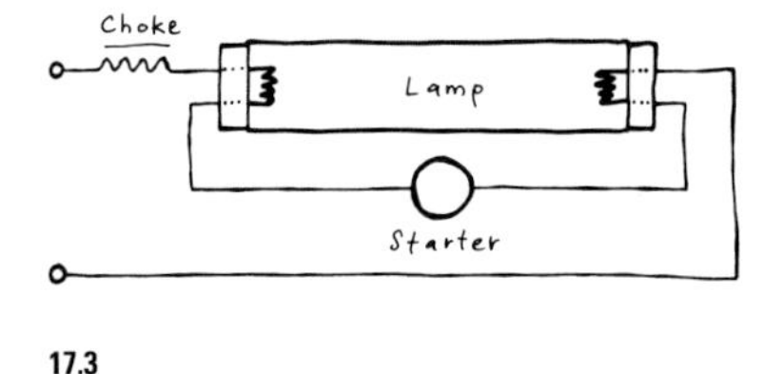

17.3

both visually (speed of ignition and degree of flicker) and in terms of energy consumption (power used in the control circuitry). The most common control circuit is a wire-wound inductive choke which is connected with the lamp and a glow-switch starter (Figure 17.3).

When the supply is switched on, the mains voltage is too small to ignite the lamp but it does produce an arc in the starter, which heats up a bimetal electrode, causing it to bend and make contact with a second electrode. This now completes the circuit and current flows through both the lamp's electrodes and heats them. However, the completed circuit now means that there is no heating arc in the starter switch and so the bimetal electrodes cool and separate. This disrupts the flow through the choke, and as this flow collapses a high voltage transient pulse is generated which is sufficient to ionise the gas in the lamp and thus ignite it.

More energy efficient lighting systems use high frequency electronic starter circuits which offer a more precise and controlled heating and ignition cycle. Mains supply frequency of 50 Hz is converted to a high frequency of around 30,000 Hz, which enables a dramatic reduction in choke size and control circuit energy losses (down by 20 to 25 per cent). Light output is also steadier and lamp life is increased.

Luminaires

A light fitting, or *luminaire*, is needed to connect the lamp to an electricity supply, support it in place and protect it from the environment it is illuminating. In addition, the luminaire will act as an optical control system to ensure that the light emitted from the lamp is dispersed correctly to achieve the desired light distribution in a space. Although luminaires are frequently chosen by designers for their aesthetic qualities, the correct choice of luminaire can have a significant impact upon the energy and visual performance of a lighting scheme.

Luminaires control the direction of light flow by using one or more of the processes of reflection (mirrored and light coloured surfaces), refraction (changing light direction at the junction of two materials) and diffusion (incident light is scattered in many directions). Figure 17.4 shows these processes, and typical luminaire materials would be steel, aluminium and mirrors for reflectors, glass for refractors and plastics for diffusers. Glare control elements, such as baffles and parabolic louvers, will also be part of a luminaire's optical control system.

Three key parameters influencing the photometric performance of a luminaire are the light output ratio (LOR), the luminous intensity distribution and the spacing to height ratio (SHR). The LOR is the ratio of the total lumen output from the luminaire to the total lumen output from

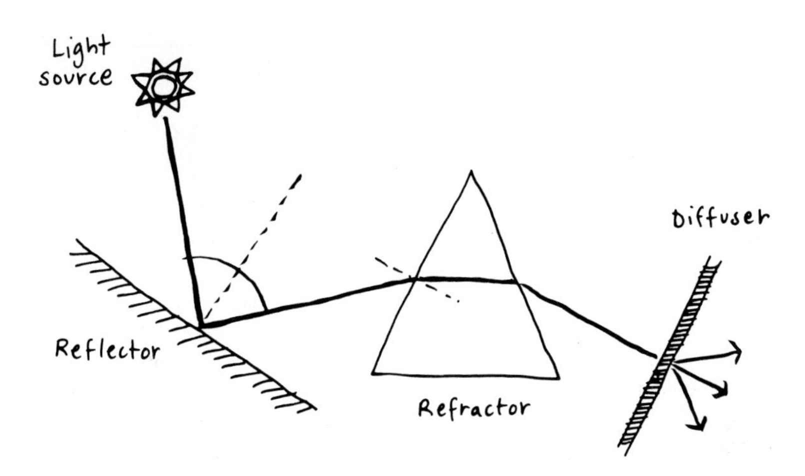

17.4

the lamp. Light absorption and loss can take place within the luminaire and at the surfaces close to the luminaire. If the tungsten bulb in Figure 17.5 emits 1,000 lumens and the luminaire + bulb emits 600 lumens then the LOR is 600/1000 or 0.6. For a lighting scheme wishing to be energy efficient the LOR should be high (although this may create glare problems).

The luminous intensity distribution indicates how the light flux from the luminaire is directed. It is often shown as a polar diagram which indicates contour lines of light intensity in candelas per 1,000 lumens of lamp output (which can be adjusted for actual lumen output) on a protractor showing angles of direction. Measurements of luminous intensity are made by rotating a photocell through 360° around the axial and transverse axes of the luminaire. Figure 17.6 shows a typical luminous intensity polar chart for a rectangular luminaire housing a fluorescent tube and baffles, which is directing all of its light downwards.

If the distance between luminaires in a lighting scheme is too large then the illuminated working plane may exhibit areas of relative darkness and the visual appearance may not seem uniform. To avoid this the ratio of the spacing between luminaires to the mounting height of the luminaires above the working plane (SHR) must not exceed limits given by the luminaire manufacturers. Typically, for a narrow beam of light SHR is less than 0.5, for a medium beam it is 0.6 to 0.9 and for a broad beam SHR can be 1.0 or greater.

Photometric data for both lamps and luminaires are readily available from manufacturers' catalogues. These are normally high quality paper

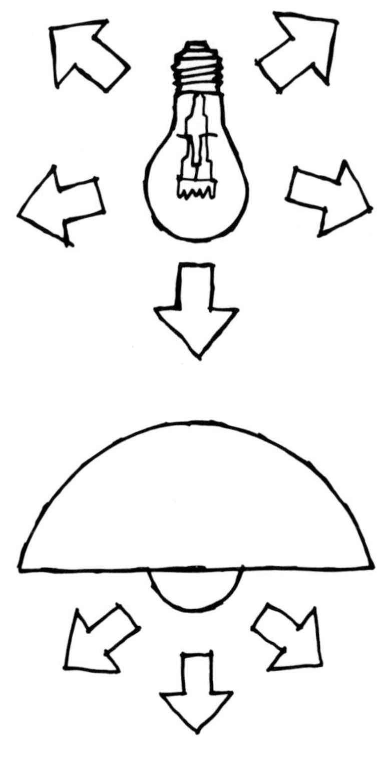

17.5

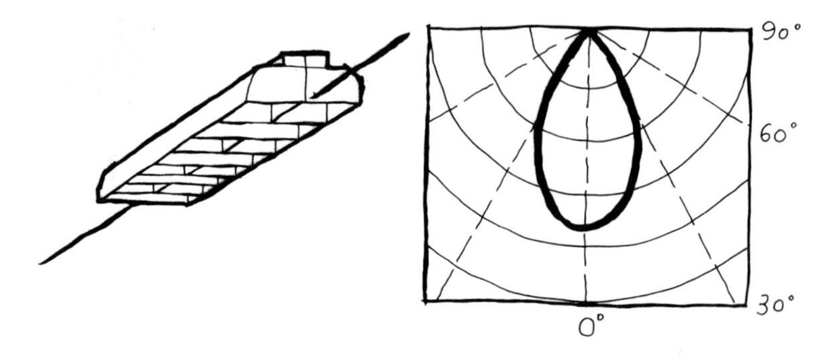

17.6

or electronic publications which also show numerous examples of lighting schemes for a range of building types.

Lumen design method

The lumen design method is the most common procedure for estimating how many lamps / luminaires laid out in a regular pattern will be needed to illuminate uniformly a space to a specified level. The lumen method equation is:

$$N = \frac{E \times A}{UF \times LLF}$$

where

N = required total number of lamp lumens installed to produce E, lumens
E = average illuminance over the horizontal working plane, lux
A = area of the horizontal working plane, m^2
UF = Utilisation Factor for the horizontal working plane, dimensionless
LLF = Light Loss Factor, dimensionless

The value of E depends upon the task being undertaken. Recommended values are available from lighting guides produced by, for example, CIBSE, IES and CIE. Typical values for E are shown in Table 17.1

The Light Output Ratio (LOR) describes how much light comes out of the luminaire. However, some of this light will be absorbed by the ceiling and walls before reaching the working plane. The Utilisation Factor (UF) is the ratio of the total light flux reaching the working plane to the total light flux emitted by the lamp. The UF indicates how effectively the

Table 17.1 Recommended task illuminance values

Type of space	*Recommended value of E (lux)*
Corridors, auditoria	100
Foyers, dining rooms	200
Libraries, teaching spaces	300
General offices, shops	500
Supermarkets	1000

luminaire and room combine to direct light onto the working plane. UF values are given in manufacturers' catalogues in terms of the reflectances of the room surfaces and the geometry of the room, as defined by the Room Index RI. For a room of length L and width W and a lamp mounted at a height H above the working plane the Room Index is given by

$$RI = \frac{L \times W}{(L + W) \times H} \quad \text{or} \quad \frac{L}{2H} \quad \text{for a square room}$$

The Light Loss Factor (LLF) reflects the fact that over a period of time the light output from a lamp decreases (LLMF – Lamp Lumen Maintenance Factor), the luminaire gets dirty (LMF – Lumen Maintenance Factor) and the room surfaces get soiled (RSMF – Room Surface Maintenance Factor). LLF is calculated from

$$LLF = LLMF \times LMF \times RSMF$$

Lamp manufacturers provide values for LLMF and LMF whilst appropriate data for RSMF can be found in CIBSE and IES lighting guides. Typical values of LLF for a very clean air conditioned office with downward lighting may be as high as 0.95 whereas an uplighter in an industrial environment could have a value of 0.4. If no information is available for LLF then a value of 0.8 can be used as an approximation.

Lumen design example calculation

The lumen design method might look complicated but most of the numbers required are readily available from manufacturers' catalogues once a lamp/luminaire combination has been chosen. In this example a naturally ventilated office, measuring 6m × 6m × 3m high and in a suburban setting, is to be lit to create an illuminance of 500 lux on a working plane which is 0.85m high. The luminaire is to be 2.85m above the floor (a mounting height H of 2.0m and a Room Index of 2.5). A louvered rectangular luminaire similar to that shown in Figure 17.6 is to be used and contains a 58W fluorescent tube, which emits 4,500 lumens.

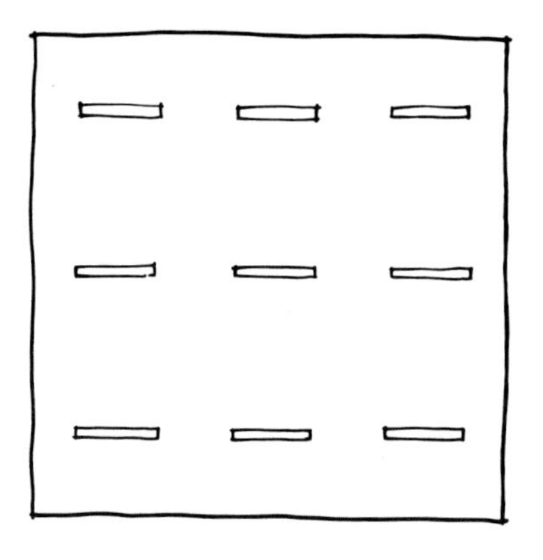

17.7

Manufacturers' data gives a Utilisation Factor of 0.6, an LLF of 0.8 and a maximum SHR of 1.75. Substituting these values into the lumen method equation gives

$$N = \frac{E \times A}{UF \times LLF} = \frac{500 \times 36}{0.6 \times 0.8} = 37{,}500 \text{ lumens}$$

Therefore, 37,500 lumens need to be installed to achieve 500 lux on the working plane. As the lamp in the luminaire emits 4,500 lumens then 37,500/4,500 or 8.3 luminaires will be needed. This figure is rounded up to 9 luminaires and could be laid out as shown in Figure 17.7.

The spacing for the 9 luminaires in the 6 x 6 room is 6/3 or 2.0. As the mounting height is 2.0 then the SHR is 2/2 =1.0 (which is within the maximum SHR value of 1.75) and so the layout should produce an even lighting distribution.

Chapter **18**

Energy efficient lighting design

Introduction

Good lighting design attempts to put the right amount of light in the right place at the right time in order to enable people to perform visual tasks safely, comfortably and efficiently. In addition, the lighting design should enhance the visual appearance of a space and, through the use of controls and daylight, be as energy efficient as possible. In this chapter the planning considerations for lighting design are discussed, together with ways in which lighting energy usage can be minimised.

The lighting design process

Lighting design is concerned with both the quantity of light and the quality of light. The quantity of light required to perform tasks is relatively easy to calculate but the visual quality of a space is much more difficult to predict – lighting design is often described as both an art and a science. It is a useful exercise, when a space appears pleasingly lit or poorly lit, to analyse the visual components in the space (windows, luminaire types and layout, surface colours and textures) to see how they are contributing to the overall impression of the visual environment.

The lighting design process typically has five stages:

1 visual objectives
2 visual specification
3 general planning
4 detailed planning
5 post occupancy evaluation

Visual objectives

This is the initial information gathering stage that attempts to determine for what the lighting is needed. Factors to be considered include:

- space function, use and style;
- building materials and finishes;
- age of occupants;
- tasks to be done in space;
- times of occupancy;
- visual appearance, impact and mood (i.e. prestigious, vibrant, relaxing, clean);
- priorities and restraints (financial, energy and environmental strategies).

Visual specification

This involves specifying the visual objectives in terms of parameters that can be assessed in some way. For some objectives which are not physically measurable, such as visual impact and mood, this is difficult and can only be described in terms of lighting schemes which have succeeded in creating the required atmosphere/impact in other designs. For example, to make a space appear large and vibrant the room surfaces would have a high reflectance and be lit brightly and evenly. To make a space appear small and intimate, narrow beam point source luminaires would produce high contrast pools of light and dark. The task illuminance is one of the simplest parameters to specify and values for most tasks and settings are available in lighting design guides. Other quantifiable factors that can be specified include colours, budgets and glare risk.

General planning

At this stage it is now possible to consider how the lighting scheme will integrate with the architectural design. The interaction between daylight and electric light is a key consideration. People prefer to live and work in rooms with windows and daylight and so the daylight environment should be designed first (see Chapter 19) and then the electric lighting needs estimated. In Chapter 15, Table 15.1 indicated how the Average Daylight Factor can be used to assess how much of the time electric lighting will be needed in a space. Other issues relating to daylight – electric light integration include:

- luminance balance between the daylit perimeter and the electric lit interior;
- colour rendering compatibility;

- glare problems;
- choice and use of daylight-sensitive lighting controls;
- night time appearance of the space.

Lighting schemes can be divided into three approaches – general, localised and local. In a general lighting scheme an approximately uniform distribution of illuminance across the working plane is achieved through the regular layout of luminaires, as shown in Figure 18.1.

The advantages of a general lighting scheme are that they are simple to plan, require no link with task location and offer great flexibility. The disadvantages include a bland appearance to both the lighting and the light fittings and that energy is wasted illuminating the entire space to a task level that may only be required in a few specific locations.

In a localised lighting scheme luminaires are arranged to provide the required illuminance in work areas together with a lower level of background illuminance for circulation areas – see Figure 18.2.

The advantages of localised lighting schemes are that they use less energy than a general scheme and can be cheaper to install. Conversely, they are less flexible as they are linked to a task position and maintenance is important as losing one luminaire can impact upon a large work area.

18.1

18.2

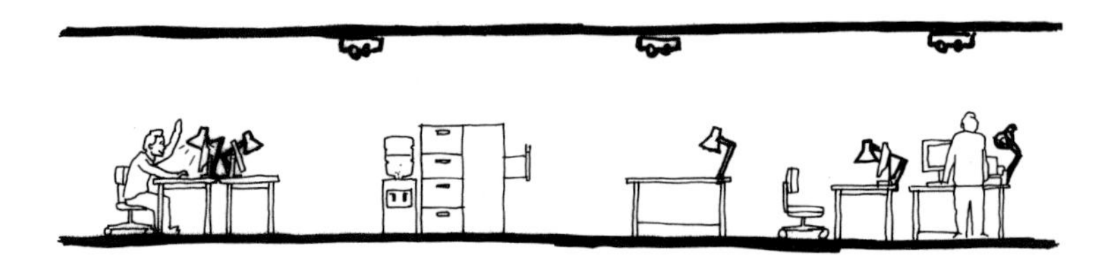

18.3

In a local lighting scheme task illumination is provided specifically over the small area involving the task and the immediate surroundings. A general lighting scheme (operating at a much lower illuminance level just for circulation and non-critical tasks) is also installed, as shown in Figure 18.3. The advantages of this scheme are it is an energy efficient way to provide good task lighting and that an individual lamp can be switched off when not needed. Disadvantages include a lack of flexibility, local luminaires can be expensive and there are potential glare and shadow risks at the task.

Detailed planning

After the general lighting design has been determined it is necessary to perform detailed calculations for a variety of parameters such as the number of luminaires required, glare risk and capital and energy costs. Most of these calculations will need to be performed by a lighting designer or engineer, but for a small general lighting scheme it is possible to estimate the lighting requirements using the lumen design method. The lumen design method is the most common procedure for estimating how many lamps / luminaires laid out in a regular pattern will be needed to illuminate uniformly a space to a specified level. The lumen design method was described in Chapter 17.

Post occupancy evaluation

Post occupancy evaluation (POE) has become an important feature of environmental design to investigate if a building performs as was intended and whether building occupants are satisfied. Lighting is one area of POE where the success or otherwise of a scheme can be relatively quickly assessed. Physical measurements of light levels can reveal if task illuminances are being achieved and users' perceptions of the visual environment can be ascertained through surveys. Systems to control the use of electric lighting can be checked against observations, occupant behaviour and electricity consumption data.

Energy efficient lighting

Globally, electric lighting consumes approximately 20 per cent of the world's generated electricity. In buildings electric lighting typically accounts for around 50 per cent of total electricity use in offices, 25 per cent in hospitals and 15 per cent in schools and homes. Energy efficiency in electric lighting involves the correct choice of lamp, luminaire and control strategy (so lighting is supplied only when it is needed). The choice of lamp will depend upon several factors, such as size, appearance and colour properties, but for energy efficiency the key parameters are luminous efficacy and lamp life. Using compact fluorescent lamps or metal halide lamps instead of tungsten lamps can produce energy savings of up to 80 per cent and reduce maintenance costs. The choice of luminaire will also be influenced by a range of issues but for energy efficiency the luminaire should have a high light output ratio (with a distribution that is projecting most of the light on to the task) and be easy to clean.

Electric lighting control systems are important for energy efficiency, with suitable controls typically reducing lighting energy consumption in offices by 30 per cent to 50 per cent. There are four basic types of control: manual, timed switch off with manual override, occupancy linked and daylight linked. The choice of control for a space will depend upon the number of people in the space and the pattern of occupancy. Studies have shown that with just manual controls the first people to enter a space in the morning tend to switch the lights on and that they will then be left on all day until the last person leaves. Although manual switching is not energy efficient, it is important that people do have, at

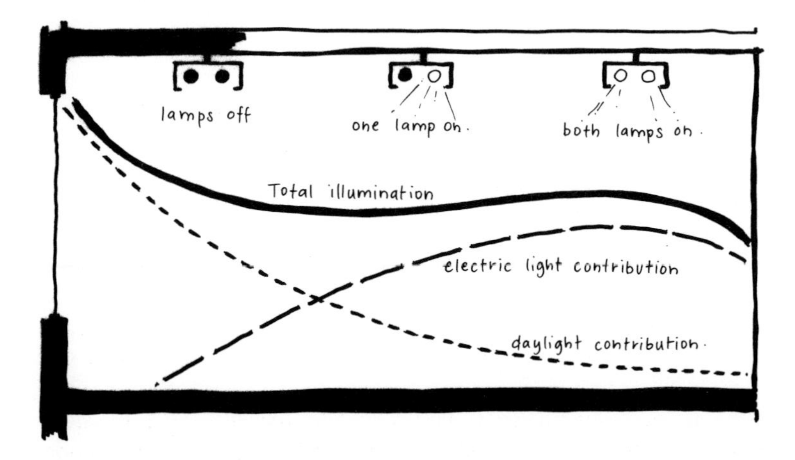

18.4

least as an override, control over their lighting environment, particularly for their own local task lighting. Timer controls switch lighting on and off during periods of the day to coincide with activity and are most useful where relatively fixed patterns of work take place – again, local manual overrides must be available. Occupancy linked controls typically use infra red, acoustic, ultrasonic or microwave sensors to detect movement or noise in a space, and if none is sensed then the lights are switched off. A time delay is built into the system before switch off to allow for occupants being still or quiet. Daylight linked controls use photocells to measure the light levels in a space and then either switch off or dim one or more rows of lamps situated parallel to the window wall to maintain a reasonably uniform illuminance across the space. Figure 18.4 shows a typical arrangement.

Achieving an energy efficient lighting scheme is one of the most effective ways of developing a sustainable building design. Although it does not have the high visibility of a photovoltaic array or a green roof, a successful lighting installation will achieve significant energy savings over a period of many years.

Chapter 19

Design examples

Introduction

The visual environment in a space contributes hugely to a person's impression of the quality of the architecture of that space. It is an interesting exercise; whether a space appears pleasingly lit or poorly lit, to identify the visual components (windows, luminaire types and layout, surface colours and textures) and try to understand how they are contributing to the overall impression of the visual environment. In this chapter some design examples of successful lightings from different building types are described and some of their key features analysed.

Offices

Offices are functional spaces that require consistent levels of good quality lighting designed to control glare. At the same time, it is beneficial from productivity and psychological viewpoints to provide office users with a stimulating visual environment, daylight, a view and some control over their local workspace. Many offices have a high occupancy density, a long daily period of use and are deep plan. Therefore, it is not surprising that the energy consumed by office lighting can be from 20 per cent to 40 per cent of total energy consumption. However, good office lighting design that implements energy saving measures has the potential to save significant amounts of energy.

Example: Arup Campus, Solihull, UK

Arup Campus was completed in 2001 and is a headquarters for Arup, one of the world's leading multidisciplinary built environment design and engineering companies. The campus has a total floor area of approximately 5,000m^2 and consists of two parallel two-storey buildings measuring approximately 60m long by 24m wide and orientated along a north-west to south-east axis. This orientation ensures that high levels of cool north-east sky light can enter the building's core via roof-mounted pods, which also serve as stack ventilation outlets. Gaps along the edge and centre of the first floor allow daylight to reach the ground floor and daylight also enters though side windows to light perimeter areas. Glazed openings either are minimised in size or have some form of louver system for solar and/or glare control. The electric lighting system consists of specially built luminaires that provide both uplighting and down lighting. The controls for the electric lighting are a highly developed system that uses both occupancy and daylight-linked sensors to provide electric light only when needed. Physical models in an artificial sky and computer simulations using the Radiance software were used to analyse and refine the lighting strategy. Figure 19.1 shows a section through one of the buildings and indicates the daylight strategy.

Schools

Schools are used predominantly during daytime hours and so daylight should always be the main source of lighting, with supplementary electric lighting being employed only when necessary. This approach is not only energy efficient – several studies have shown that student performance and attendance are better in schools that are predominantly daylit. It is important to be able to control lighting and glare within the classroom by, for example, having separate lighting for whiteboards, the ability to darken a room for projection and having task lighting for specialised teaching areas. The layout and dimensions of classrooms are also important considerations, both for access to daylight and for meshing with the distribution of the electric lighting arrangement.

Example: Kingsmead Primary School, Northwich, Cheshire, UK

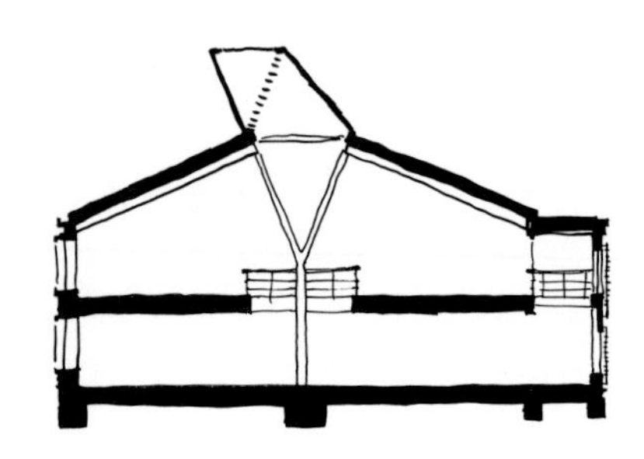

19.1

Kingsmead is one of many new sustainable schools constructed under the UK government's ambitious *Building School for the Future* programme. It was completed in July 2004 and has 250 pupils accommodated in a floor area of 1800m^2. It is a single storey building which is curved in plan with, unusually, most of the classrooms facing north. Each classroom has a controllable top-light in the deepest part of the classroom space. The architects (White Design) wanted to use natural lighting in all the main spaces, and most of the electric lights are switched off during the day. Classroom light switches are arranged in rows, allowing banks of lights to be switched on and off as required – useful for parts of the classrooms furthest away from the windows or

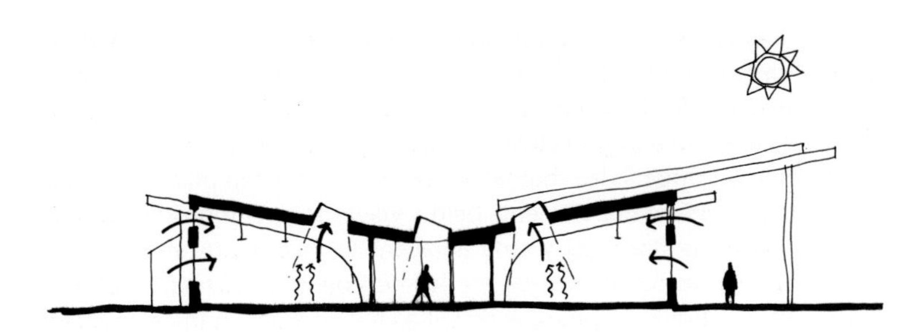

19.2

skylights. In addition, daylight sensors are linked to the electric lights, allowing lights to be dimmed automatically when adequate natural light is available. Post occupancy studies have shown that the quality of the daylit environment encourages users to keep the lights off, and, in addition, the building has scored a very high occupant satisfaction rating (in the top 10 per cent of UK buildings surveyed). Figure 19.2 is a section through the school, showing the north facing classrooms and the inverted roof for rainwater harvesting.

Hospitals

Hospitals are complex buildings to light – there is a very wide range of lighting requirements, from high lighting levels (>50,000 lux) in operating theatres to comfortable, low-stress lighting in wards and waiting areas. Many parts of a hospital will be running 24 hours per day and so lighting energy costs are high for a poorly designed lighting scheme. Hospitals can feel like enclosed spaces for both staff and patients. Good lighting and a stimulating visual environment can help, and the role of the hospital environment in healing and well-being has become more widely appreciated in recent few years. Research indicates positive impacts not just on subjective measures like patient satisfaction and staff morale but also on objective measures such as medical error rates, infection rates, staff turnover and patient length-of-stay. Some ways of ensuring efficient and satisfactory hospital lighting include providing windows to allow natural daylight into patient rooms, orientating patient rooms to exploit early-morning sun exposure, providing high lighting levels for complex visual tasks and having windows in staff areas so that staff have access to natural light.

Example: Evelina Children's Hospital, London, UK

Evelina was the first new children's hospital in London for over 100 years. It was designed by Michael Hopkins Architects and was completed in 2005. It is a seven storey building spread over 16,500m^2 and represented a radical departure from traditional hospital design. Evelina is dominated by a four storey south facing atrium that accommodates a school, a café and a large activity area. The atrium brings daylight into the hospital on three sides that penetrates into the deep plan treatment areas and outpatient departments below via large openings in the floor. Offices and three floors of wards adjacent to the atrium also receive natural light from it. The wards are located behind full-height glazing that enables patients to view the activities taking place in the atrium, as well as providing views out over London. Traditional approaches to electric lighting in hospitals were also discarded in an attempt to make the building feel less formal. For example, the main lighting in the atrium comes from 1 kW floodlights concealed on the top of the sixth floor offices that project light onto 'clouds' of adjustable mirrors suspended from the roof structure, which in turn reflect the light around the interior. This visually interesting solution also helped with maintenance and lamp replacement issues within the high space of the atrium. The eight 'clouds' in the roof structure can provide light levels of around 200 lux at atrium floor level. Two floodlights serve each cloud, with control via daylight sensors and a timer. Figure 19.3 shows a section through Evelina.

Exhibition spaces

Exhibition spaces, such as museums and art galleries, require lighting that serves two purposes – enjoyable viewing of the exhibits and a pleasing visual environment for visitors. Some key factors in such lighting schemes include the role of daylight, viewing comfort, modelling, reflections, colour rendering, conservation and safety. Daylight has excellent colour rendering but it can create problems such as glare from a bright sky in dark interiors, ultra-violet damage to exhibits and integration of daylight with artificial light in viewing areas. In many galleries daylight is predominantly used in circulation and social spaces, but it is becoming more common for controlled daylight to be brought into exhibition areas. A striking example of this is Tadao Ando's Daylight Museum in Gamo-Gun Shiga, Japan, which is lit only by natural light and closes at sunset. For the comfortable viewing of an exhibit, a balanced visual field is needed in which there is a gradual change in brightness or luminance between the exhibit, its surroundings and the background. A luminance range ratio of 10:3:1 is often found to be successful. Modelling involves highlighting the detail, colour and texture of an exhibit. Three-dimensional exhibits such as sculptures normally require dominant light with some fill lighting. Light coming from 15° to 40° above horizontal is best, but difficult to achieve with ceiling mounted luminaires. Reflections are a problem for exhibits in glass display cabinets. Possible solutions include ensuring the exhibit

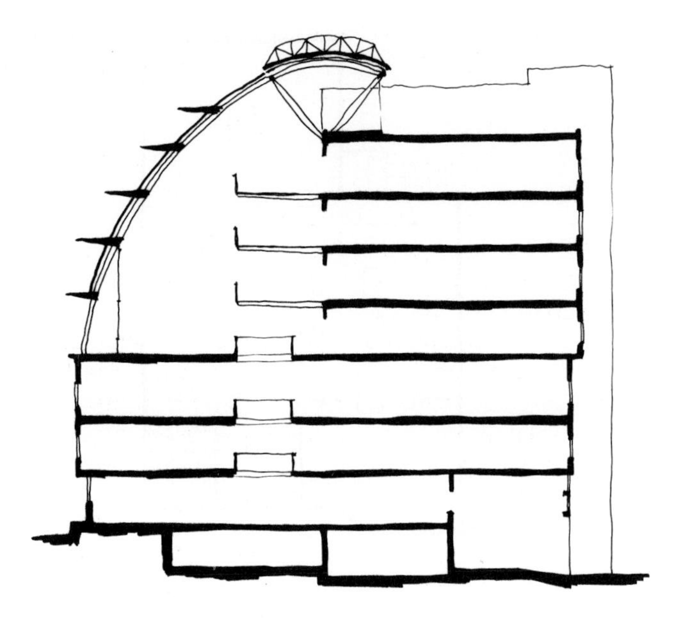

19.3

case is well lit compared to its surroundings, tilting the reflecting surface a few degrees and placing dark or neutral screens between exhibits. Conservation of delicate exhibits is obviously a critical consideration. Exhibits can be badly damaged by too much light, too much ultra violet radiation or too long an exposure to light. In order to conserve exhibits, light switching, UV filters and daylight control might be needed. Conservation needs, or the desire to create an interesting ambience, may lead to light levels in some exhibition spaces being very low. As darkness and brightness adaptation can take significant periods of time to achieve then it is important to allow sufficient time and space for people to adapt visually as they move between light and dark spaces.

Example: The New Art Gallery, Walsall, UK

The New Art Gallery at Walsall (designed by Caruso St John Architects) was completed in 2000 and houses the historic Garman Ryan Collection, together with high quality facilities for contemporary temporary exhibitions and education spaces. The building has a floor area of around 5,200m^2 spread over six storeys consisting of large rectangular galleries and a tower. The cladding material is neutrally coloured terracotta tiles. For galleries housing the permanent Garman Ryan Collection a considerable amount of the lighting is by natural daylight from side windows (the large gallery areas arranged vertically above each other mean that

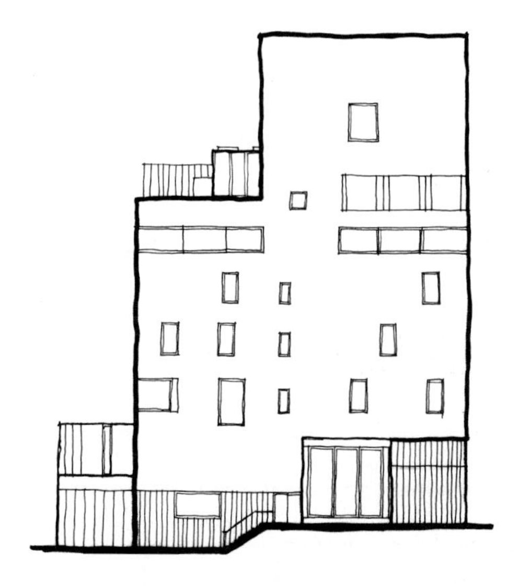

19.4

skylights could not be used). Side-lighting can be quite inflexible, is at lower illuminance levels than roof lighting and can produce asymmetric lighting conditions, leading to reflections on artworks hung opposite side windows. By placing the windows in some galleries off-centre the asymmetric nature of the side-lighting was emphasised but allowed art work in different media in the collection (such as robust canvas oil paintings and more delicate paper-based works) to be hung in the same gallery but on different walls. A window depth of 600mm, together with metal sputtering on the window glass, was chosen to give suitable light distribution and diffusion. White material blinds with a light transmission value of 10 per cent provide control of the amount of daylight entering the spaces, and are lowered when the daylight levels exceed a fixed limit or when direct sunlight irradiates the windows. The artificial lighting in these spaces is also located off-centre as with the natural lighting strategy. Hanging diffuse-glasshouse fluorescent lamp luminaires provide ambient lighting when daylight is insufficient, with electric light levels being dimmed or raised automatically in response to daylight levels. The lighting levels throughout the Temporary Exhibition rooms had to meet conservation standards set by art lending institutions. A layered clerestory window system was devised with electric lighting and motorised blinds located in the cavity between light-diffusing layers of glass. The blinds adjust so that permitted light levels are not exceeded, and the electric lighting is automatically dimmed to supplement daylight when required and to illuminate the spaces at night. The diffusing windows are located above head height, eliminating the risk of reflections off exhibits. Figure 19.4 shows the east elevation, the tiled exterior and the asymmetric nature of the glazing.

Part **4**

Bibliography

Cuttle, C. *Lighting by Design*, Architectural Press (2003).

Egan, M.D and Olgyay, V. *Architectural Lighting*, 2nd edn, McGraw-Hill (2002).

Moore, F. *Concepts and Practice of Architectural Daylighting*, Van Nostrand Reinhold (1991).

Phillips, D. *Lighting Modern Buildings*, Architectural Press (2000).

Phillips, D. *The Lit Environment*, Architectural Press (2002).

Phillips, D. *Daylighting*, Architectural Press (2004).

Tregenza, P. and Loe, D. *The Design of Lighting*, E & FN Spon (1998).

Verges, M. *Light in Architecture*, Tectum (2007).

Webliography

http://www.enermodal.com/Canadian/pdf/DaylightingGuideforCanadianBuildingsFinal6.pdf Daylighting guide for Canadian commercial buildings (2002) (accessed 14 March 2008).

http://www.learn.londonmet.ac.uk/packages/synthlight/handbook/index.html SynthLight Handbook (2004) (accessed 14 March 2008).

http://windows.lbl.gov/daylighting/designguide/dlg.pdf Tips for daylighting with windows (1997) (accessed 14 March 2008).

Part 5

Acoustic design and the aural environment

Chapter **20**

Basic principles of sound

Introduction

The reader who might have an interest in sustainability may wonder about the reasons for giving the issue of noise some coverage in a book dealing with technology and sustainability in the built environment. Although the link between noise and architectural technology is fairly straightforward, its relationship with sustainable developments needs to be clarified. Most publications on environmentally conscious design approaches tend to emphasise the issue of energy, which does not apply directly to the aural environment. Noise, however is closely related to sustainability in many ways.

In urban areas, the proliferation of new mixed developments for commercial and housing use meant that what once were industrial estates in the suburbs are now located adjacent to where people live and work. This can cause noise nuisance. With the increased interest in urban regeneration, the need to deal with noise issues as part of a sustainable way of living has never been greater. If sensible land use is to be adopted and if high density housing is part of a sustainable future, then noise related issues become very relevant to the sustainability agenda. The choice of materials and techniques used to mitigate noise effects have a direct bearing on our built environment, both in terms of resources and environmental conditions.

Although the case of urban area was highlighted here, rural areas also have their own problems with noise, particularly, transportation, and wind farm noise.

This section will discuss various aspects of design that relate to sound and noise, and offer some guidance that would enable future designers to consider solutions that would help promote sustainability. In order to give some understanding of the sonic and aural environment, the principles associated with sound and noise are reviewed. This is followed by a discussion of methods and techniques used to mitigate the effect of noise.

Physics of sound

One of the functional requirements of spatial design is to provide the right conditions for hearing and enjoying the sounds as well as the right conditions for peace and quiet. Before those conditions are discussed further, a review of the physical principles of sound would be helpful.

Sound is an aural sensation, which is caused by fluctuations in the pressure of the air reaching the eardrum. Those fluctuations in the air are caused by some source of vibration, which can be either from some solid object (e.g. a string) or from turbulence in a liquid or gas (e.g. whistle). Acoustics (from the Greek akoustikais) is the science of sound which also translates to science of small amplitude mechanical vibrations.

What the human ear can hear depends on the physical characteristics of the sound. These are frequency (number of vibrations per second measured in Hertz and abbreviated to Hz), wavelength (the distance travelled by the sound during the period of one complete vibration, measured in metres and abbreviated to m) and their product, which gives the speed of sound (measured in metres per second abbreviated to m/s). For everyday application the speed of sound in the air is taken as 340 m/s.

Decibel

The unit used to measure sound levels is the decibel (abbreviated to dB). The sub-multiple deci- is used because the original unit (Bel) named after Alexander Graham Bell) is rather large. The decibel scale is a logarithmic scale and has been devised to reflect the way the human ear responds to stimuli. The dB level can be derived from either the sound intensity (abbreviated to I) or the sound pressure (abbreviated to p). The way the human ear perceives sounds is by comparing the intensity or pressure of the sound wave to a *reference value* that represent the threshold of hearing. These two quantities have their values as follows:

Reference intensity I_0 = 1 pico-Watt/m^2 = 10^{-12} W
Reference pressure p_0 = 20 μPa
(micro-Pascal = 20 x10^{-6} Pa or 2 x10^{-5} Pa)

The two equations used to derive the sound level from the quantities above are as follows:

$$\text{Sound intensity level: SIL} = 10 \times \log \frac{I}{I_0} \quad \text{(in dB)}$$

$$\text{Sound pressure level: SpL} = 20 \times \log \frac{p}{p_0} \quad \text{(in dB)}$$

All this theory is not crucial to the non specialist in acoustics. However it is worth remembering that because of the logarithmic nature of the decibel scale, there are practical implications that the designer needs to bear in mind. One of these is the way the cumulative effect of different sounds is heard by the human ear simultaneously. The combined effect of any two sounds is given by an increment based on the difference between the two sounds. The increment is added to the higher of the two levels and would represent the combined sound level. The nomogram given in Figure 20.1 demonstrates how two sound levels can be combined.

The range of everyday sounds that the human ear can hear varies between lower and upper thresholds (see Figure 20.2). Our ears can detect a 1dB change in the sound level. In practice however, a 3dB change is considered the smallest difference that is significant. Table 20.1 shows the effect on hearing of various sound level changes.

Auditory response and loudness

The sensitivity of the human ear to sound is affected by the frequency at which the sound is generated. This is important to the designer, as the design of solutions to noise associated problems rely on identifying the nature of the noise nuisance including its frequencies.

Human hearing is least sensitive to low frequencies (bass). For example, a 60dB sound at 1,000Hz would be perceived by the human ear in

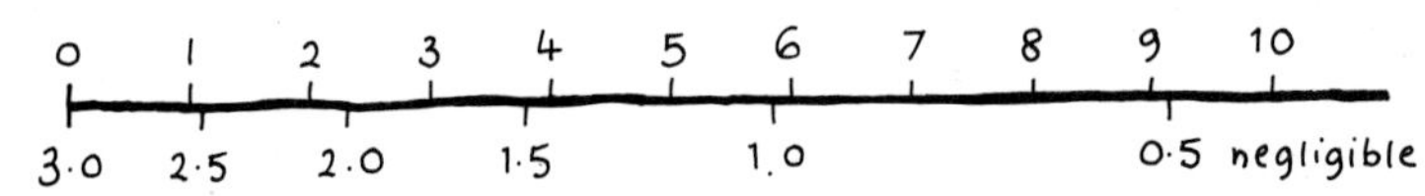

20.1

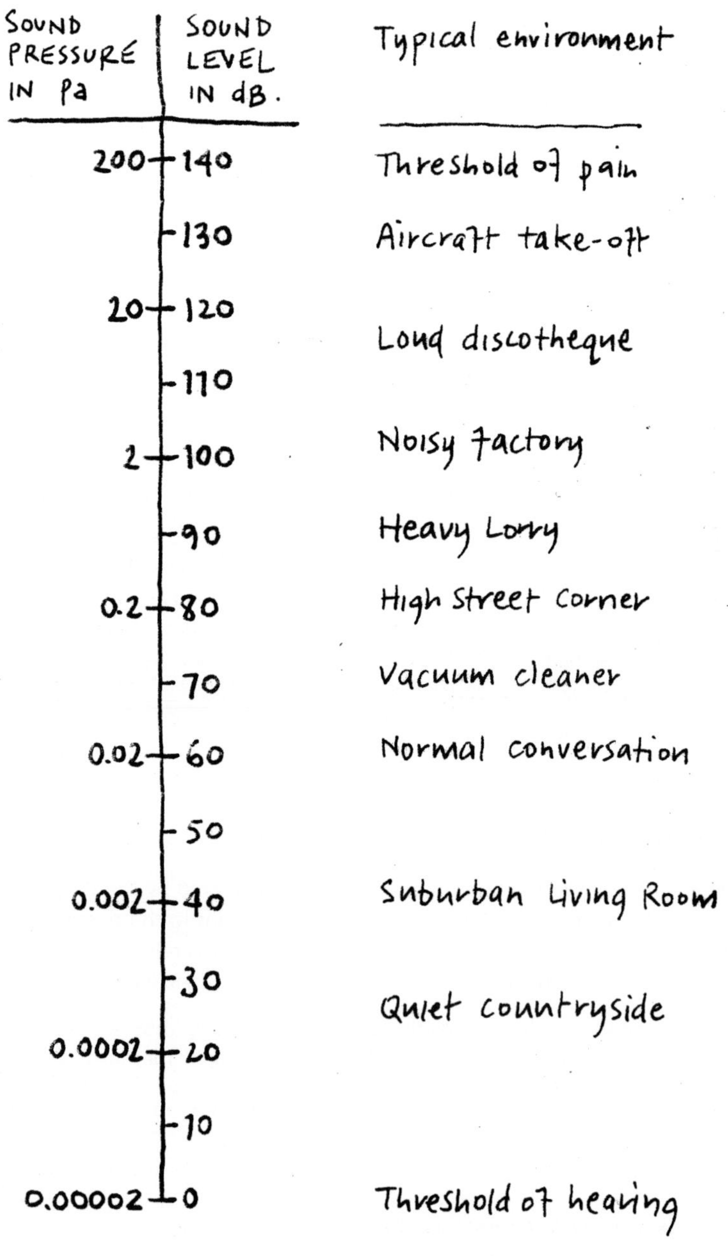
SOUND PRESSURE IN Pa
SOUND LEVEL IN dB.
Typical environment
200
140
Threshold of pain
130
Aircraft take-off
20
120
Loud discotheque
110
2
100
Noisy factory
90
Heavy Lorry
0.2
80
High Street Corner
70
Vacuum cleaner
0.02
60
Normal conversation
50
0.002
40
Suburban Living Room
30
Quiet countryside
0.0002
20
10
0.00002
0
Threshold of hearing

20.2

Table 20.1 Effect of changes in sound level on hearing

Change in decibel level	*Effect on hearing*
+/– 1dB	Negligible
+/– 3dB	Just noticeable
+ 10dB	Twice as loud
– 10dB	Half as loud
+ 20dB	Four times louder
– 20dB	One quarter as loud

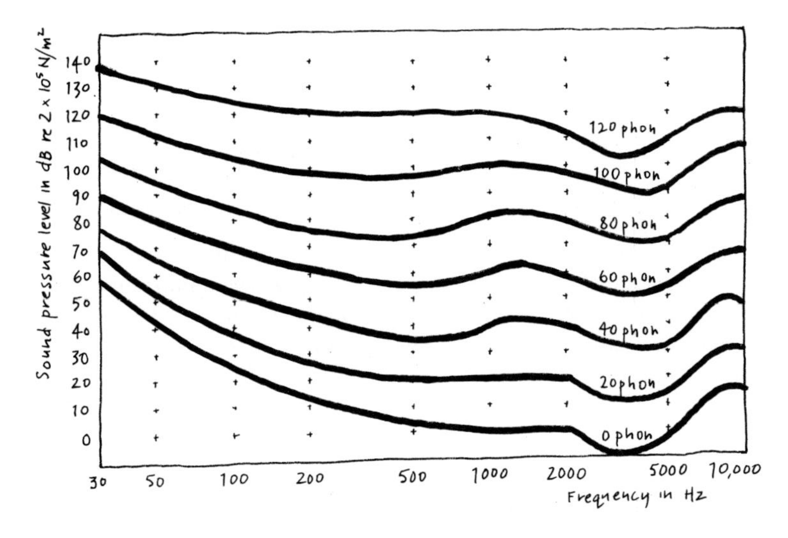

20.3

the same way as an 80dB one at 50Hz.The way the ear responds to noise at various frequencies leads to the development of *equal loudness contours* (see Figure 20.3). The contours, show how the human ear is most sensitive between 2kHz and 5kHz and that its sensitivity is reduced at lower frequencies. The unit used to indicate the loudness is the *phon*. Each of the two sound levels mentioned above (60dB at 1,000Hz and 80dB at 50Hz) would produce the same effect, which is 60 phon loudness.

Since the phon level cannot be measured directly, as it is to do with the subjective response of the human ear, sound level meters are provided with mechanisms to provide such correction. One such mechanism, which is relevant to architectural acoustics, is the 'A' weighting scale

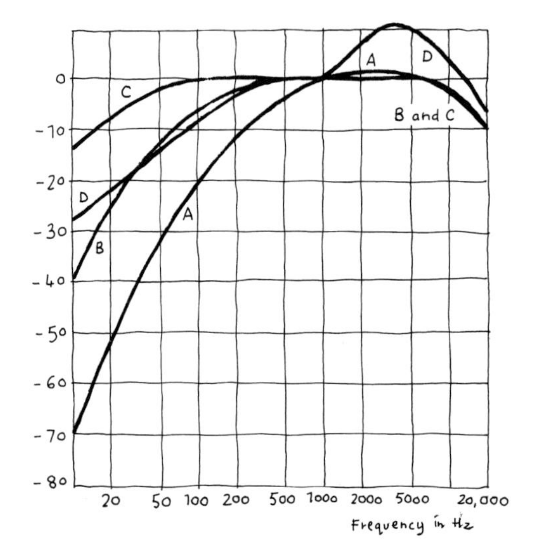

20.4

which produces sound levels expressed in A-weighted decibel or dB(A) (see Figure 20.4). On close inspection, the A-weighting curve is a close approximation to the 40 phon loudness contour. Most of the architectural acoustics applications make use of this scale, including performance criteria and statutory requirements.

Chapter **21**

Noise in the external environment

Noise

So far the discussion has been focused on the nature of noise as a physical phenomenon and how the human ear perceives it. This chapter will look at the behaviour of sound particularly in the external environment. The discussion would be of interest to both students and practitioners of design as it would shed light on ways that can lead to dealing with noise successfully as part of the design process. Before that can be undertaken, it is worth clarifying the difference between sound and noise. From a purely physical point of view, both sound and noise are the same as they are both random vibrations. From a subjective point of view however, there is a difference. One person's enjoyable sound (loud music with a distinct bass) is another's noise. Noise therefore can be defined as unwanted sound.

Sound propagation

When a sound or noise travels from the point where it was generated (source) to the point where it is heard (receiver) its level (how loud it is) will decrease as its energy is spread over a wider area. The rate of reduction in sound level due to distance travelled varies according to the type of source generating the sound.

For a point source (a source that is off the ground and is radiating in all directions), the energy of sound is radiated equally in all directions covering an area of a sphere that has the source at its centre and a radius equal to the distance from source to receiver. Under these conditions, the sound intensity is inversely proportional to the square of the distance (see Figure 21.1). For example if the distance is increased by a factor of 2, the surface area over which sound is spread increases by a

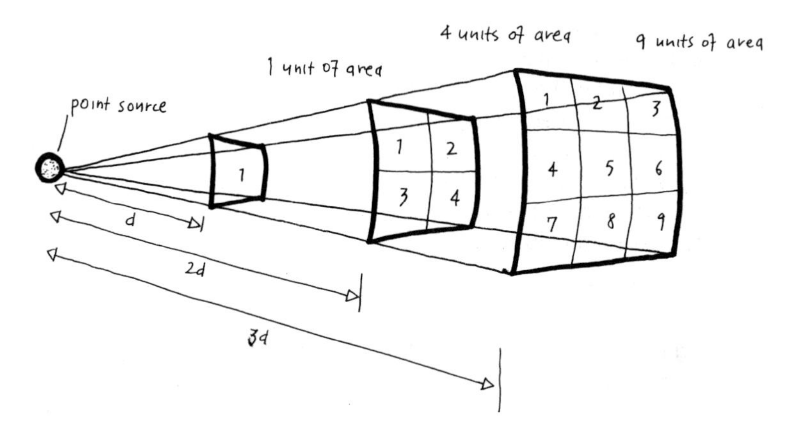

21.1

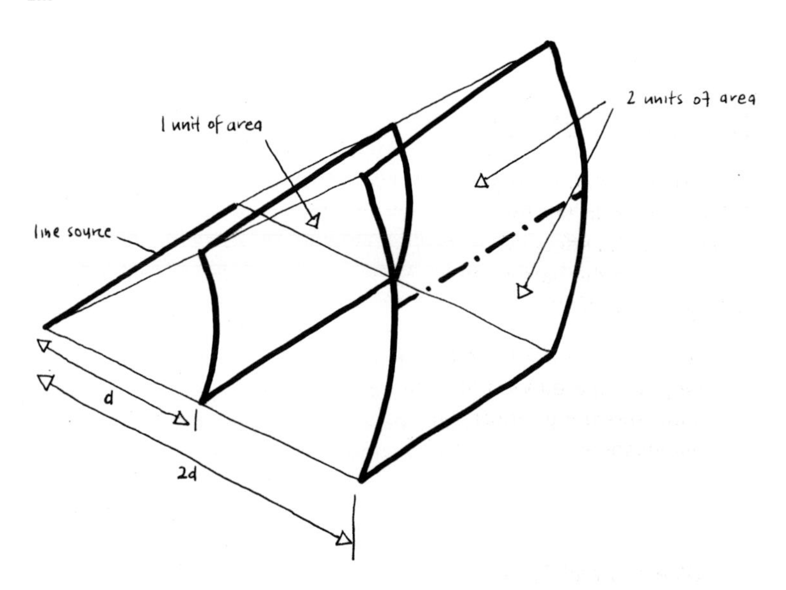

21.2

factor of 4, the sound energy will decrease by a factor of 4 and the dB level will be reduced by 6dB (10 x log 4). If the source of sound is located on the ground and emitting its sound energy in a hemisphere, the above relationship is true but only for half a sphere. In other words, doubling the distance would only result in a 3dB sound attenuation. A single car on a paved hard surface would be approximated to such a condition.

When the sound is generated from a line source, the sound energy spreads out in the shape of a cylinder for which the radius is equal to the distance from the source to where the sound is heard (see Figure 21.2).

For this type of source, the sound intensity decreases in inverse proportion to the distance from the source. For each doubling of the distance the sound level will decrease by 3dB. Where the source is close to the ground and the intervening surface (between source and receiver is hard), the reduction in noise level is about 1.5dB. A typical line source would be free flowing traffic on a busy road heard at a point not too close to the road so that the noise is coming from more than just the vehicle passing the observer.

The principles of sound propagation clearly show that distance from the source of sound will not, by itself, provide enough sound reduction. Moving the position of a building away from the road would not provide much sound reduction within the area of most building plots, and other methods need to be explored. Further discussion of some of these methods will follow later.

Reduction of noise by barriers

Barriers are often used to shield away the noise and reduce its effect. These can be in the form of, fences, walls, vegetation, earth mounds and so on. The effect of a barrier in mitigating noise depends primarily on the size of the barrier, its location with regard to the source and the nature of its surface.

- For a rigid barrier to be effective in screening noise, it needs to be large compared with the wavelength of the noise. For any significant screening effect, the following relationship needs to be established:

  $$\frac{H^2}{\lambda D_s} \geq 2$$

  Where H and D_s are as shown in Figure 21.3 and λ is the wavelength of the sound.

- The noise attenuation by a barrier can be approximately estimated from the mathematical formula based on the work of Maekawa (Smith *et al.* 1996) which gives the sound reduction due to a thin rigid barrier between source and receiver as:

  $$E_b = 10\log\left(3 + \frac{40\delta}{\lambda}\right)$$

  where; δ is the sound path difference as illustrated in Figure 21.4. The advantage of such a formula is that it can be applied to any combination of barrier dimensions and position with regard to source and receiver.

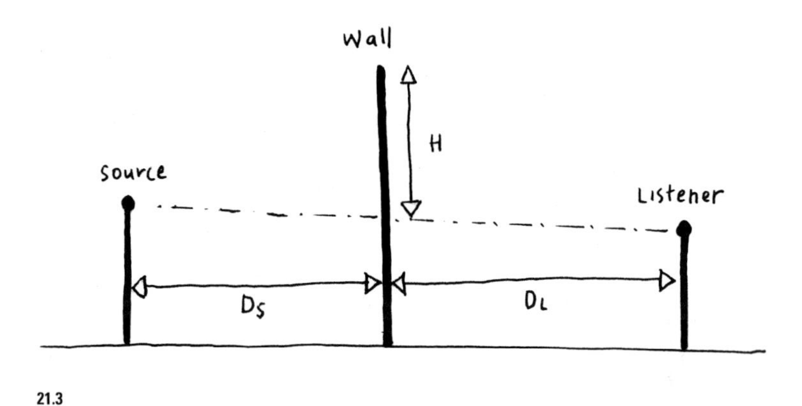

21.3

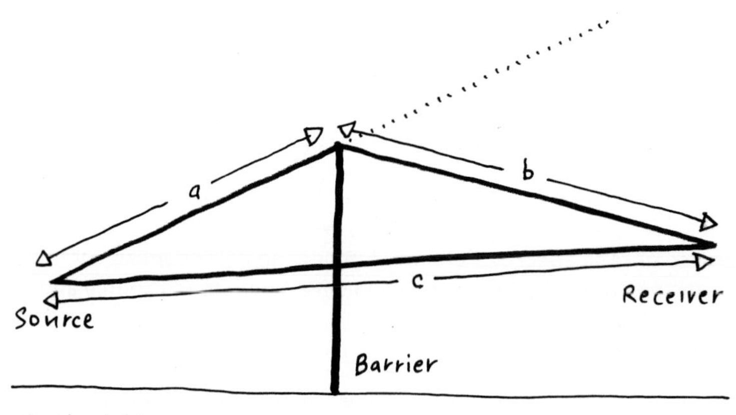

21.4

Since no specific data regarding the material of the barrier is required to estimate its performance, pre-prepared graphical data such as that shown in Figure 21.5 can be used to read off noise attenuation of a barrier at any given frequency.

The discussion above is only meant as a way of providing general guidance to the architect/designer in order to consider the possible attenuation effect of the barrier-distance combination at an early design stage. For detailed assessment of barrier performance and noise effects, the input of a specialist acoustician would be required.

Landscape

Noise attenuation due to shrubs and trees is limited compared to hard barriers. However, their presence affects the noise reduction process by

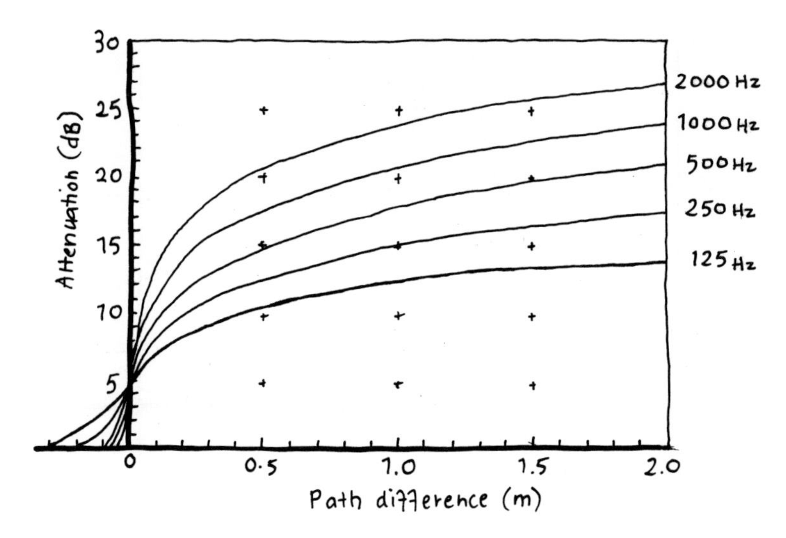

21.5

providing some absorption of sound energy in contact with the foliage near the soft ground associated with vegetation.

The use of earth mounds and cuttings as barriers to noise is gaining popularity among designers. Although an earth mound of a certain height would give slightly less attenuation than a hard barrier of a similar height, it is still worth considering given other advantages that it offers particularly its environmental credentials. Research work by Ekici and Bougdah (Bougdah *et al.* 2006) has shown that an earth mound such as that described in Figure 21.6 can attenuate road traffic noise by up to 16dB at some 50m away behind it at a height of 1.5m above the ground. These conditions represent typical distances from the edge of a major highway to nearby buildings and their external spaces. Placing 0.5m high strips of hard thin material on top of the mound has resulted in an improvement of over 3dB in sound attenuation. The mound was studied under hard surface conditions, and using soft ground conditions and vegetation would result in even further improvements in performance.

Noise rating

One area, which designers need to be familiar with, is the rating of noise. This is because often the debate at an early design stage, or even planning stage, is about such issues as noise and whether or not it could be a problem. In order to be able to fully contribute to that debate,

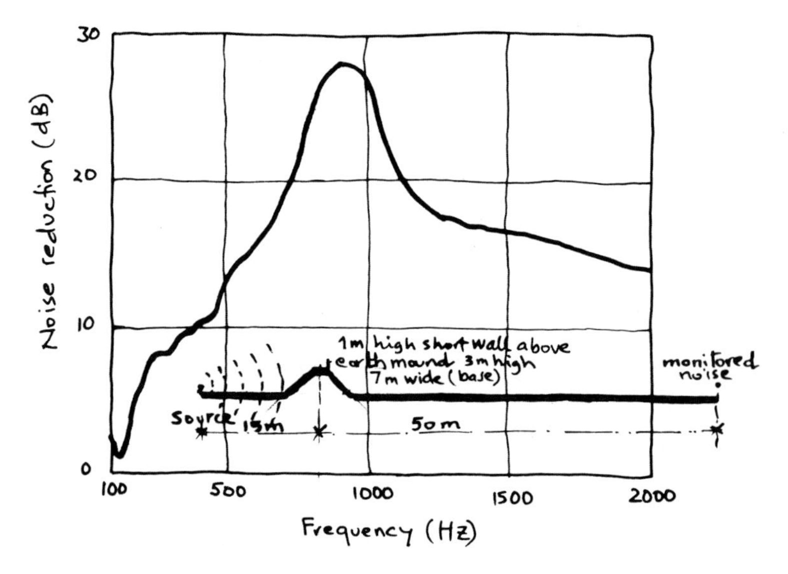

21.6

it would be helpful for designers to be familiar with some of the criteria used by planning authorities to decide on thc outcome of planning proposals. Noise rating criteria are numerous and varied, but two such criteria that are used quite often are the dB(A) scale, the *Noise Criterion* scale and the *Noise Rating* scale.

The *phon* scale has been discussed previously. Its drawback, however, is that it applies to pure tones, or sounds generated at a single frequency. Most of the noise we hear everyday is complex and usually contains a number of frequencies. An A-weighted sound level dB(A) can be used often to describe such a complex noise. This description, however is only sketchy and does not give the full picture as the dB(A) is a weighted average. For a complete description of the noise climate, there is a need for a third octave analysis that would describe the full noise spectrum (see Figure 21.7) which then can be rated for its noisiness.

The Noise Criterion or NC curves were developed from results obtained from interviews with office workers, industrial workers and people in public spaces. These are mainly used in the United States. The primary concern for the NC curves is the interference of noise with speech intelligibility. The NC rating of a noise under consideration is determined by plotting the octave-band sound pressure levels of the sound on the family of NC curves (see Figure 21.8). For the noise to achieve a particular NC rating, the spectrum should be as close as possible to the curve but not any higher.

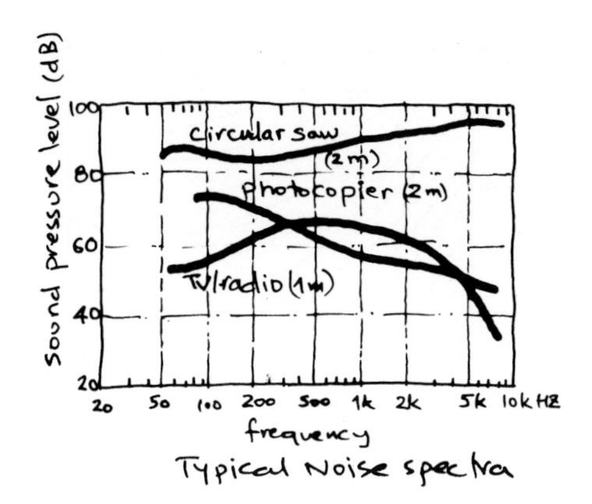

21.7

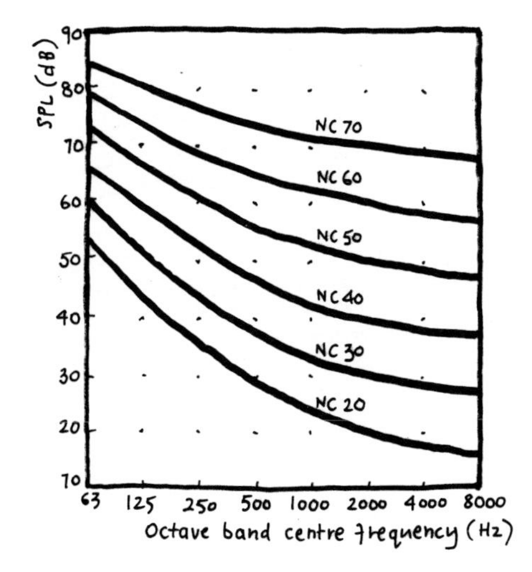

21.8

The Noise Rating curves are similar to the NC curves but have more tolerance for low frequency noise (see Figure 21.9). They are used in the UK for several purposes including assessment of acceptability of noise for hearing preservation and avoiding annoyance. Although the noisiness of a given noise climate has a subjective element to it, it seems to have a correlation with the NR rating. Table 21.1 shows how various NR levels are generally judged.

Although the dB(A) and NR scales are different in how they describe the noise, however, for practical purposes, the dB(A) value can be taken to be between 4 and 6 units above the equivalent NR number, depending on the spectrum.

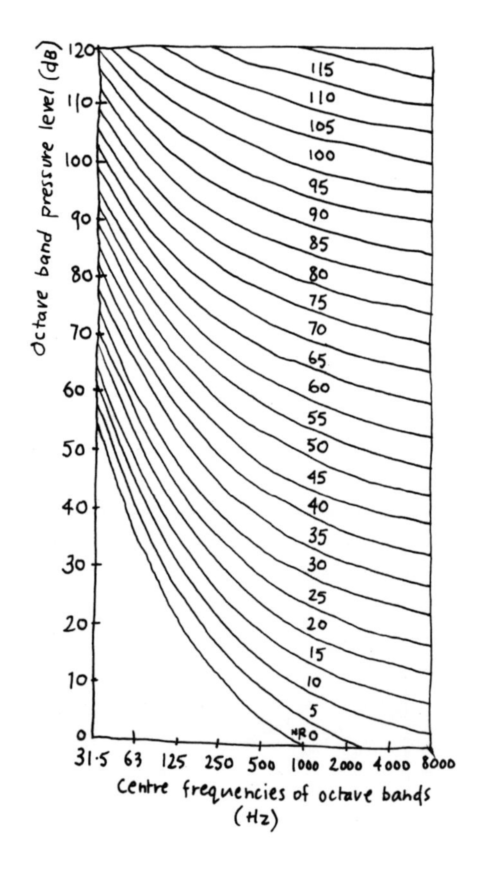

21.9

Table 21.1 Typical NR values

NR rating	*Description*	*Typical examples*
NR20–25	Very quiet	TV studios/bedroom
NR30–35	Quiet	living room/classroom
NR40–45	Moderately noisy	Conference room
NR50–55	Noisy	General office
NR60 +	Very noisy	

Practical issues

Although the architect/designer is not required to know the various engineering analysis methods that acousticians use, it would be worth his/her while to be familiar with some general rules of thumb that can be made use of at an early design stage. The use of such rules is particularly useful to establish the merits of sites to be developed and the severity or otherwise of the noise issue. The following guidance may prove to be useful.

When estimating the reduction in sound level with distance from the source, the following rules can be used:

- For a point source radiating in all directions, sound attenuation at a distance d metres away is given as: *Attenuation* = 10 log $(4\pi d^2)$
- If the sound is radiated over non-absorbent ground, attenuation is estimated as: *Attenuation* = 10 log $(2\pi d^2)$
- For a line source, the two equations given above would be modified as follows:

  Sound radiated uniformly: *Attenuation* = 10 log $(2\pi d^2)$
  Sound radiated over non-absorbent ground:
  Attenuation = 10 log (πd)

Thin rigid barriers, such as fences and walls can be used as means to attenuate noise. Their effectiveness depends primarily on their physical size and location with regard to the source and receiver. The path difference equation given previously can be used to estimate their performance. If these barriers are used, two issues need to be borne in mind; first, they need to be free from gaps in their surface and second, their visual impact needs to be considered.

Whenever possible, 'green' barriers consisting of earth mounds and cuttings topped up by evergreen vegetation ought to be used instead of rigid barriers. To estimate their performance, it can be approximated to that of an equivalent thin barrier and worked out using the method explained previously.

Chapter 22

Sound insulation

Sound insulation and design

Although sound insulation shares a common concern with other aspects of design in specifying materials that provide a certain level of performance, it is the one area where workmanship is extremely important in order for the specified materials to achieve their stated performance. This chapter will deal with some technical and practical issues of sound insulation so that the reader can:

- appreciate how sound is transmitted within buildings;
- be familiar with the principles of sound control and their application;
- be aware of typical sound insulation requirements of building regulations.

Noise transfer

Sound energy is transferred into and between different parts of buildings by means of various mechanisms. From a designer's point of view knowing the type of sound being considered would help identify ways of dealing with it. As far as noise transfer is concerned, there are two types of noise; airborne sound and impact sound. In order to illustrate the difference between the two types of sound, let us consider two adjacent rooms separated by a partition (see Figure 22.1). The room where the sound is generated is referred to as the source room. The room where the sound is heard by an observer is referred to as the receiving room.

Airborne sound is sound energy that travels in the air before reaching the partition that will attenuate it. Typical examples of airborne sound

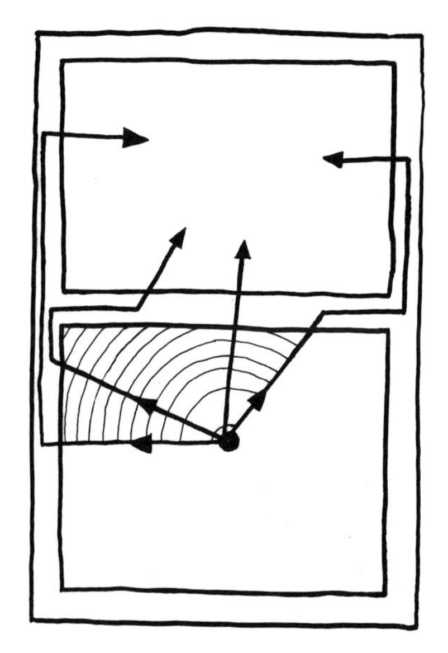

22.1

include voices, musical instruments and traffic noise. As Figure 22.1 illustrates, the sound transmitted into the receiving room reaches its destination by various paths. Those other than through the separating partition are referred to as flanking paths. The level of sound reaching the receiving room will depend on the characteristics of the separating wall as well as the conditions of adjoining surfaces that make up the flanking paths. These issues will be discussed further later on in the chapter.

Impact sound is generated in the structure of the room (walls, floor, etc.). It travels through the various flanking paths first, then through the air before it reaches the receiver (see Figure 22.2). In order to reduce the sound level at receiver, the sound is dealt with at source by means of isolation. Further discussion of this will follow.

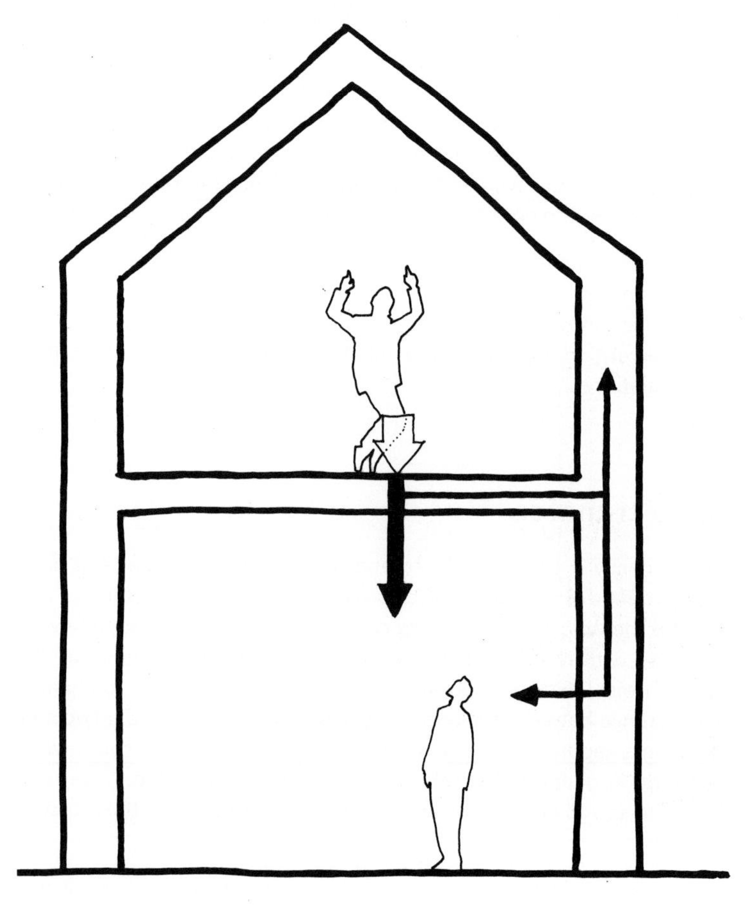

22.2

Statutory requirements

Standards for sound insulation vary from one country to another. In the UK there are various standards for different parts of the country. The Building Regulations for England and Wales has its counterparts in Scotland (Building Standards) and Northern Ireland (The Building Regulations, Northern Ireland). The designer is reminded to check which regulations apply and which version is current.

Part E of The Building Regulations 2000, England and Wales, deals specifically with the resistance to the passage of sound within and between adjoining buildings used as dwellings and for residential purposes. The sound insulation of the building envelope is dealt with separately under a British Standard (BS8233) that puts a limit on indoor ambient noise levels inside various types of buildings. The focus of the building regulations, on the other hand, is the separating elements between dwellings. These include separating walls and separating floors as indicated in the diagram in Figure 22.3. Walls are required to meet sound insulation standards for airborne sound while floors are required to meet both airborne and impact sound.

For airborne sound insulation, the criterion used is $D_{nt,W}$, which stands for weighted standardised sound level difference in dB. In other words, it is the sound that is prevented from passing from one room to another due to the presence of the intervening element (wall or floor). This criterion is a single-number quantity that characterises airborne sound insulation

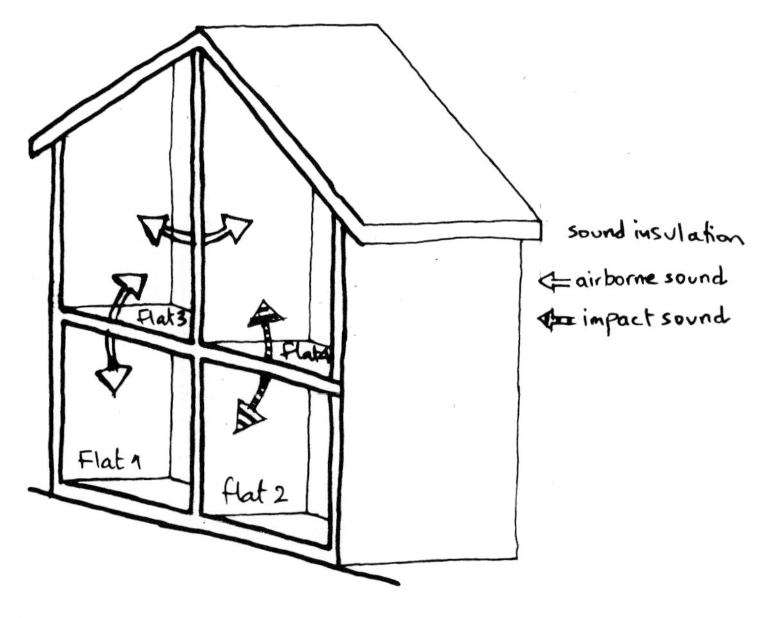

22.3

between rooms using a particular noise spectrum. To correct for the effect of the spectrum, a correction factor C_{tr} is used. For the purpose of building regulation compliance the criterion is given as $D_{nt,W} + C_{tr}$.

For impact sound insulation, instead of using a level difference between source and receiver, an actual maximum sound level that is not to be exceeded in the receiving room is specified. The $L'_{nT,W}$ or weighted standardised impact sound level is used as the performance criterion.

A summary of the sound insulation standards for separating walls and floors is given in Table 22.1 below. For a complete set of performance standards, the approved document Part E of the Building Regulations should be consulted (ODPM 2004)

For the designer, it is not merely being aware of the standards, but also being able to design solutions to deal with sound insulation. The practical guidance section will shed more light on the subject.

Controlling noise during the planning stage can be an effective tool for reducing noise effects. To this effect, the reader's attention is drawn to planning legislation and guidance that national and local governments use. An example of such guidance is the Planning Policy Guidance 24: Planning and Noise, which applies to England and Wales (Department for Communities and Local Government 1994); and its equivalent statutory guidance that exists for the rest of the UK. The purpose of this statutory document is to guide local authorities on the use of their powers to minimise the impact of noise for sensitive developments. The main feature of the guidance is the use of four noise exposure categories for residential developments and setting noise levels for each of the categories.

Noise exposure categories (NECs)

The guidance has made provision for four noise exposure categories. Any proposal for residential development near a source of sound would

Table 22.1 Sound insulation standards (after ODPM 2004)

Separating element	*Airborne sound insulation $D_{nt,W} + C_{tr}$ dB* (*Minimum values*)	*Impact sound insulation $L'_{nT,W}$ dB* (*Maximum values*)
Purpose built dwellings		
Walls	45	n.a.
Floors	45	62
Dwellings formed by material change of use		
Walls	43	n.a.
Floors	43	64

need to be assessed against one of the four categories and dealt with accordingly. According to PPG24 (ODPM 2004), the four categories are as follows:

Table 22.2 Noise exposure categories (NECs)

NEC	*Guidance*
A	Noise need not be a determining factor in granting planning permission, although the noise level at the high end of the category should not be regarded as a desirable level.
B	Noise should be taken into account when determining planning applications and, where appropriate, conditions imposed to ensure an adequate level of protection against noise.
C	Planning permission should not normally be granted. Where it is considered that permission should be given, for example because there are no alternative quieter sites available, conditions should be imposed to ensure a commensurate level of protection against noise.
D	Planning permission should normally be refused.

Each of the four NECs is allocated recommended noise levels for various sources during the daytime and night-time. These are as follows:

Table 22.3 Limiting noise levels for NECs

Noise levels corresponding to the Noise Exposure Categories for new dwellings

	Noise Exposure Category			
Noise source	*A*	*B*	*C*	*D*
Road traffic				
07.00–23.00	<55	55-63	63–72	>72
23.00–07.00	<45	45-57	57–66	>66
Rail traffic				
07.00–23.00	<55	55-66	66–74	>74
23.00–07.00	<45	45-59	59–66	>66
Air traffic				
07.00–23.00	<57	57-66	66–72	>72
23.00–07.00	<48	48-57	57–66	>66
Mixed sources				
07.00–23.00	<55	55-63	63–72	>72
23.00–07.00	<45	45-57	57–66	>66

Physics of sound insulation

Understanding the basic principles behind sound insulation can help designers devise solutions to noise problems. This section will discuss the main mechanisms involved in sound insulation. Sound insulation depends on four general principles. These are: mass, completeness, flexibility and isolation. The following sections give some insight into these sound insulation techniques.

Mass

Heavyweight materials and constructions transmit less sound than lightweight ones. The highly packed particles of a dense material restrict the size of sound vibrations inside it and as a result, the amplitude of the sound waves re-radiated into the air at the other face of the material are restricted. In other words, less sound energy travels through dense materials. This is referred to as the *mass law* and it stipulates that the sound insulation of a single leaf partition is proportional to its mass per unit area (otherwise known as surface density). The following points are part of the interpretation of this law:

- The single leaf description extends to composite construction such as plastered masonry, as long as the layers are bonded together.
- According to the theory, a doubling of mass would increase the sound insulation by 6dB. In practice, however, a 5dB increase is likely to be the case.
- The same rule applies to the doubling of the frequency.

As Figure 22.4 demonstrates, the mass law does not hold good for all the frequencies. Towards both the lower and upper end of the frequency spectrum, the performance of partition is controlled by what is

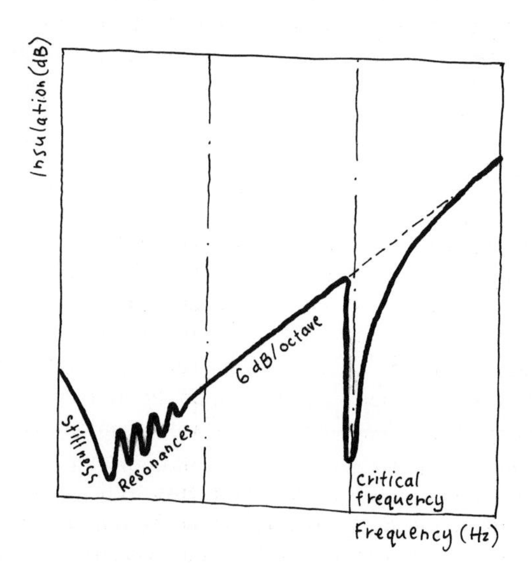

22.4

referred to as resonance and coincidence effects respectively. These are highly specialist areas of engineering and usually dealt with by an acoustician.

Completeness

When sound energy hits an obstacle such as a dense wall, it would try to circumvent it to find a way through, and the presence of small gaps in the structure become more significant to the overall sound insulation. The completeness of a structure and hence its ability to provide good sound insulation, is affected by air tightness and uniformity of mass.

The presence of small gaps in the structure resisting the noise will reduce its sound insulating ability. This is particularly an issue for air-borne sound. For instance the presence of a crack, which in size represents only 0.008 per cent of the total area of a brick wall will cause its sound insulation to be reduced from 50dB to 40dB. If the size of the crack were to be increased to 0.1 per cent, the sound reduction of the wall will fall to 30dB.

The overall performance of a structure to resist the passage of sound is greatly affected by the presence of small areas with low sound insulation, as the combined performance would be closer to that of the area of poorer performance. For instance a poorly sealed door with an area occupying 25 per cent of a wall which otherwise would have a sound insulation value of 45dB would bring it down to 23dB. Although openings such as doors and windows are necessary in a building, being aware of the uniformity principle can reduce their negative impact on the overall sound insulation of the structure. Further guidance will be discussed later.

Flexibility

The stiffness of a partition is a physical property that depends upon the elasticity of the material that makes up the partition and the way this is fixed around the edges. High stiffness can cause loss of sound insulation at both high and low frequencies as shown in the mass law diagram. These losses are caused by both resonance and coincidence effects. Loss of insulation due to resonance occurs when the frequency of the sound passing through the partition is the same as the natural frequency of the partition itself. This is particularly a problem in the cavities of floating floors and dry-lined constructions (see Figure 22.5). In such cases, the mass of the panel (in kg/m^2) multiplied by the depth of the cavity (in metres) ought to be more than 0.5 to keep the resonance frequency below 100Hz. The table below illustrates some typical examples.

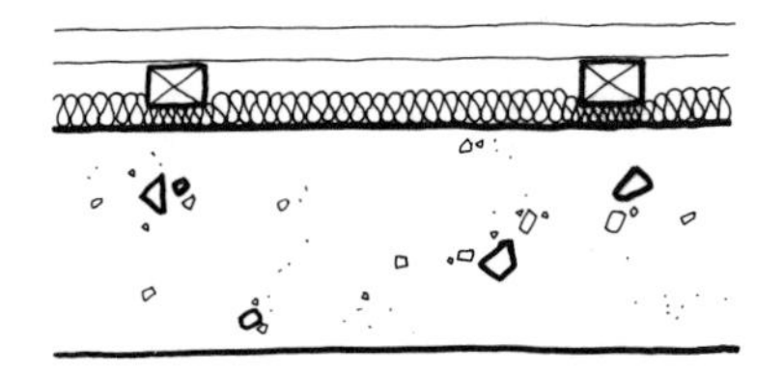

22.5

Table 22.4 Resonant frequency for some typical constructions

Mass-air-resonance

Resonant frequency of a panel $f_{res} = \dfrac{60}{\sqrt{(m \times d)}}$ Hz

m: mass per unit area (kg/m^2)
d: depth of separation (m)

Construction	Air gap *d* (m)	f_{res}	$m \times d$
19 mm chipboard	0.05	72	0.700
22 mm floorboards	0.05	85	0.500
50 mm screed	0.006	72	0.690
19 mm plasterboard	0.025	87	0.365
19 mm chipboard	0.006	207	0.084

Rule of thumb: always keep $m \times d > 0.5$

Above a certain frequency known as the critical frequency, the behaviour of a partition in controlling noise no longer obeys the mass law. A loss of insulation is caused at and above the critical frequency due to coincidence between the sound wave and the wave of flexing and bending vibrations in the partition. Different materials would have different critical frequencies. This is rather a specialist subject and the architect is encouraged to seek specialist advice.

Isolation

Isolating two adjacent structures from each other will reduce the sound energy passing from one side to another. This method of providing sound insulation can be as effective as heavy construction but using lightweight materials. Lightweight forms of construction work on this principle. In practice however, they have some inherent problems if the detailing is not carefully considered. For isolation to work, the two structures need to be in minimal contact with each other as sound insulation due to isolation can easily be undone by flanking transmission. The cavity separating the two structures needs to be wide enough to avoid the effect of resonance as described previously.

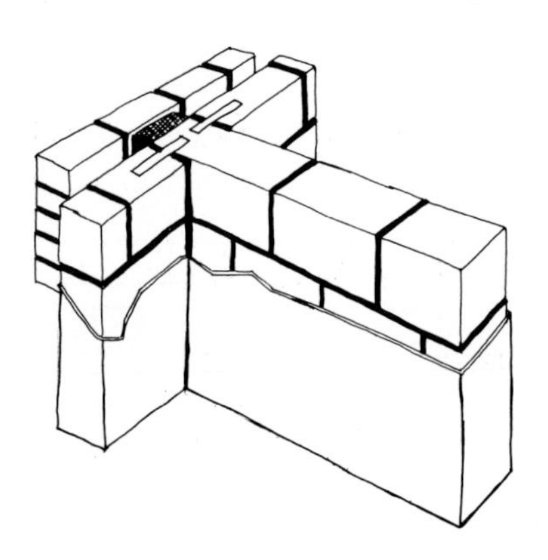

22.6

Practical guidance

The provision of good sound insulation is often reduced to meeting statutory requirements imposed by building codes and regulations. From a designer's point of view, such an issue needs to be considered as a design objective where creativity, knowledge of materials and good detailing are called upon to achieve design solutions that go beyond just a mere compliance.

Statutory requirements tend to offer well-described standard forms of construction that have been proven to offer the required minimum level of sound insulation. Of course the designer is reminded to refer to those forms of construction as a basis on which alternative design solutions can be developed. To highlight this point, the following example is used. Take a wall construction that would have to meet the requirements of Part E of the Building Regulations (England), one of the standard forms of construction would be a solid masonry one with plaster on both sides (Figure 22.6). For this type of construction, the sound insulation is provided by means of the mass of the material. Usually a mass per unit area of around 400 kg/m^2 is required. Although the standard solutions cover 'conventional' masonry only (concrete blocks, bricks and cast concrete), the designer can use the same principle of mass with other alternative or novel methods of construction. Such methods can include, rammed earth, stone masonry, and wattle and daub. A second approach to sound insulation offered by the standard forms of construction rely on the principle of isolation as seen in Figure 22.7. The main feature of this construction is the use of two independent frames with a minimum distance between inside linings of 200mm and the use of absorbent material. The double frame construction can be applied to non-standard forms of construction with success, provided that care is taken to close gaps in the construction when detailing and the workmanship during construction is of a high standard.

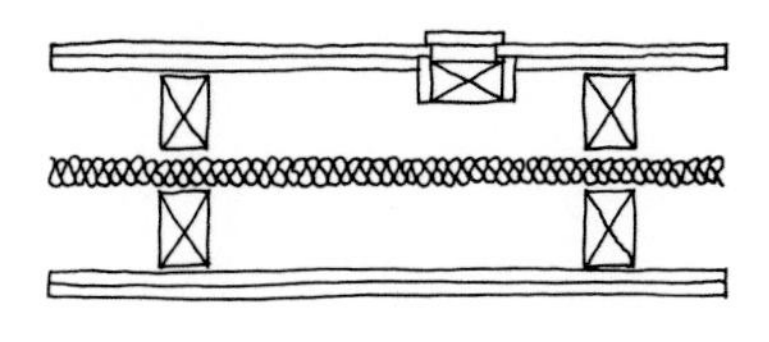

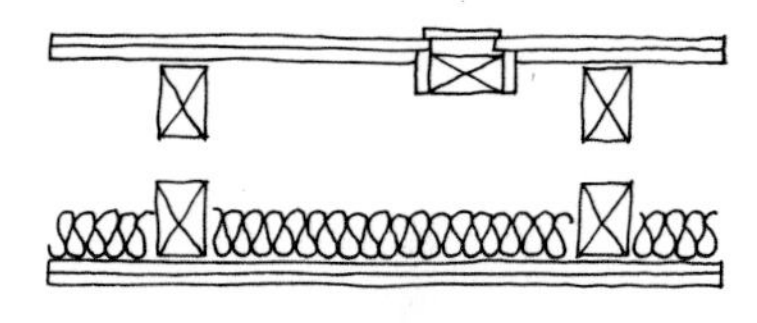

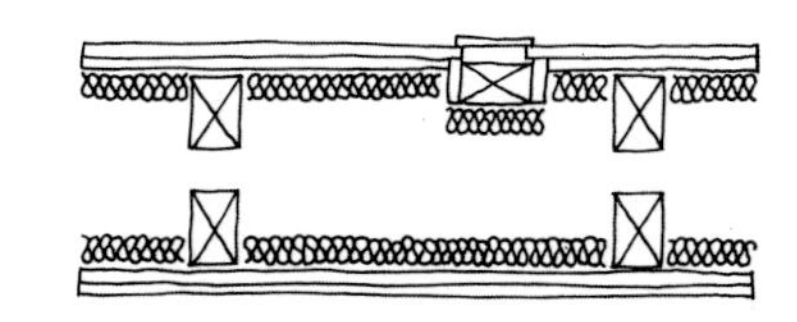

22.7

The second area of sound insulation that Part E deals with is separating floor construction. The regulations offer three standard forms of floor construction (see Figure 22.8). The designer can use these as a basis for some non-standard solutions that would meet the sound insulation requirements as well as any other design requirements.

When designing for sound insulation, detailing is an extremely important part. The provision of either mass or isolation or a combination of both, will not, necessarily, guarantee the sound insulation if junctions between various components are not air tight. Detailing for sound insulation can be complex and the designer is encouraged to seek specialist advice. Among the literature that one might find useful is the series of technical manuals published by the Building Research Establishment.

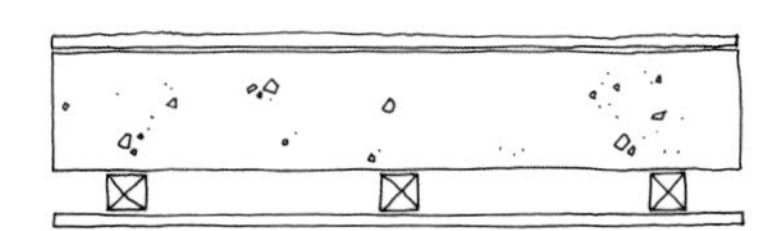

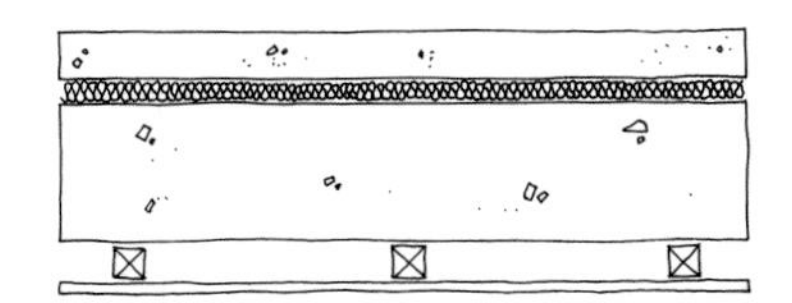

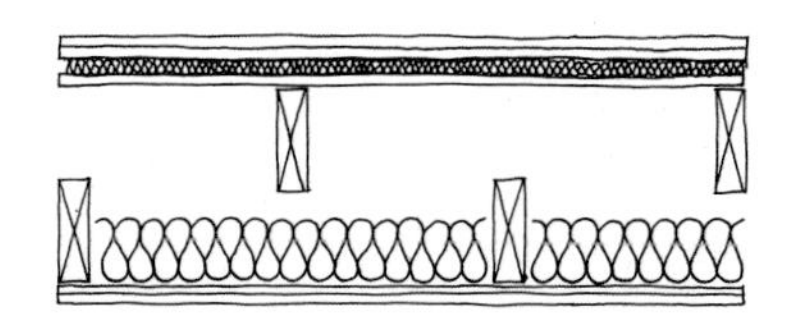

22.8

Chapter **23**

Room acoustics

Introduction

While sound insulation dealt with the control of noise transfer from room to room or from inside to outside, room acoustics is a different area of intervention that designers may find themselves involved in. Acoustics is concerned with the quality of sound inside a space and the provision of the best conditions for the production and reception of sounds for performance purposes. It is often described as an art. However in order for the 'artist acoustician' to be successful, they need to match their creative imagination to some technical know how. This chapter will introduce some of the technical aspects of acoustics to allow the reader to:

- Understand the mechanisms of sound behaviour in rooms. These include, absorption, reflection and reverberation.
- Appreciate the effect of space geometry (form, shape, size, etc.) on the quality of sound.
- Familiarise themselves with the general requirements for good acoustic performance.

Requirements for good acoustic conditions

The primary objective of acoustic design is to provide the optimum acoustic conditions within an enclosed space and enable occupants to enjoy the quality of the sound(s) being performed. The role of the designer is to use materials and design techniques to enhance the quality of the sound in the space. In general terms this objective can be described by means of a number of general requirements. These include:

- The sound inside a room is usually produced at a certain location. The seating positions need to take this into account in order that an adequate amount of sound reaches all parts of the room, particularly those seats furthest from the source. Furthermore, an even distribution of the sound energy around the room is very desirable. Otherwise acoustical defects would reduce the acoustic performance of the space.
- Noise other than that intended in the room needs to be kept to an acceptable level that prevents masking of the performance sound.
- Echoing or reverberation in the room must be controlled in order to achieve optimum reverberation time for the required use of the room.
- Acoustical defects, which are likely to affect the acoustic conditions in the room, need to be avoided. These include: long echoes, flutter echoes and sound concentration.

Some of the design techniques used to achieve these requirements will be discussed in the forthcoming sections. The discussion will focus mainly on reflection and absorption, as they play the largest roles in the behaviour of sound in enclosures.

Reflection

Sound can be reflected in the same way as light, with the angle of incidence being equal to the angle of reflection. Figure 23.1 demonstrates that. But for that to hold true, the size of the reflecting surface must be at least equal to the wavelength of the sound. In practice this would mean a reflector size of 6.8 m for a sound at 50Hz and 3.4m for a sound at 100Hz and so on. When using reflection as a means to control the spread of sound inside a room, it is worth remembering that reflections *near* the source can be useful, while those at a *distance* from it may be troublesome.

Types of reflectors

As mentioned above, the size of reflectors affects the nature of the reflected sound energy. However, though that is a general comment that applies to all reflectors, it is not the only geometrical criteria that determine their reflective behaviour. The following paragraphs will describe various reflector geometries as well as some of the reflection effects that can exist inside an acoustic enclosure.

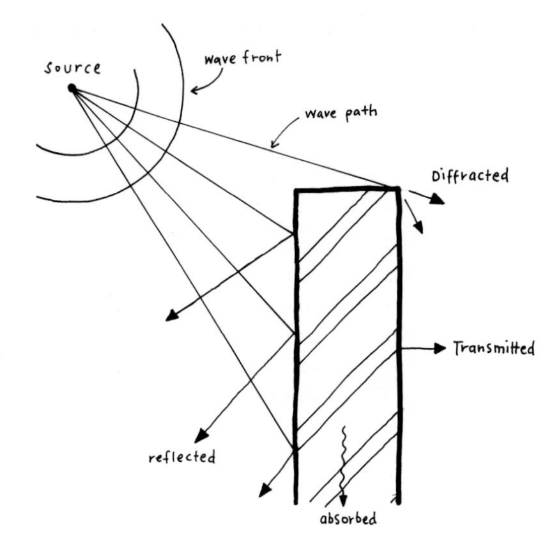

23.1

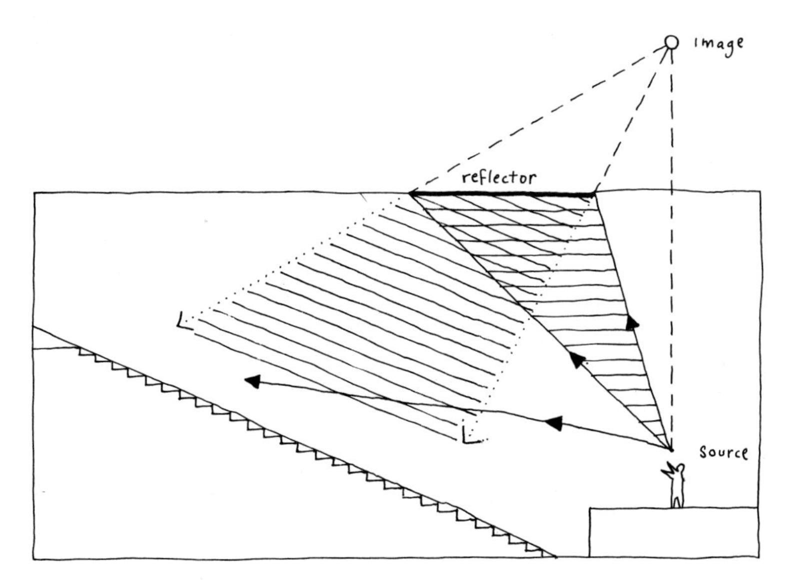

23.2

Planar reflectors

If we take the example shown in Figure 23.2, the sound energy that arrives at the back of the hall is made up of two components, the direct sound source and the reflected sound. The extra sound energy (reflected one) will help reinforce and enhance the sound signal heard at the far end of the room. Planar reflectors with adjustable mounting are often used above a stage to redirect sound into the audience. For such reflectors to be effective, they need to be wide enough for reflections to cover the full width of the room.

Curved reflectors

Although the rules of reflection described above apply to curved reflectors, their geometry gives varying effects. Figure 23.3 illustrates the effects of curved reflectors. Among these are the focusing effect of a concave surface (inward curve) and the diffusing effect of a convex one (outward curve). While the former may cause loud sounds, the latter can lead to dead spots. Convex reflectors can be used to distribute sound energy over larger areas.

When the curves have tight radii, such as those of the ornamental and elaborate plasterwork, the effect is a random scattering of sound, which is beneficial in large interiors such as halls and cinemas.

Concave surfaces tend to focus sound hence the need to consider the radius of such curvature. In order to avoid acoustic defects the focal point needs to be outside the area of acoustic significance (for example seating area in a hall). Shallow domes are preferred to deep ones as their focal point would be outside the enclosure.

Echoes

An echo is a reflection, which is heard sometime after the original sound. This can lead to lack of clarity. If the reflected sound is delayed by more than 50 milliseconds, it is likely to create confusion between the direct and reflected sounds, particularly for speech. In order to avoid such situation, the difference in the distance travelled from source to destination, between the direct and reflected sound needs to be kept less than 17m.

Another type of echo is what are known as flutter echoes, which are perceived as a buzz when sound is decaying. They are caused by multiple reflections from parallel hard reflecting surfaces. This can be a problem particularly in small rooms. Using absorbing and dispersing surfaces can alleviate it.

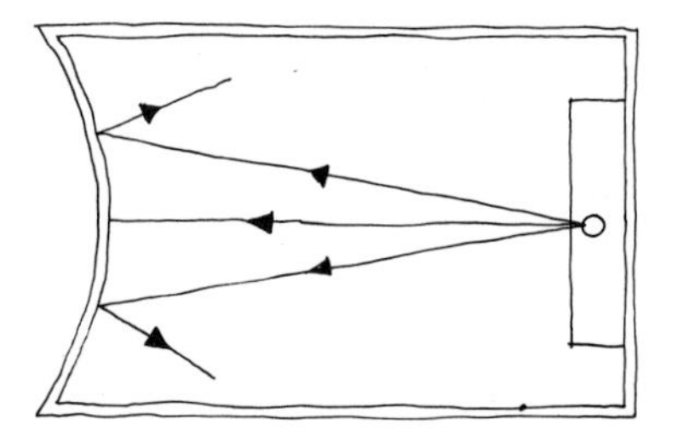

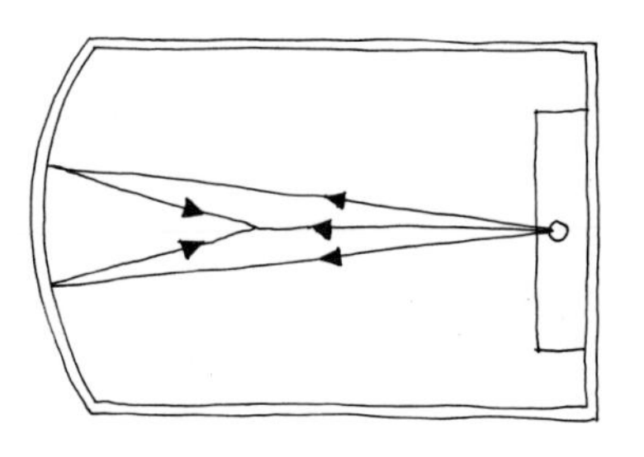

23.3

Standing waves

When the distance between two parallel walls in a room is a multiple of half the wavelength of the sound, multiple reflections will cause standing waves, which are detected as large variations in the sound level at various positions. This can be a problem particularly with low frequency sound in small rooms. In such cases, parallel reflecting surfaces are to be avoided. If planning and construction issues require parallel walls, for instance, they can be treated with dispersing and/or absorbing surfaces.

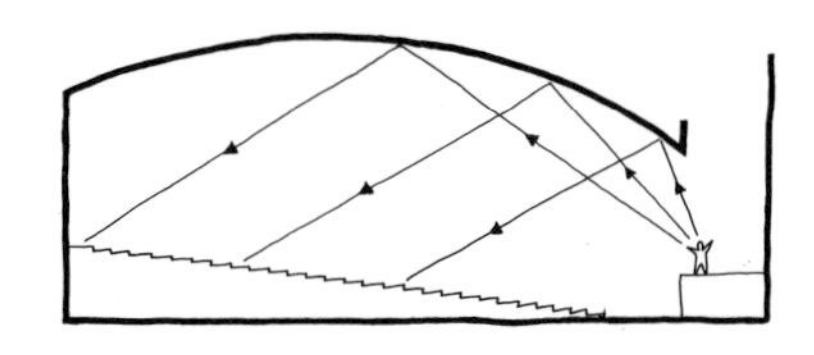

23.4

Shape of interior

So far the discussion has focused on the effects of surface geometry and reflection characteristics of surface materials on the behaviour of sound and its quality. The quality of acoustics inside a hall, for instance, is also affected by the shape of the interior space, particularly for halls with capacity larger than 1,000 seats. Given the acoustic requirements as well as other functional criteria, three basic shapes of auditoria are usually found. These are rectangular, fan and horseshoe shaped.

23.5

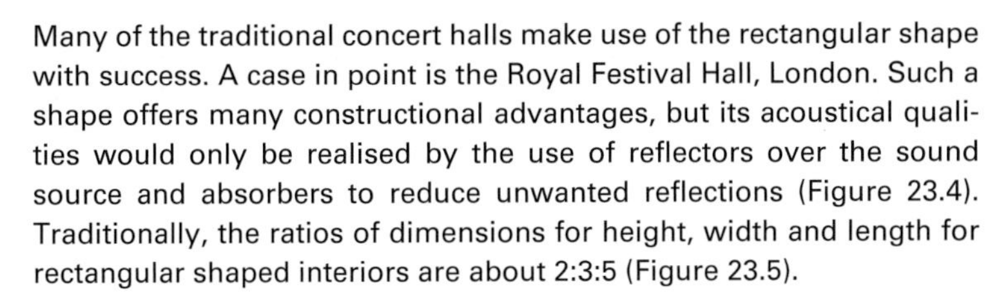

Many of the traditional concert halls make use of the rectangular shape with success. A case in point is the Royal Festival Hall, London. Such a shape offers many constructional advantages, but its acoustical qualities would only be realised by the use of reflectors over the sound source and absorbers to reduce unwanted reflections (Figure 23.4). Traditionally, the ratios of dimensions for height, width and length for rectangular shaped interiors are about 2:3:5 (Figure 23.5).

The fan shaped interiors are preferred for halls seating more than 1,000 people so that more of the audience is seated closer to the sound source (Figure 23.6). For this shape of halls, it is advisable to avoid having concave surfaces at the end of the hall, and that reflections from the side walls are corrected by means of large diffusers or absorbent material when those reflections are not needed.

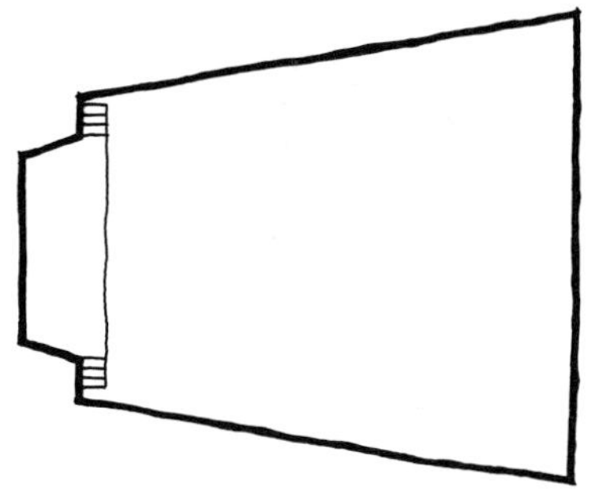

23.6

A horseshoe shaped plan is a common occurrence in traditional opera houses. The shape offers even more proximity to the stage and intimacy. The concave shape of the end wall is broken up by tiers of boxes. These provide absorbent surfaces. The absorption provided by the audience is ideal for opera as clarity is more important than fullness of tone. On the other hand such halls would not suit orchestral music.

Absorption

The ability of a material to absorb sound energy is often exploited to control the behaviour of sound inside a room and improve its quality. It involves a reduction in the sound energy reflected from a surface.

This is particularly useful when the need to control echoing inside a room is a design requirement. The amount of sound absorption afforded by a material is described in terms of an absorption coefficient with a numerical value, which is always less than one. The higher the coefficient, the more absorption the material provides. The coefficient can vary according to the frequency of sound. This is important as different materials have different absorption coefficients at different frequencies. The role of the designer is to match materials specified to the frequencies of sound to be controlled.

In order to assess the total absorption inside an enclosed space, knowledge of the materials and surface areas they cover is required. The effective absorption of a material in use is given by the product of its surface area multiplied by its absorption coefficient. For instance, a floor with an area of $15m^2$ has a carpet finish with an absorption coefficient of 0.5 at 500Hz. Its total absorption is given as 15 times 0.5, which is equal to $7.5m^2$ sabins (or units of absorption). The total absorption of the room is the sum of the absorption values provided by each of the surfaces that make the enclosed space as estimated in the example above.

Types of absorbers

Knowledge of materials and their behaviour is an important tool at the disposal of the designer. From an acoustical point of view, the designer would find it helpful to know how various materials would behave with regard to sound absorption. Materials and components used for sound absorption fall into one of three general categories; porous absorbers, panel absorbers and cavity absorbers.

Porous absorbers

These consist of materials with a cellular structure having a network of interlocking pores. Typical examples include: fibreboard, fibreglass and mineral wool. The presence of air in the cells helps convert some of the sound energy into heat (which is insignificant from a thermal point of view). Such materials are characterised by effective absorption at frequencies above 1kHz. Their low frequency absorption can be improved slightly by increasing the thickness of the material as illustrated in Figure 23.7. A similar improvement in performance can be achieved by incorporating an air gap when mounting the material. Porous absorbers are available as either acoustic plasters or acoustic tiles as well as blankets (glass wool).

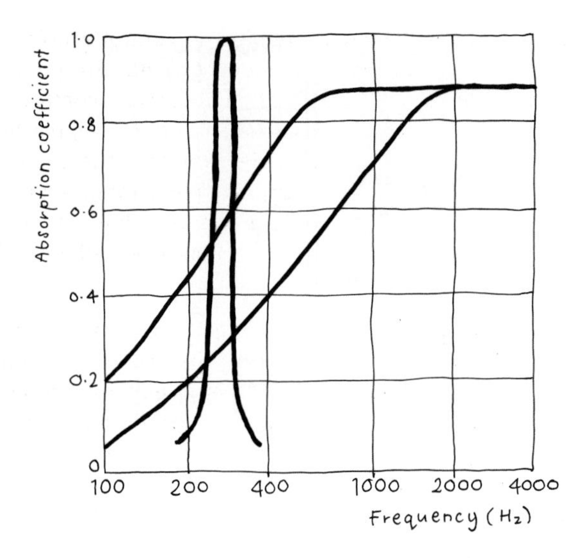

23.7

Panel absorbers

These are also referred to as membrane absorbers. They consist of thin panels or sheets of fixed materials mounted with a space behind them (see Figure 23.8). The space can either be left empty or, for increased performance, can be filled with a porous blanket. Just like porous absorbers, the performance of these absorbers is frequency dependent. It is normally in the range of 50 to 500Hz (see Figure 23.7). The frequency at which maximum absorption occurs (resonant frequency) can be assessed from the formula:

$$f_{res} = \frac{60}{\sqrt{(m.d)}}$$

where m is the mass of the panel (in kg/m^2) and d is the air gap (in m) as indicated in Figure 23.8. Ether of these two variables or both can be specified with values that can achieve the required frequency at which absorption is a maximum.

Cavity absorbers

These absorbers are also known as *Helmholtz resonators*. They are similar to panel absorbers in the way they enclose a cavity, but they differ in that the cavity has a narrow surface opening onto the room air (see Figure 23.9). The opening of the cavity acts as an absorber when air is forced to vibrate by a passing sound wave. The cavity can either be empty (just air) or it can contain an absorbing material. A cavity

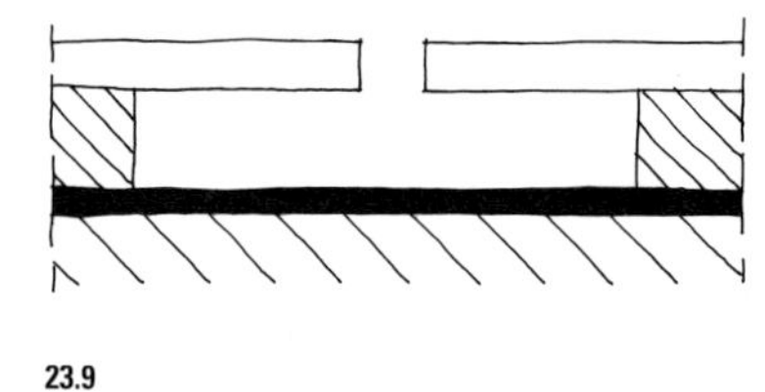

23.9

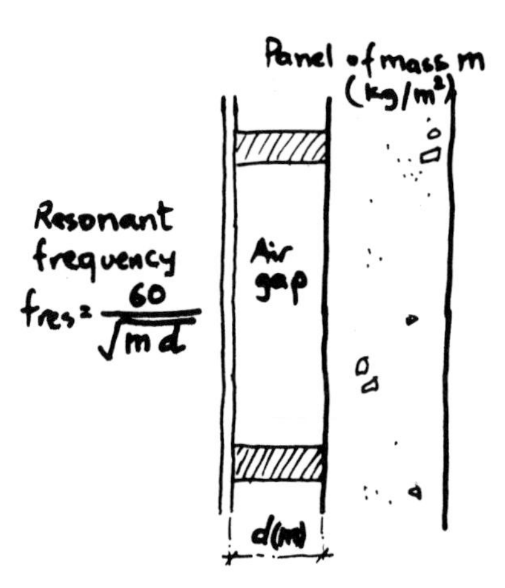

23.8

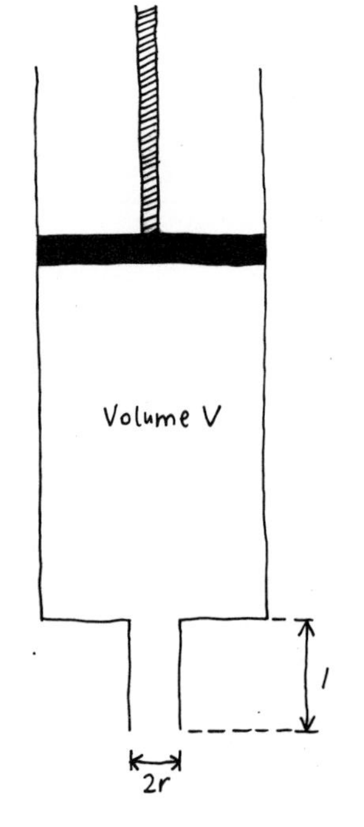

23.10

absorber can have a high absorption coefficient over a narrow frequency range (refer to Figure 23.7). The dimensions of the resonator can be manipulated to tune it to a given frequency at which absorption is a maximum (resonant frequency of the system). For a resonator with a narrow neck, such as that shown in Figure 23.10, the resonant frequency is given by the following equation:

$$f_{res} = \frac{cr}{2\pi}\sqrt{\left[\frac{2\pi}{(2l + \pi r)V}\right]}$$

where c is the speed of sound, r is the radius of the neck and the remainder of the parameters are as shown in Figure 23.10.

If the cavity has no neck, the equation is simplified to:

$$f_{res} = \frac{c}{2\pi}\sqrt{\left[\frac{2r}{V}\right]}$$

Absorbers in practice

Products used in practice can behave as a combination of more than one of the types described above. Take the case of acoustic tiles, for example. The basic material of the tile such as fibreboard is porous and would absorb sound at higher frequencies. The tile can sometimes contain holes, which make it behave as a cavity absorber. If the tile is mounted with an air space behind it (as in the case of suspended ceilings), it would also act as a panel absorber.

Reverberation

Inside certain enclosures of large volume and hard internal surfaces, one's voice is heard after they stop talking. This is known as reverberation and should not be confused with echoes. While in the case of echo the reflections of the original sound are heard by the listener as separate sounds, for reverberation, the reflections reach the listener too quickly and are perceived as an extension of the original sound. This description can lead us to the definition of reverberation as the continuation of sound caused by rapid multiple reflections between the various surfaces of an interior (Figure 23.11). Reflected sound will mix with direct sound to form what is known as reverberant sound. The degree to which an interior is reverberant would determine the acoustic environment in that interior. This is usually quantified by means of *reverberation time*. In order to explain this design criteria let us consider the following scenario. A room of given dimensions and surface finishes has a certain source of sound operating inside it. At some point, the source of sound is switched off. The sound heard by an observer inside the room does not stop instantaneously, but fades away with time in a similar way to that shown in Figure 23.12. The time taken for the sound to decay by 60dB is what is known as reverberation time. The time taken for sound to decay will depend on the following factors:

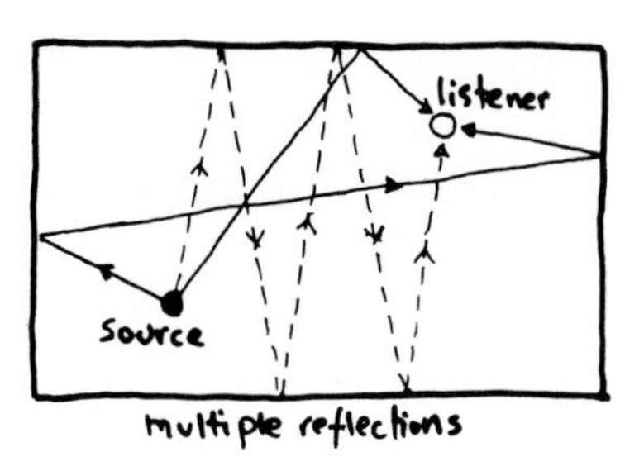

23.11

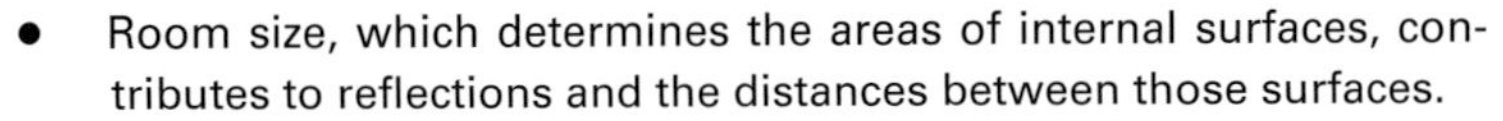

- Room size, which determines the areas of internal surfaces, contributes to reflections and the distances between those surfaces.
- Amount of sound absorption on the internal surfaces.
- Frequency of sound.

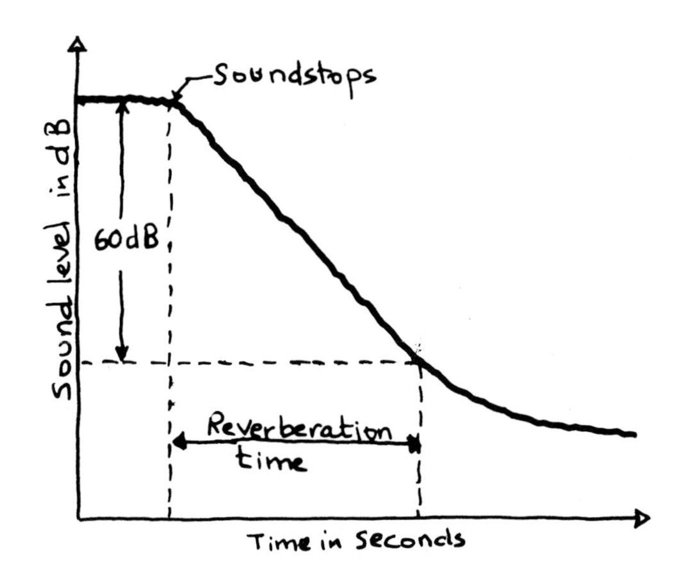

23.12

Reverberation time is an important parameter to consider when designing interiors as it helps describe the acoustical qualities of a room. For an existing interior, the reverberation time can be measured using a generated sound and recording its decay rate. At design stage however, the reverberation time can be estimated using various formulae that make use of the characteristics of the room identified above. As the sound absorption of any material is frequency dependent as has been discussed previously, the reverberation time is estimated for any given frequency.

Sabine formula

This formula works on the assumption that the decay of sound is continuous. It is commonly used for estimating reverberation time for rooms without excessive absorption. The formula is given as:

$$t = \frac{0.16 \times V}{A}$$

Where t is the reverberation time in seconds (s), V is the room volume in cubic metres (m^3) and A is the total absorption of the room surfaces in m^2 sabins. This latter one is worked out for each different surface finish, by multiplying its surface area by its absorption coefficient and adding up the values for all the various surface finishes. The presence of an audience in the room will affect the amount of absorption and hence the reverberation time. To allow for the effect of the audience, an absorption value of 0.46 is allowed for every person to be seated in the room. For a full explanation on how this calculation method can be carried out, the reader is referred to the example given in the next chapter.

Eyring formula

In certain specific applications, such as broadcasting studios, where the amount of surface absorption is high, reverberation time is better predicted using the Eyring formula, which gives more accurate estimates. The formula is given as:

$$t = \frac{0.16 \times V}{-S \log_e(1 - \bar{\alpha})}$$

Where t is the reverberation time (in s), V is the room volume (in m³). S is the total of the area surfaces (in m²); log_e is the natural logarithm and $\bar{\alpha}$ is the average absorption coefficient of the surfaces in the room.

Optimum reverberation time

In practice, reverberation times vary according to the room size and the type of activities that take place inside it. This can vary from a fraction of a second for a small room to a few seconds for a large interior such as a church (St Paul's Cathedral has a reverberation time of 11 seconds). From an acoustic quality point of view, different activities would require different reverberation times. As a rule of thumb, speech requires between 0.5 and 1 second's reverberation time. For clarity of speech, it is necessary to have short reverberation times otherwise speech will be blurred due to the continuing presence of reverberant sound that will mask some syllables. Music on the other hand would require between 1 and 2 seconds. Longer reverberation time enhances the quality of music, which can sound dry or dead when heard under shorter reverberation times.

Optimum values of reverberation times for an enclosed space can be estimated from the formula suggested by Stephens and Bates (after Crocker 1997:1128):

$$t = K(0.118\sqrt[3]{V} + 0.1070)$$

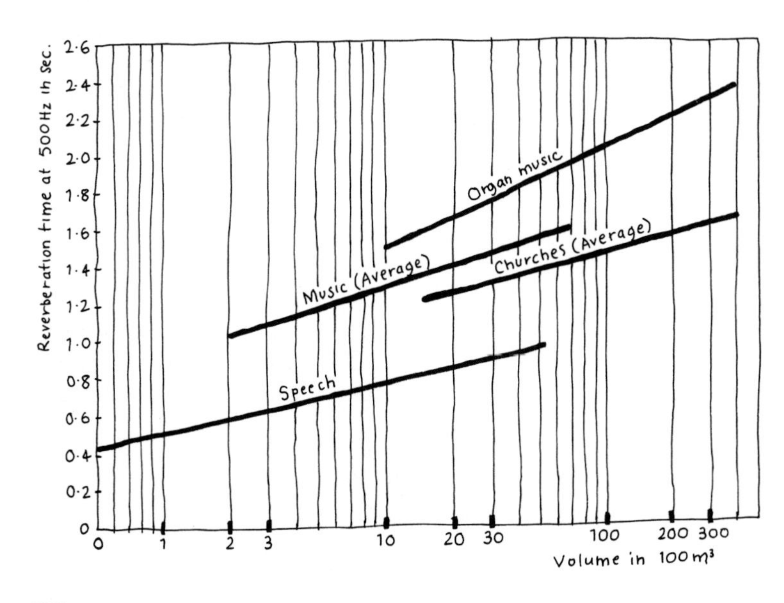

23.13

Where V is the room volume, the constant K takes the following values according to the proposed use: for speech K=4, for orchestra K=5, and for choirs and rock bands K=6. At lower frequencies, the calculated value needs to be increased by an increment ranging from 40 per cent at 250Hz to 100 per cent at 63Hz.

Alternatively, graphical data such as that shown in Figure 23.13 can be used.

Chapter **24**

Design examples

Barrier effect

In this example, the reader will be guided through the steps involved in assessing the noise screening potential of a barrier. In the following example, a new building site is the source of noise and the likely noise level in an adjoining housing development needs to be assessed. The noisiest source on the new site is a compressor with an output of 104dB(A) at 500Hz when in operation. The centre of the compressor is 0.5m above the ground. In order to assess the risk of annoyance to the neighbours in the adjoining development, the noise level from the site is assessed at the nearest back garden on the development. For the noise level to comply with local authority requirements, its level must not exceed 50dB(A) outdoors. This level is taken to be at a height of 1.5m above the ground. The site is to be surrounded by a 2.5m high fence at a distance of 5m from the offending source and 30m from the edge of the nearest garden. The ground between the source of sound and where the noise is assessed is assumed to be hard, flat and level.

Step 1: graphical representation of the data

Both the sound propagation and screening effect of the barrier are affected by the geometrical positions of the source, receiver location and barrier. In this case drawing a section such as that in Figure 24.1 will be the first step in the analysis.

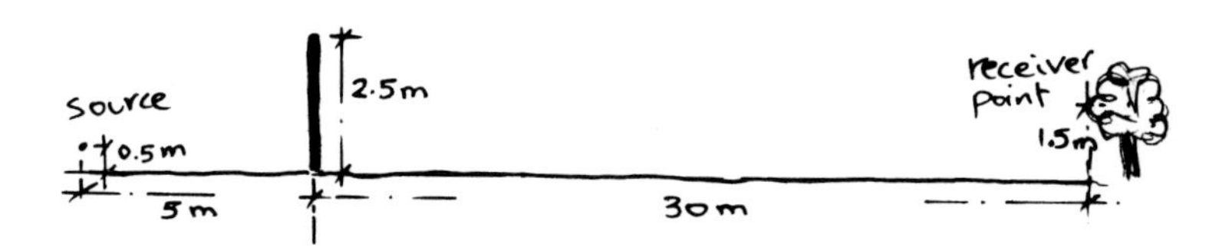

24.1

Step 2: sound attenuation due to propagation over distance

Taking the sound source as a point source, radiating over hard ground and using the equation discussed in Chapter 21, attenuation due to distance is worked out as:

$$Attenuation = 10log\,(2 \times \pi \times 35^2) = 39 \text{ dB(A)}$$

Step 3: barrier attenuation

Referring to Figure 24.1, the distances *a, b* and *c* need to be calculated.

$$a = \sqrt{5^2 + 2^2} = 5.39\text{m}$$
$$b = \sqrt{30^2 + 1^2} = 30.02\text{m}$$
$$c = \sqrt{35^2 + 1^2} = 35.01\text{m}$$
$$\delta = a + b - c$$
$$\delta = 5.39 + 30.02 - 35.01 = 0.4$$

Using the Maekawa formula (see Chapter 21), barrier attenuation E_b is given as:

$$E_b = 10log\left(3 + \frac{40\delta}{\lambda}\right)$$

With λ being the wavelength of sound at 500Hz which is calculated as:

$$\lambda = \frac{speed\ of\ sound}{frequency} = \frac{340}{500} = 0.68\text{m}$$
$$E_b = 10log\left(3 + \frac{40 \times 0.4}{0.68}\right) = 14 \text{ dB(A)}$$

Step 4: noise level at receiver location

$$L_{receiver} = 105 - 39 - 14 = 52 \text{ dB(A)}$$

This exceeds the local authority criteria hence there is a need for extra measures to further reduce the site noise. Increasing the fence height to 3m and starting the process again would give a noise level of 50dB.

Reverberation time in a room

Worked example

A lecture room is 20m long by 12m wide by 5m high and has the following surface areas and absorption coefficients at 500Hz:

Table 24.1 Characteristics of surfaces in the room under consideration

	Area	*Absorption coefficient*
Walls: fair faced concrete blocks	320 m^2	0.3
Floors: carpet on concrete	240 m^2	0.5
Ceiling: acoustic tiles	240 m^2	0.75

It is required to calculate the reverberation time at 500Hz, when the room is occupied by 150 people.

For each of the various surface finishes, the absorption is calculated as: absorption = area x absorption coefficient

Table 24.2 Working out of acoustic absorption units

	Area	*Absorption coefficient*	*Absorption (m^2 sabins)*
Walls: fair faced concrete blocks	320 m^2	0.08	25.6
Floors: carpet on concrete	240 m^2	0.2	48
Ceiling: acoustic tiles	240 m^2	0.1	24
Audience	150 people	0.46 each	69
Total absorption			166.6

Using the Sabine equation above and substituting for the room volume and the total absorption, the reverberation time *t* is calculated as:

$$t = \frac{0.16 \times 12 \times 20 \times 5}{166.6} = 1.15 \text{ seconds}$$

If the reverberation time is to be shortened, the walls need to be covered with a certain amount of absorbent material of known absorption coefficient and the above calculation is repeated to include the added absorption, and a new reverberation time is achieved.

Large performance halls

This section will review the main acoustic features for three performance halls with a view to giving the reader an insight into the practicalities of acoustic design and demonstrate how some of the fundamentals of acoustic design are applied. The choice of examples is to reflect the developments in acoustics and the diversity of design approaches based on the use of the halls and their shapes. The first of the three was designed before auditorium acoustics became a science. The second example reflects the advances in acoustical design from the mid-1930s to the 1960s. While the first two examples are of concert halls, the last one represents the more recent approach to the multi-purpose use of amphitheatres.

Royal Albert Hall, London

For a building erected for the advancement of the Arts and Sciences, the Royal Albert Hall has certainly provided valuable lessons for the science of acoustics, but not in the way it was intended. When it opened in 1871, it was unique both in style and scale. The elliptical plan measuring some 70m at its widest point, had layers of boxes surrounding it (Figure 24.2). A dome of iron and glass is used to cover the largest unsupported roof span at the time (Figure 24.3). Given its sheer volume of 86,650m^3 surrounded by concave focusing surfaces, the hall was never going to be without problems. The echo from the dome marred the opening royal speech by the then Prince of Wales (later to become King Edward VII). In an effort to deal with the problem of echo, a huge velarium, weighing 1.25 tons, was stretched underneath the roof. Despite the efforts to experiment with various heights, the problem persisted. By the 1920s an alternative treatment of 4,000m^2 of suspended felt was abandoned on

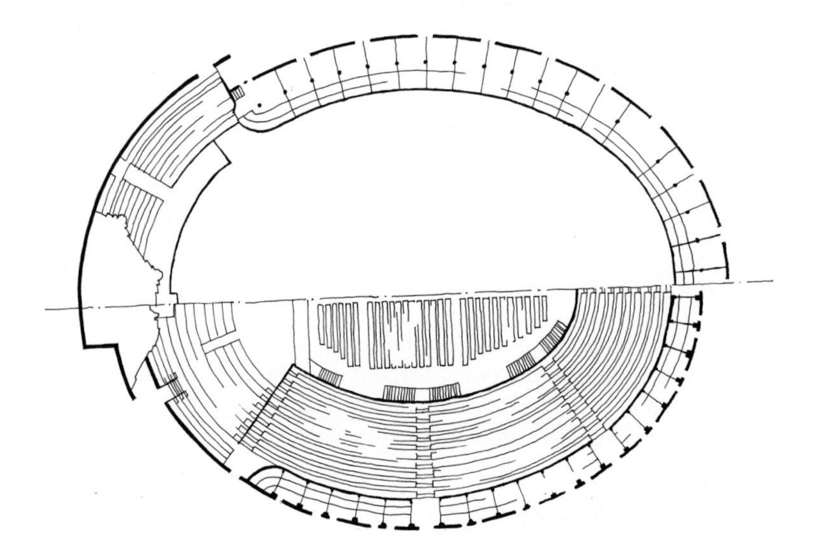

24.2

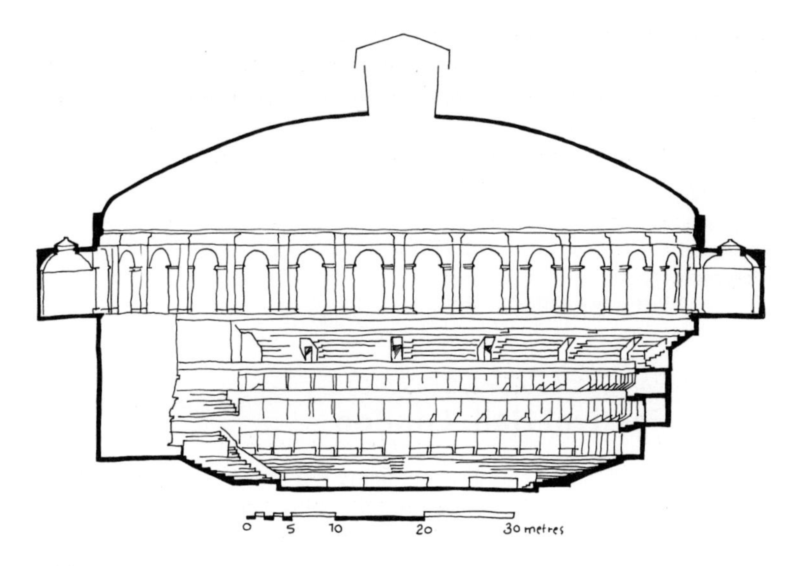

24.3

the grounds of affordability. The next stage in the search for a cure to the echo problem came after the Second World War. The velarium was replaced with an inner dome, of fluted aluminium, which had a perforated lower skin and mineral wool backing. This solution improved the acoustic conditions but echo was still heard around the perimeter of the dome. The final part of the solution to the echo problem came in 1970, when 134 diffusers were suspended as illustrated diagrammatically in Figure 24.4. The diffusers have also contributed to reducing the reverberation time for such a huge volume as their upper side was treated with absorbent. Furthermore they provide early reflections for some seats with otherwise might not receive them.

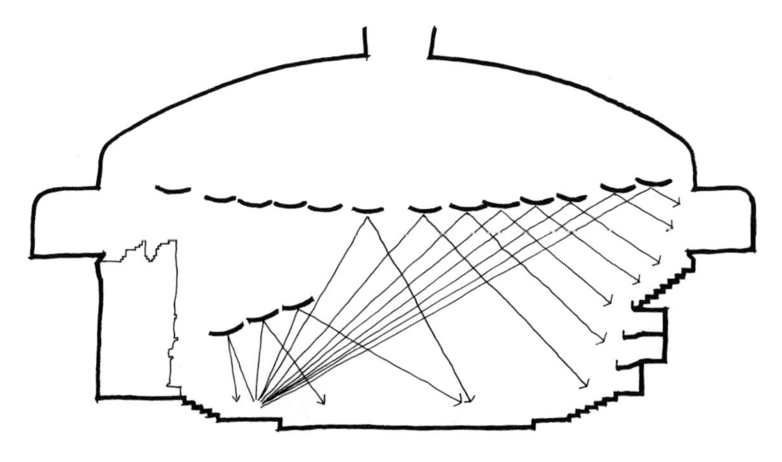

24.4

The Royal Albert Hall in detail:

Completion date	1871
Architect	Captain F. Fowke, and later Lt Colonel and H.Y.D.
Acoustic consultant Scott	
	–
Volume	86,650m^3
Seating capacity	5,090seats
Total length	67m
Mean width	47m
Mean height	36m
Mean occupied reverberation time	2.5s

Royal Festival Hall, London

Apart from its historic significance, being the only permanent building among the exhibition structures for the 1951 Festival of Britain, the Royal Festival Hall is considered by many as a landmark in acoustic design. Completed in 1951, with an internal volume of 21,950m^3 and a capacity to seat 2,645, the design of the hall used many features that became an established standard in large concert halls. Some of these features are briefly reviewed in the following paragraphs.

Having considered a fan shape for such a large interior, the designers favoured a traditional rectangular shape that had built itself a good reputation in halls such as the Stadt-Casino, Basel (1876), the Grosser Tonhallsaal, Zurich (1895) and the Liverpool Philharmonic Hall (1849–1933). But having a larger capacity hall than many classical rectangular ones meant that some features were experimented with. These include:

- The width of the Royal Festival Hall was extended to 32m, which is more than any of the classical halls and the walls enclosing the lower stalls splay out (see Figure 24.5).
- The side balconies were omitted (due to poor visibility) and replaced by a single deep balcony facing the stage as shown in the section in Figure 24.6.
- The use of a polished wood reflective canopy above the stage improved the acoustic conditions for the performers. As a result they can hear themselves and their colleagues.
- In order to accommodate the requirements of both choral and instrumental music, the designer opted to design for a long reverberation time combined with a profiled ceiling to give enhanced early reflections. This latter feature constitutes a departure from the high ceiling associated with rectangular classical halls.

The Royal Festival Hall was designed for a reverberation time of 2.2 seconds, but in reality this was only 1.5 seconds, until it was corrected by means of assisted resonance. But even with its lower than expected

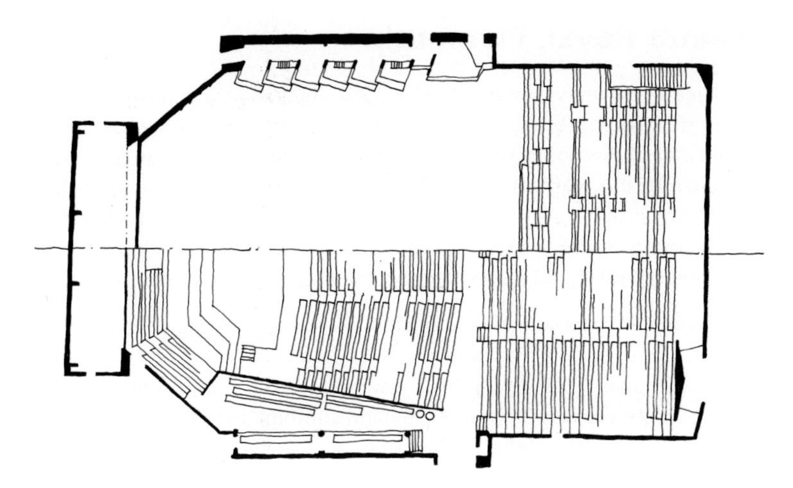

24.5

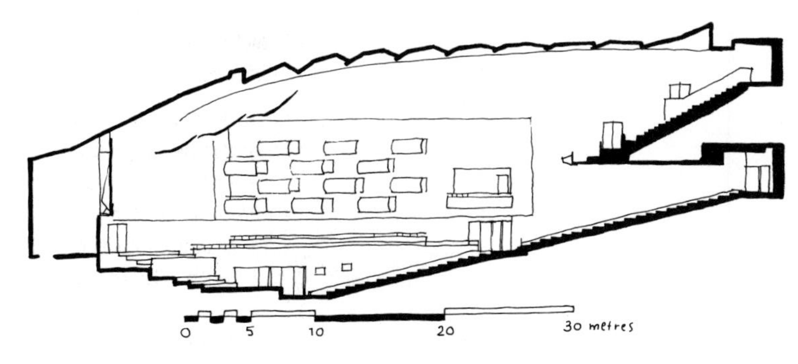

24.6

reverberation time, it always divides opinions from both the arts and the sciences. However, despite that shortcoming, it is still considered as a landmark in large concert hall design.

The Royal Festival Hall in detail:

Completion date	1951
Architect	London County Council Architects
Acoustic consultants	H. Bagenal, P.H. Parkin, W.H. Allen
Volume	21,950m^3
Seating capacity	2,645 seats
Total length	52m
Mean width	32m
Mean height	15m
Mean occupied reverberation time	1.8s

Theatre Royal, Plymouth

The Theatre Royal was completed in 1982. Its design was a response to a very demanding brief for a large multi-purpose performance space for the city of Plymouth which up until then was without one as a consequence of the wartime bombing. The brief called for an auditorium that allows small-scale repertory theatre and large-scale productions as well as opera and musicals. The seating capacity was specified to be in the range of 750–1,200 depending on the nature of the performance.

The architects' response was to design the space with the characteristic acoustics for theatre performance and use an electronic system to modify them for music. This option was deemed easier than modifying the music acoustics to suit drama. The design combined elements from both theatres and concert halls. The adoption of a fan shape plan helped to keep distances from the stage short (see Figure 24.7). This was

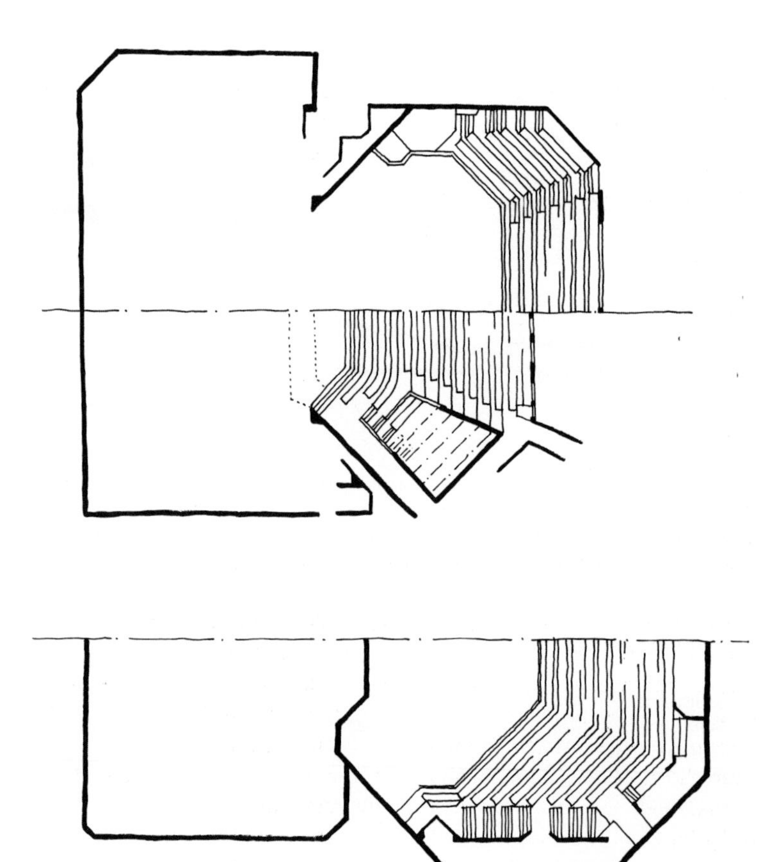

24.7

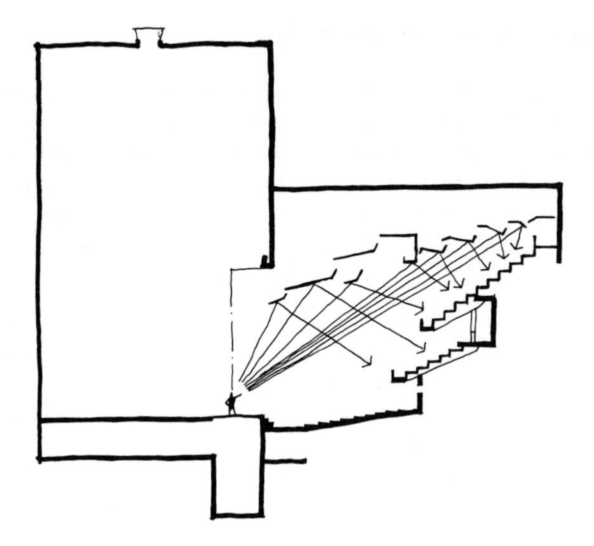

24.8

combined with highly raked balconies of seating (Figure 24.8). The suspended elements of the ceiling are used to control early reflections and to block off the upper circle seating when not in use.

Although the design for theatrical performance has been more successful than for musical performance, the Theatre Royal, Plymouth has demonstrated that a multi-purpose auditorium can be achieved.

The Theatre Royal Plymouth in detail:

Completion date	1982
Architect	Peter Moro Partnership
Acoustic consultants	Sound Research laboratories
Volume	6,490m^3
Seating capacity	1,271 seats
Total length	23m (excluding fly tower)
Mean width	26m
Mean height	13m
Mean occupied reverberation time	0.8s (for speech), 0.9s (for music)

The three case studies presented in this section show that acoustic design is a collaborative process to which different specialists have an input. For it to be successful it needs to consider the important design issues in a holistic way right from the beginning of the process. The reader is also reminded that most of the issues relating to acoustic qualities emanate from choice of materials and their locations inside an interior. Knowledge of materials' acoustic properties is very useful to the designer. Not only will s/he be able to specify the right materials for the task in hand, but s/he would also be able to identify the range of alternative materials from which a specification can be undertaken.

Part **5**

Bibliography

Barron, M. *Auditorium Acoustics and Architectural Design*, E&FN Spon (1993).

Bougdah, H., Ekici, I., Kang, J. An investigation into rib-like noise reducing devices, *Journal of the Acoustical Society of America*, Vol. 120(6): 3714–22 (2006).

Crocker, M.J. (ed.) *Encyclopaedia of Acoustics*, John Wiley & Sons, Inc. (1997).

Department for Communities and Local Government, Planning Policy Guidance 24: Planning and Noise, HMSO (1994).

Lord, P. and Templeton, D. *Detailing for Acoustics*, 3rd edn, E & FN Spon (1996).

McMullan, R. *Environmental Science in Building*, 5th edn, Palgrave (2002).

Office of the Deputy Prime Minister, The Building Regulations 2000: Approved Document E, NBS (2004).

Smith, B.J., Peters, R.J. and Owen, S. *Acoustics and noise control*, 2nd edn, Addison Wesley Longman (1996).

Part 6
Sustainable building design

Chapter **25**

Environmental impacts of buildings

Introduction

Buildings have a major impact upon the physical environment. The materials used to construct and maintain buildings and the energy used to service them, coupled with a typical life expectancy of 50 to 100 years, ensure that buildings create a significant environmental load. In this chapter some of these impacts are highlighted and a number of ways of reducing these impacts discussed

Energy impacts

Buildings use energy to heat, cool, light, ventilate and service internal spaces. In most industrialised countries the energy used by buildings will typically represent around 50 per cent of total energy consumption, as shown in Figure 25.1

As most of this energy comes from the burning of fossil fuels then buildings are also responsible for approximately 50 per cent of CO_2 emissions into the atmosphere. In addition, this burning also produces, globally, 10 per cent of methane emissions, 25 per cent of NO_x emissions and 25 per cent of SO_x emissions. Therefore, buildings are a major contributor to global warming, climate change, air pollution and acid rain production. In the past the refrigerants used in building air conditioning systems and the manufacture of some building insulations materials released chlorofluorocarbons (CFC) into the atmosphere where they depleted the ozone layer (the ozone hole) that protects the Earth's surface from harmful UV radiation. This process had been going on for over 50 years before the problem was recognised and the 1987 Montreal Protocol led to the successful phasing out of CFC production.

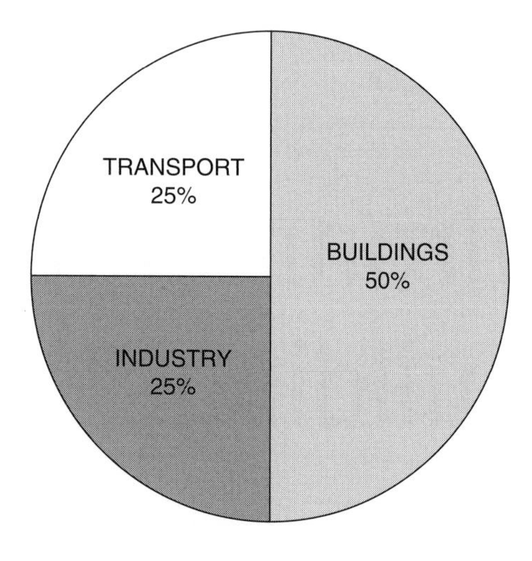

25.1

The success of the Montreal treaty has not been emulated by the 1997 Kyoto Treaty on reducing carbon emissions.

Although some energy is used by buildings in material production, construction, maintenance, demolition and removal, over the life of a building most energy is used by the building services (called the operating energy). Therefore, the single most effective way of reducing the environmental impact of a building is to make it as energy efficient as possible. Parts 2 and 3 of this book have discussed some of the key parameters for low energy design (insulation, air tightness, passive solar gain, efficient services and use of renewables) and so they will not be repeated here. An excellent example of this energy efficient design approach in action is demonstrated in the PassivHaus construction standard for dwellings, which was developed in Germany but which is now widely applied. A dwelling that achieves the PassivHaus standard typically includes very high levels of insulation with nominal thermal bridging, planned use of internal and solar gains, exceptionally high levels of air tightness and good indoor air quality produced by a very efficient whole house mechanical ventilation heat recovery system. A PassivHaus does not require traditional heating or active cooling systems to achieve comfort and the small annual heating load is usually met by a compact unit that integrates heating, hot water and ventilation provision. Table 25.1, which is adapted from PassivHaus UK (www.passivhaus.org.uk), compares PassivHaus and typical current UK dwelling standards, and Figure 25.2 shows an insulation detail to meet UK Building Regulations and what is needed to satisfy PassivHaus requirements.

The Passive House Planning Package (PHPP) is a computer-based design tool that can be used to check that a design is meeting the PassivHaus standard. PHPP is available from the Passive House Institute

Table 25.1 PassivHaus and typical UK energy standards for dwellings

Feature	*PassivHaus standard*	*UK common practice*
Compact form and good insulation	External fabric limit U-value ≤ 0.15 W/m²/K	External fabric limit U-value ~ 0.25 – 0.35 W/m²/K
Southern orientation/ shade considerations	Passive use of solar energy is a significant factor in PassivHaus	Some consideration but the improved energy savings are often overlooked.
Energy-efficient window glazing and frames	Windows (glazing and frames, combined) U-Values ≤ 0.80 W/m²/K	Windows (glazing and frames, combined) typically U-Values ~ 1.8 – 2.2 W/m²K
Building envelope air-tightness	Air leakage permeability less than 1 m³/hr/m² @ 50 Pa	Air leakage permeability 7 to 10 m³/hr/m²@ 50 Pa.
Passive preheating of fresh air	Fresh air may be brought into the house through buried ducts and preheated by 5°C	The majority of dwellings do not achieve good enough air tightness to warrant whole house ventilation system - thus trickle vents, extract fans or passive stack ventilation are commonly used
Heat recovery using an air-to-air heat exchanger	Heat in the exhaust air is transferred to incoming fresh air (heat recovery over 80 per cent)	
Energy-saving household appliances	Low energy refrigerators, stoves, freezers, lamps, washers, dryers, etc.	Low-energy bulbs provided in new dwellings – supplied appliances not generally A-rated
Total energy use for space heating and cooling	Less than 15 kWh/m²/yr	Typically 55 kWh/m²/yr

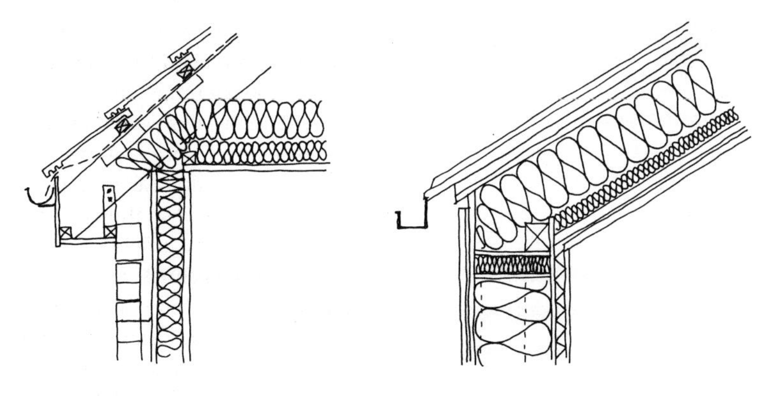

25.2

(http://www.passivehouse.com/) or the PassivHaus UK website. A rigorous onsite quality control procedure is another important aspect of the PassivHaus approach to ensure that very high levels of air tightness and thermal insulation are achieved in the completed dwelling.

Material impacts

Buildings are constructed from a variety of natural and manufactured materials and there are substantial energy and environmental impacts associated with the acquisition, processing, transport, use and disposal of these materials, as outlined in Figure 25.3.

The total amount of primary energy used during the lifetime of a material from extraction to disposal is called the embodied energy, which has units of MJ/kg of material. Calculating embodied energy is a difficult task because it partly depends on the criteria used in the analysis. In addition, embodied energy values do not necessarily reflect other beneficial aspects of a material. For example, steel requires huge amounts of energy in terms of its initial production, and so has a very high embodied energy. However, steel is also highly recyclable (50 per cent of the steel in the world is recycled) and so it is possible to consider it a sustainable material despite its high embodied energy. Figure 25.4 shows the embodied energy for some common materials used in buildings.

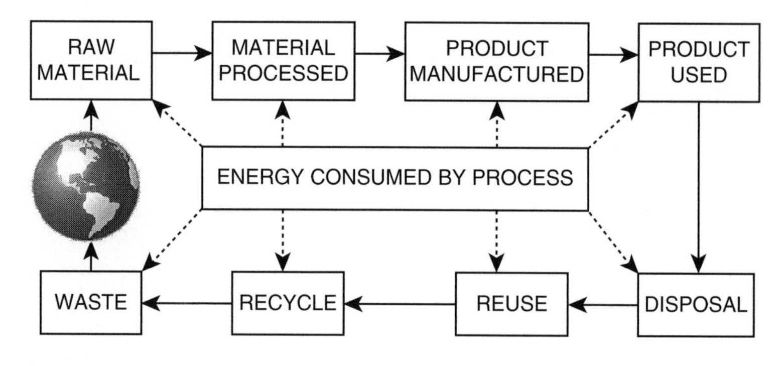

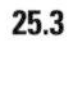

25.3

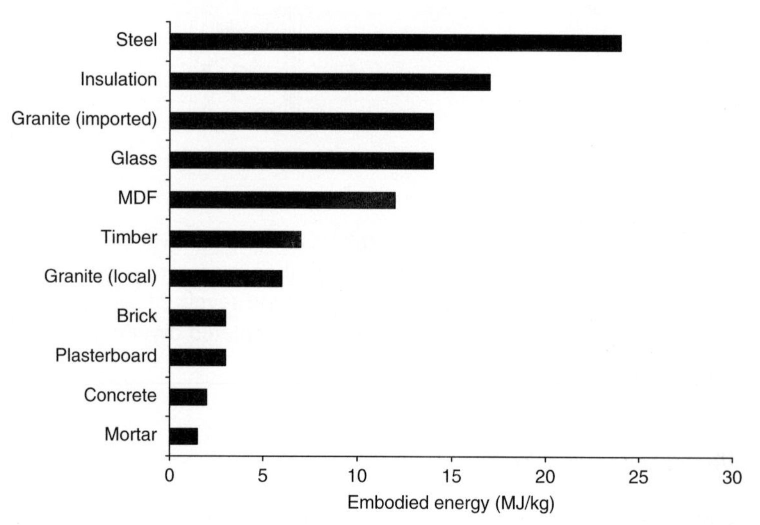

25.4

The embodied energy of over 400 materials is available from the University of Bath at http://www.bath.ac.uk/mech-eng/sert/embodied/. The Building Research Establishment's *Green Guide to Specification* is one of the most comprehensive sources of information on the environmental impact of construction materials and components. The Green Guide contains more than 1,200 specifications employed in various types of building and uses an A+ to E ranking system, where A+ represents the best environmental performance/least environmental impact and E the worst environmental performance/most environmental impact. The latest edition of the Green Guide is available on line at http://www.thegreenguide.org.uk/index.jsp.

There are several ways of reducing the embodied energy of a building. Transport is a major component of embodied energy and so using local materials and locally produced building components can have a significant impact. Figure 25.4 shows that locally quarried granite has an embodied energy of 6 MJ/kg whilst the value for imported granite is 14 MJ/kg. Long lasting materials that will not rot or corrode quickly (relative to the life of the building) are also beneficial as any replacement carries a large energy overhead. In general, natural building materials such as timber, stone, rammed earth and straw bales, have lower embodied energies than their manufactured equivalents. The recovery, reuse and recycling of materials and components in buildings will obviously help reduce a building's embodied energy, and the BRE Office of the Future, described in Part 2, is an excellent example of this approach, reclaiming and reusing 96 per cent of the materials from the demolished building that previously stood on the site. Another major benefit of reducing the amount of materials brought to a building site is the impact on waste generation. Waste is a significant problem for the construction industry. The UK construction industry consumes more than 400 million tonnes of materials each year and generates over 100 million tonnes of waste. Annually, around 30 million tonnes goes straight to landfill, costing companies hundreds of millions of pounds in landfill tax. UK Government targets are to halve landfill waste by 2012 and eliminate it all together by 2020. Waste can also be reduced drastically by the use of standard components and modular construction based around the on-site assembly of pre-fabricated elements that are manufactured in factories. There is little cutting or mixing of materials and so off-cuts of timber or pieces of plasterboard do not finish up in waste skips. The Huf House, Scania-Hus and Baufritz are typical domestic examples of this modular approach to building, and many of these designs have strong environmental credentials.

Water impacts

Water is obviously a basic element of life, and people and processes consume large volumes of water in buildings. The demand for water continues to grow. In the UK, for example, population numbers have not grown significantly in the last 50 years but water consumption has increased by around 75 per cent. During the same period average rainfall fell by 8 per cent. The environmental impacts of water use are significant and include extraction from rivers and boreholes, flooding of land for reservoirs, overloading of existing sewage systems and energy and chemical use to treat water. Usable water is a scarce resource globally, and despite the Earth being seen as a blue planet, 97 per cent of the Earth's water is seawater, 2.7 per cent is held in polar ice and only 0.3 per cent is usable water. Climate change scenarios suggest that some parts of the world will experience previously unknown drought conditions and this had led to speculation that water, as a commodity, will become the oil of the twenty-first century. For all of these reasons it is important that sustainable building design should attempt to conserve, harvest and reuse water.

Although collected water in most developed countries is treated to make it drinkable only around 4 per cent of water consumed in dwellings is used as drinking water. Figure 25.5 shows how water is used in dwellings, and demonstrates how large amounts of non-potable water (such as directly collected rainwater) could be used for tasks such as flushing toilets and washing. Rainwater harvesting is becoming an increasingly important feature of sustainable buildings, but it does have design consequences such as requiring large storage tanks, oversized gutters, pitched roofs, suitable roof materials, easy access to clean gutters and higher costs.

Water that has already been used for washing, laundry or bathing is called grey water and is normally drained into the sewer system. A sustainable alternative is to collect this grey water, filter it and then return it to a

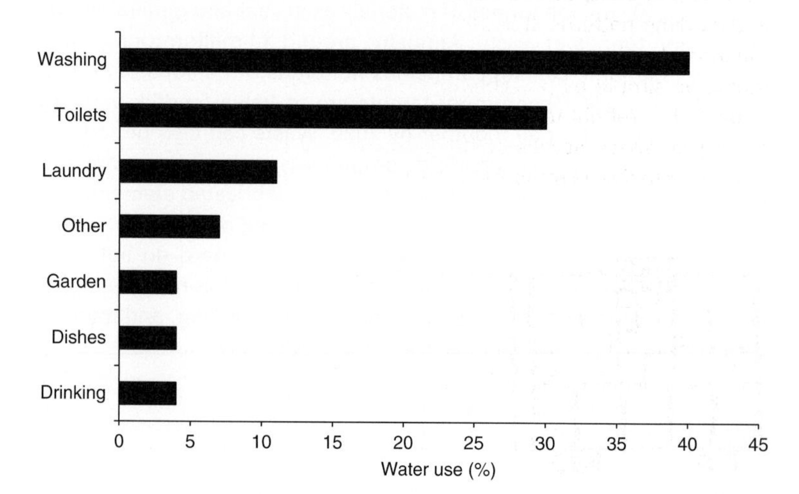

25.5

storage tank to be used for toilet flushing or garden watering. This approach requires separate toilet and other wastewater plumbing systems to be installed. It is also possible to treat foul water from toilets sustainably by using reed beds to collect the foul water and then allowing microorganisms living on the reed root system to clean the contaminated water. Other ways to use water sustainably include self-closing taps, low flush toilets, compost toilets, showers, efficient washing equipment and permeable paving to feed groundwater. The Hockerton Housing Project near Nottingham in the UK is a sustainable housing scheme that has made extensive use of some of the water saving measures outlined here – see http://www.hockertonhousingproject.org.uk/

Design impacts

Buildings that have to be demolished after a relatively short period because they are no longer fit for purpose are self evidently not sustainable. Most of the materials and all of the energy used to construct the building will normally be lost during demolition. There are many reasons why buildings are demolished: they may become too expensive to heat; there may be structural or material faults; their initial function may no longer be appropriate or they may have become socially unacceptable. Apart from making a building energy efficient, the other key approach to designing a sustainable building is to ensure that it is adaptable and reusable.

Designing buildings that are adaptable and flexible starts with a consideration of the plan, section, structural design and building services. The floor layout is particularly important to allow for changing circumstances and uses, such as ageing, disability, family growth and living and working patterns. It is useful to group together spaces with similar functions (such as bathrooms and kitchens) and to keep structural elements as simple as possible. Internal partitions should be able to be relocated or rebuilt to make rooms bigger or smaller without compromising on space access or function. For example, Figure 25.6 shows three alternative layouts for the same floor plan to create a variety of

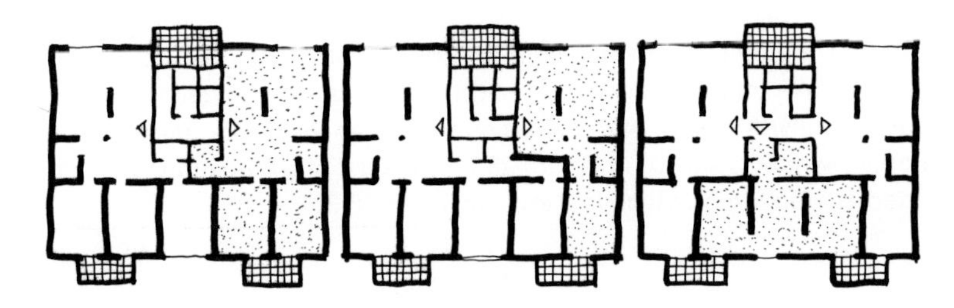

25.6

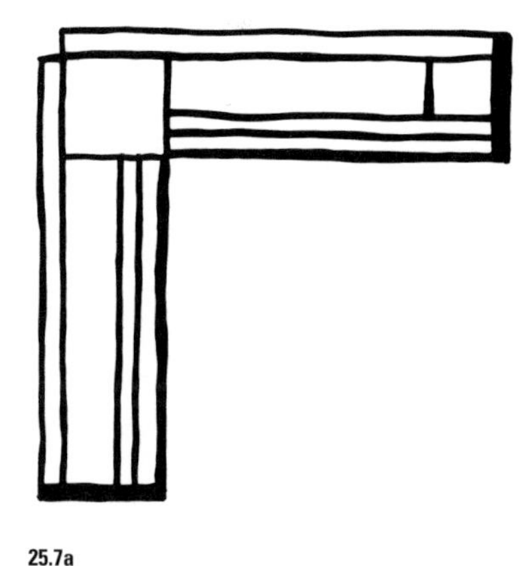

25.7a

25.7b

Table 25.2 Connection types, benefits and drawbacks (adapted from Morgan and Stevenson, 2005)

Type of connection	*Benefits*	*Drawbacks*
Screw fixing	• easily removable	• limited reuse of both hole and screws • cost
Bolt fixing	• strong • can be reused a number of times	• can seize up, making removal difficult • cost
Nail fixing	• speed of construction • cost	• difficult to remove • removal usually destroys a key area of element
Welding	• very strong	• difficult to separate • requires energy
Mortar	• can be made to variety of strengths	• mostly cannot be reused, unless clay • strength of mix often overspecified making it difficult to separate bonded layers
Resin bonding	• strong and efficient • deal with awkward joints	• virtually impossible to separate bonded layers • resin cannot be easily recycled or reused
Adhesives	• variety of strengths available to suit task	• adhesive cannot be easily recycled or reused, many are also impossible to separate
Riveted fixing	• speed of construction	• difficult to remove without destroying a key area of element

bedroom and living spaces. Part M of the UK Building Regulations places some requirements on building design to ensure flexibility so that all building users, including those with disabilities, can access and enjoy a building's facilities.

The process of planning a building for the reuse of its materials and components is called designing for deconstruction. Deconstruction is not simply the opposite of construction – it requires a detailed consideration of how the elements in the building are distributed, accessed and connected at the planning stage before the building is built. The most successful way to design for deconstruction is to minimise the number of building elements (fewer and larger), detach services from structure (around, not through) and decrease the number of connections (fewer and stronger). The design of connections is probably the single most important factor as this determines how easily elements can be separated and what condition they will be in afterwards. Morgan and Stevenson (2005) identify three types of connection – direct (interlocking), indirect (linked by an interim component) and infilled (glued or welded). An indirect connection is the most likely to be deconstructed successfully Morgan and Stevenson give an example for wooden panels, which is shown in Figure 25.7, and a list of connection types, an adapted version of which is shown in Table 25.2.

Chapter **26**

Environmental assessment of buildings

Introduction

As the significance of the environmental performance of buildings grows so the need for systems that can assess environmental performance becomes more important. The basic aim of any building environmental assessment scheme is to set criteria against which to rate a building and then to provide a score or descriptive rating for that building. This rating can be used to show the building's environmental credentials and can have commercial value in terms of promoting a sustainable, eco-friendly image. In addition, a rating system allows a comparison to be made between the performances of similar building types. Although most assessment schemes were originally voluntary and optional, there is a trend in some countries to make assessment and rating mandatory to complement existing legislation on the minimum standards required by regulations and codes. In this chapter the basis of assessment systems is discussed and then some examples of such systems are described.

Basis of assessment systems

There are typically four key elements to an assessment system. The first element consists of identifying those environmental criteria that will be used in the procedure. These criteria are chosen for their impact upon natural, human and built environments and their contribution to sustainable development. There are some obvious criteria for buildings, such as energy use, materials and waste management, but there are also more subjective items that can be included, such as health and well-being. The choice of environmental criteria may reflect prevailing conditions or construction customs in a particular country and so, for example, a rating system developed in the UK may be adopted but modified by a country with a different climate. The second assessment element relates to how the criteria will be scored – for instance, percentage values, credits or points per criterion met. The third, and possibly most important issue, is the weighting given to the criteria to determine what proportions they will contribute to the final score. For example, in the UK's Code for Sustainable Homes (CSH) system energy and CO_2 related issues can be awarded up to 29 credits and have a weighting of 36 per cent of the total possible score whereas waste issues can gain up to seven credits with a weighting of 6 per cent of the total possible score. By contrast, the current version of the USA's Leadership in Energy and Environmental Design (LEED) rating system allocates one credit for each individual environmental criterion and then simply adds up all the credits awarded (although this changes to a weighted approach in the LEED 2009 version). The final element of an assessment system considers how the individual scores are combined and then described to give a building a single score overall rating. Some schemes use a descriptive approach ('good', 'very good', 'excellent' or 'outstanding'). Others use star ratings and the LEED system draws parallels with medal awards (certified, silver, gold and platinum).

BREEAM (UK)

BREEAM (Building Research Establishment Environmental Assessment method) was the world's first building environmental rating system and was released in the UK in 1990. It is not only the longest established but also the most widely used environmental assessment tool for buildings. More than 115,000 buildings have been certified under BREEAM and it has been adopted and adapted by many countries. BREEAM assesses the performance of buildings and awards credits in the following sections:

- Management: overall management policy, commissioning site management and procedural issues.
- Health and Well-being: indoor and external issues affecting health and well-being.
- Energy use: operational energy and carbon dioxide (CO_2) issues.
- Transport: transport-related CO_2 and location-related factors.
- Water: consumption and water efficiency.
- Materials: environmental implication of building materials, including life-cycle impacts.
- Waste: control and management.
- Land Use and Ecology: greenfield and brownfield sites, ecological value, conservation and enhancement of the site.
- Pollution: air and water pollution issues.

Each environmental section covers a variety of topics and has a prescribed number of credits assigned to it. For example, under Health and

Well-Being for an office assessment there are 14 credits available in total that relate to topics such as amount of daylight, background noise levels and thermal comfort. The credits awarded are then adjusted using a set of environmental weightings, which are shown for BREEAM 2008 in Table 26.1. These weightings indicate the relative importance of the environmental parameters in the overall assessment. A BREEAM assessment is carried out by a qualified assessor who will have attended a BRE accredited training course.

The weighted credits are then added together to create a single overall score. The building is then given a BREEAM ranking according the overall score, as listed in Table 26.2.

BREEAM is updated every two years in response to feedback, building developments and legislative changes. The 2008 version included significant developments in terms of mandatory post-construction assessment, the introduction of an 'outstanding' rating, credits for innovation and the introduction of mandatory standards. Another innovation for BREEAM 2008 is that all of the Assessor Manuals are now freely available and downloadable (BREEAM 2008) for all of the non-domestic building types covered by BREEAM (offices, retail, education, prisons, courts, healthcare, industrial and specialised bespoke buildings). Table 26.3 shows an example of a rating calculation taken from the BREEAM Offices 2008 Assessor Manual.

Table 26.1 Environmental weightings in BREEAM 2008

Environmental Parameter	*BREEAM 2008 Environmental Weighting*
Management	0.12
Health and well-being	0.15
Energy	0.19
Transport	0.08
Water	0.06
Materials	0.125
Waste	0.075
Land use and ecology	0.10
Pollution	0.10
Total	1.000

Table 26.2 BREEAM 2008 rating scores

Score (%)	*BREEAM Rating*
< 30 %	Unclassified
≥ 30 %	Pass
≥ 45 %	Good
≥ 55 %	Very good
≥ 70 %	Excellent
≥ 85 %	Outstanding

Table 26.3 Example of BREEAM 2008 office calculation

BREEAM section	*Credits achieved A*	*Credits available B*	*% of credits achieved C=100(A / B)*	*Section weighting D*	*Section Score C x D*
Management	7	10	70 %	0.12	8.40 %
Health and well-being	11	14	79 %	0.15	11.79 %
Energy	10	21	48 %	0.19	9.05 %
Transport	5	10	50 %	0.08	4.00 %
Water	4	6	67 %	0.06	4.00 %
Materials	6	12	50 %	0.125	6.25 %
Waste	3	7	43 %	0.075	3.21 %
Land use and ecology	4	10	40 %	0.10	4.00 %
Pollution	5	12	42 %	0.10	4.17 %
				Total score	54.87 %
				Innovation credits achieved	1 %
				Final BREEAM score	55.87 %
				BREEAM Rating	Very Good

Although BREEAM is not a design tool, it is possible to deduce from the Assessor Manuals those features that will contribute to a good rating. However, a good rating should be the natural consequence of a well-developed sustainable design rather than the contrived outcome of a building that has been designed to tick certain rating boxes.

Code for Sustainable Homes (UK)

The Code for Sustainable Homes (CSH) is a development from the original BREEAM procedure for dwellings, called Ecohomes, and was introduced in 2007. The code is an environmental assessment rating method for new homes in England, and from 1 May 2008 all new homes must have a code rating. The code assesses environmental performance in a two stage process (design stage and post construction) and uses a stars and levels system to rate the overall sustainability performance, ranging from one ★ (Code Level 1) to six ★★★★★★ (Code Level 6). One star is the entry level (a standard above the current Building Regulations) and six stars is the highest level – indicating an exemplar for sustainable development with zero carbon emissions. The UK Government set a target that, from 2016, all new dwellings must be built to zero carbon standards (Code Level 6) - to be achieved through the incremental increase of energy standards in Building Regulations (see Table 26.4).

The code measures the sustainability of a home against nine environmental impact categories, where each category relates to a number of environmental issues, as listed in Table 26.5. There are four un-credited mandatory, minimum performance standards that have to be met before a code rating can be given (shown as *[M_u]* in Table 26.5). There are

Table 26.4 Timetable for Level 6 dwellings in the UK (adapted from CLG 2008b)

Date	*2010*	*2013*	*2016*
Energy efficiency improvement of the dwelling compared to UK 2006 Building Regulations Part L	25 %	44 %	Zero carbon
Equivalent rating standard in Code for Sustainable Homes	THE CODE FOR SUSTAINABLE HOMES Code level 3	THE CODE FOR SUSTAINABLE HOMES Code level 4	THE CODE FOR SUSTAINABLE HOMES Code level 6

Table 26.5 Environmental impact categories, issues (adapted from CLG 2008a)

Categories	*Environmental issues*
Energy and CO_2 emissions	Dwelling emission rate *[M_c]* Building fabric Internal lighting Drying space Energy labelled white goods External lighting Low or zero carbon (LZC) technologies Cycle storage Home office
Water	Internal water use *[M_c]* External water use
Materials	Environmental impact of materials *[M_u]* Responsible sourcing of materials – building elements Responsible sourcing of materials – finishing elements
Surface water run-off	Management of surface water run-off from developments *[M_u]* Flood risk
Waste	Storage of non-recyclable waste and recyclable household waste *[M_u]* Construction site waste management *[M_u]* Composting
Pollution	Global Warming Potential (GWP) of insulants NO_x emissions
Health and well-being	Daylighting Sound insulation Private space Lifetime homes – accessible and adapatable design *[M]*
Management	Home user guide Considerate constructors scheme Construction site impacts Security
Ecology	Ecological value of site Ecological enhancement Protection of ecological features Change in ecological value of site Building footprint

two credited mandatory issues which are considered to be very important to meet (shown as *[M_c]* in Table 26.5) and one credited mandatory issue relating to Level 6 Lifetime Homes (homes designed to be accessible and adaptable to meet the changing needs of current and future occupants – marked *[M]* in Table 26.5). The environmental impact categories and the credits associated with these categories in the code are weighted in terms of the relative impact new housing makes to each code category and the potential to mitigate a category's environmental impacts at the design and construction stages. Table 26.6 shows the credits and weightings used in the code and Table 26.7 shows an example of how individual credits are distributed in a category (in this case the Energy and CO_2 emissions category).

To calculate a code rating the number of credits achieved by the new dwelling in each category is divided by the total number of credits available in that category and then multiplied by the category weighting factor. This gives percentage point scores for each category (rounded

Table 26.6 Total credits and weightings factors (adapted from CLG 2008a)

Categories of environmental impact	*Total credits in category* *A*	*Weighting factor (% points contribution)* *B*	*Approximate weighted value of each credit* *B/A*
Category 1 – Energy and CO_2 Emissions	29	36.4 %	1.26
Category 2 – Water	6	9.0 %	1.50
Category 3 – Materials	24	7.2 %	0.30
Category 4 – Surface Water Run-off	4	2.2 %	0.55
Category 5 – Waste	7	6.4 %	0.91
Category 6 – Pollution	4	2.8 %	0.70
Category 7 – Health and Well-being	12	14.0 %	1.17
Category 8 – Management	9	10.0 %	1.11
Category 9 – Ecology	9	12.0 %	1.33
Total	–	100.0 %	–

Table 26.7 Available credits for Category 1 energy and CO_2 emissions (adapted from CLG 2008a)

Category 1 energy and CO_2 emissions	*Available credits*	*Category weighting factor*
Dwelling emission rate	15	
Building fabric	2	
Internal lighting	2	
Drying space	1	
Energy labelled white goods	2	
External lighting	2	
LZC energy technologies	2	
Cycle storage	2	
Home office	1	
Category total	29	36.40 %

down to two decimal places). For example, if a house achieved in the energy and CO_2 emissions category a total of 18 credits, then the percentage points score for this category would be (18/29) x 36.40 = 22.59 points. The point score from each category is added to give a total percentage point score that is rounded down to the nearest whole number. The relationship between scores and level ratings are shown in Table 26.8, and an example of a CSH calculation is given in Table 26.9. The whole CSH process is shown schematically in Figure 26.1

A full description of the code and a summary are given in CLG (2008a, 2008b) and the full calculation procedure is explained in a CLG Technical guide (2008c)

Other worldwide rating systems

More and more countries around the world are developing their own environmental rating systems that are adapted for their specific requirements.

Table 26.8 Total percentage scores and code level (adapted from CLG 2008a)

Total percentage points score (equal to or greater than)	*Code levels*
36 points	Level 1 (★)
48 points	Level 2 (★★
57 points	Level 3 (★★★)
68 points	Level 4 (★★★★)
84 points	Level 5 (★★★★★)
90 points	Level 6 (★★★★★)

Table 26.9 Example of code for sustainable homes assessment

CSH category	*Credits achieved A*	*Credits available B*	*Weighting factor C*	*Percentage point score (A/B) × C*
Energy CO_2 emissions	19	29	36.4 %	23.85
Water	4	6	9.0 %	6.00
Materials	14	24	7.2 %	4.20
Surface water run-off	2	4	2.2 %	1.10
Waste	4	7	6.4 %	3.66
Pollution	2	4	2.8 %	1.40
Health + well-being	8	12	14.0 %	9.33
Management	4	9	10.0 %	4.44
Ecology	5	9	12.0 %	6.67
			Total Percentage point score	60.65
			Rounded whole number	60
			Code for sustainable homes rating	Level 3 (★★★)

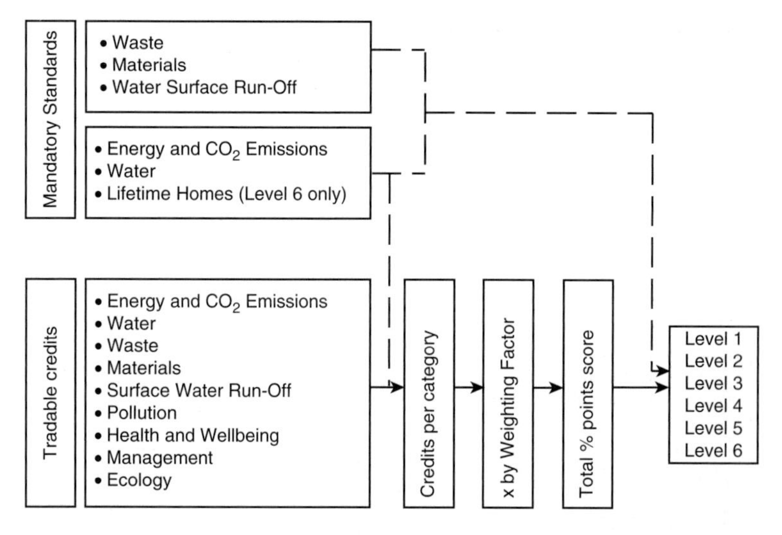

26.1

Most of these systems are modelled on the original BREEAM approach of specifying environmental categories, awarding scores and then bringing the scores together in to one rating. In the USA the Leadership in Energy and Environmental Design (LEED) Green Building rating System™ was released in 1998 and is run by the US Green Building Council (USGBC 2008). LEED-NC (New Construction) version 2.2 (LEED 2005) is structured into six categories, each of which is assigned a number of credits / points, as shown In Table 26.10. A version 3 of LEED, to be called LEED 2009, proposes some changes to the points allocation of LEED credits (LEED 2008).

There are prerequisites for each category that have to be met before any certification level can be awarded. The number of credit points achieved and the overall rating are determined by a third-party assessor. The overall rating scale for LEED is shown in Table 26.11.

Table 26.10 LEED credit and points categories

Category	*No. of credits*	*Maximum number of points possible*
Sustainable sites	8	14
Water efficiency	3	5
Energy and atmosphere	6	17
Materials and resources	7	13
Indoor environmental quality	8	15
Total number of core points possible		64
Innovation and design process	2	5
Total number of project points possible		69

Table 26.11 LEED rating score

Points score	*LEED rating*
26–32 points	LEED certified
33–38 points	LEED silver
39–51 points	LEED gold
52 or more points	LEED platinum

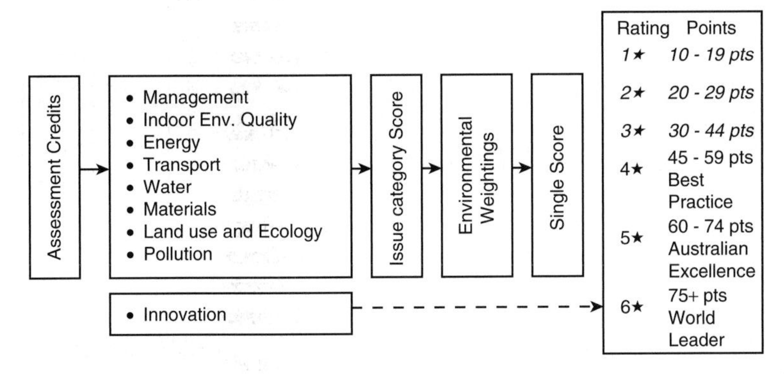

26.2

The Green Globes™ rating system from the Green Building Initiative™ (GBI 2008) is another popular rating system in the USA. Environmental impact is assessed on a 1,000-point scale, spanning seven categories, and projects are awarded one to four globes. The SBTool 07 is also used in the USA; it was developed from the 16 country International Initiative for a Sustainable Built Environment (iiSBE 2008). SBT07 provides a generic toolkit for any local organisation to develop a rating system. It gives an assessment checklist for assessing building performance with a weighting system for regional parameters such as climate, occupancy and local building codes. Design features are compared to national benchmark values and design performance is then scored and weighted as acceptable, good or best practice. In Australia the Green Star rating system for offices was launched by the Green Building Council of Australia (GBCA 2008) in 2003. It is a hybrid of BREEAM and LEED, and brings together the technical rigour of BREEAM with the commercial awareness of LEED. Over 70 per cent of new offices in Australia have been assessed by Green Star, and its basic structure and rating scheme is shown in Figure 26.2.

Chapter **27**

Climate change and building design

Introduction

Climate is, by its very nature, variable and so any attempt to predict future climates for, say, 50 to 100 years from now (the lifetime of a building) is, given the intricacy, interdependencies and uncertainties in climate modelling, a difficult and contentious area of research. What is definitely known, based upon actual thermometer measurements taken since the mid-nineteenth century, is that global air temperatures are rising. There is also a widespread scientific belief that the climate change arising from global warming is the result of increased greenhouse gas emissions from human activity. The future changes to weather patterns that might result from global warming are dependent upon a vast number of parameters, including greenhouse emission scenarios and geographical location, but the major predicted changes include drier and warmer summers, milder and wetter winters and rising sea levels. In addition, extreme climatic events such as more very hot days and heat waves, heavier periods of intense rain and a greater frequency of storms, are expected to occur. Current building construction and environmental design procedures are based on historical weather data that may well be quite different from the climatic conditions a new building of today could be experiencing 50 years from now (TCPA 2007). In this chapter the potential impacts of climate change on buildings will be discussed and some design options to make buildings more resilient to future climates considered.

Designing for the temperature effects of climate change

Global average air temperatures are likely to rise by 1°C to 6°C during the next 100 years, with the greatest warming taking place at high latitudes. Urban areas are already warmer than their surrounding countryside due to solar radiation absorption in building and road surfaces, heat emissions from transport and buildings and the lack of cooling features such as grass, trees and water. This higher temperature is called the urban heat island (UHI) effect, shown in Figure 27.1, and it is particularly evident during summer nights. In London, for example, the highest values of the UHI raised temperatures, in the region of 6°C to 8°C, are mostly experienced between 11.00 at night and 3.00 in the morning.

Global warming will add to the already higher temperatures the urban heat island effect produces in cities, meaning that urban residents will be most at risk from thermal stress. There is a strong correlation between very hot conditions and human illness and mortality, particularly for vulnerable groups such as the old and the ill. Figure 27.2 indicates the approximate relationship between average daily air temperature and the number of daily deaths in south-east England. The European heat wave of August 2003 caused an estimated 35,000 excess of deaths across Europe, and some climate change experts believe that the temperatures experienced during the summer of 2003 could be common by the 2040s and even considered cool by the 2080s.

Perceptions of thermal discomfort vary between individuals, but most people will typically feel thermally uncomfortable for indoor air temperatures above 25°C. Table 27.1 suggests some thermal discomfort criteria for a range of building types, and a building would be considered to be overheating if it experiences temperatures over the 'Warm' threshold given in the table for more than 5 per cent of occupied hours or for more than 1 per cent of occupied hours for the 'Hot' threshold.

The first stage in designing buildings to cope with a future warmer climate is to ensure that the site's microclimate is as cool as possible

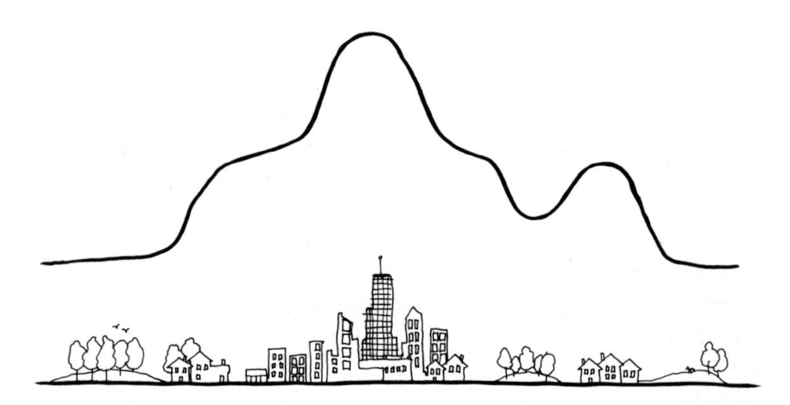

27.1

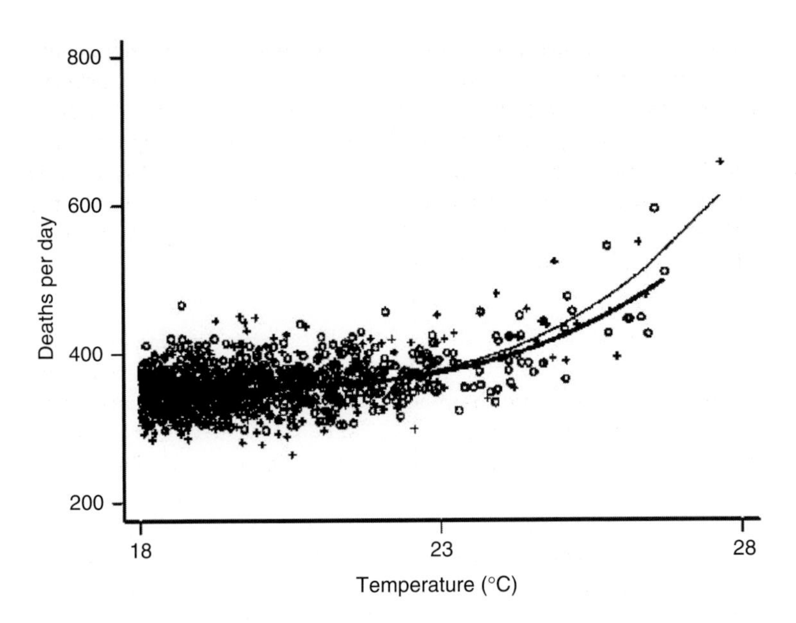

27.2

Table 27.1 Thermal discomfort criteria

Building	*'Warm' temperature threshold*	*'Hot' temperature threshold*	*Heat stress risk temperature threshold (RH 50%, healthy adult)*
Offices, schools, living areas in homes	25°C	28°C	35°C
Bedrooms in homes	21°C	25°C	

during summer months. Landscaping is important for this and green and open spaces containing grassy areas, gardens, trees, pools of water and water features such as fountains should be integrated in to the built environment. In addition, these features can improve external air quality and are a source of moisture in the generally dry urban environment. Spacing between buildings to provide shade, enhance cooling breezes and natural ventilation should be planned from knowledge of solar movements, prevailing wind conditions and architectural aerodynamics. Building surfaces, particularly roofs, should be painted or treated to have a high reflectance (or albedo) to solar radiation in order to minimise solar gain in the opaque fabric and to keep the roof and wall surfaces as cool as possible. This is routinely done in many hot areas, such as southern Europe, but is not a traditional feature of design in cooler climates. Table 27.2 gives typical reflectance values for some common building surfaces and surroundings.

Table 27.2 Typical reflectance values for building surfaces

Building surface / finish	*Solar reflectance (%)*
White paint	90
Aluminium	85
Portland stone	60
Concrete	30
Brick (red)	20
Roof tile (red)	20
Asphalt	10
Grassland	10
Black paint	5

The potential thermal impact of reflective surfaces is demonstrated in Figure 27.3, which shows the results from an analysis of predicted noon external air temperatures three days after the start of a sunny period for a range of building reflectance values.

Placing vegetation on buildings for cooling, in the form of green walls and green roofs, is becoming increasingly popular and has other environmental and constructional benefits such as low maintenance and control of storm water run-off. On very sunny days green roof temperatures may be 20°C to 40°C cooler than a traditionally constructed dark coloured flat roof. Other building fabric responses to climate change will involve solar shading, thermal mass, ventilation and insulation. The main building services considerations will include heating and cooling systems.

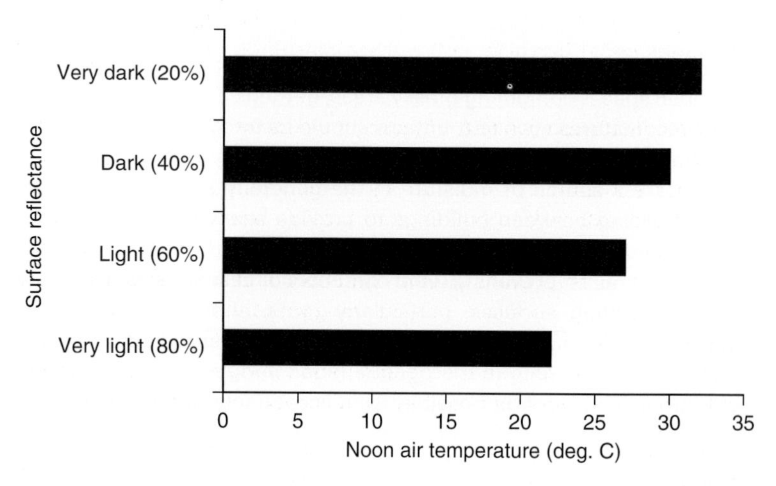

27.3

Solar gain through windows and opaque elements will usually be one of the largest heat gains in a building and so is one of the key design parameters to control in a warming climate. Shading devices can take several forms (louvers, blinds, shutters) and for best performance they should be light coloured, permeable, external and moveable. Roofs should be shaded at latitudes where the sun reaches a high altitude in its path across the sky. In climates that are already hot, building form and layout are also used to provide shade – for example, by placing buildings close together or by forming courtyards. A detailed discussion of solar shading control is given in the CIBSE publication TM37 (CIBSE 2006).

Thermal mass is related to how much heat a material can store and how rapidly that heat is transmitted through the material. Building materials such as concrete and stone are high thermal mass materials and the interiors of caves and cathedrals demonstrate how effective mass can be in keeping spaces cool on very hot days. The disadvantage of thermal mass is that the heat continues to be stored within the building fabric at night, when the UHI has its greatest impact. Night ventilation (the nighttime opening of secure louvers, vents and windows) can be used to discharge some of the stored heat, with the result that the building starts the next day a few degrees Celsius cooler than it otherwise would have been. Ventilation is also important for providing fresh air, removing stale air, controlling relative humidity and offering daytime cooling in summer. Natural ventilation strategies relate to wind driven forces (determined by wind speed and direction) and stack or buoyancy forces driven by the height between inlet and outlet ventilation openings and the indoor-outdoor temperature difference. Future wind speed and direction scenarios are currently poorly understood but it is clear that in a warming environment the potential of summer time cooling by natural ventilation, particularly by buoyancy forces, may be greatly diminished. This use of active or mechanical systems to cool buildings could increase, with consequences for energy demand and waste heat injection into the urban environment.

Thermal insulation is used in building envelopes to reduce heat losses in winter, minimise energy use and maintain thermal comfort. In summer insulation can have two contradictory impacts – it can reduce and retard external solar heat gains being transmitted through the fabric to internal rooms, but it can also impede heat generated within a room (such as solar gains through windows or casual gains from activity) from leaving the space. In a warming climate it becomes less clear how conventional insulation should be used in a future building design. As an alternative, for example, green roofs offer good winter insulation but also provide summer cooling, biodiversity and longer roof life.

A heating boiler runs most efficiently when it is operating close to full output. Heating systems are likely to require much smaller capacities in the future in response to lower winter heating loads. Consequently, the required maximum output of a boiler sized using historical weather data will need to be revised each time the boiler is replaced (say every ten years). For buildings constructed to a very high standard of insulation and air tightness, such as the PassivHaus system discussed in Chapter 25, a warming climate may remove the need for a central heating system altogether. Thermal comfort may be achievable for much of the year using just passive solar gains and casual internal gains from people and electrical equipment.

Traditional passive means of cooling buildings (natural ventilation, thermal mass, evaporation) will probably not be able to guarantee summer thermal comfort for future climate scenarios, especially in heat waves. Current active cooling systems are typically refrigerant-based air-conditioning units with a high electrical energy demand. Such units use the outdoor environment as a heat sink in to which waste heat is discharged. More energy efficient cooling systems, which include the use of chilled beams, ground water, evaporative cooling and ground-coupled cooling, have been developed and implemented into some recent low energy buildings (see GPG 2001). It seems inevitable that mechanical cooling systems will become more widely used to combat the higher indoor temperatures resulting from climate warming. However, their use should represent the final stage after all other passive cooling strategies have been designed in to the building.

Hacker *et al.* (2005) and CIBSE (2005) have analysed how effective some passive adaptive measures might be in combating overheating resulting from climate change. The environmental performance of a number of parameters, such as space heating, risk of summer overheating, need for comfort cooling and performance of mechanical air conditioning systems, were simulated for a range of building types using a current design hot weather year and future weather scenarios. The adaptive measures examined for a new build detached house included thermal mass, solar shading, a reduction of ventilation during the warm part of the day and an increase in ventilation at night. Discomfort temperature levels were taken as 28°C in the living room and 25°C in the bedroom. Figure 27.4 shows the impact of mass on overheating in a living room for an unadapted house in London for a period from the 1980s to the 2080s, expressed as the number of days in a year when indoor temperatures exceeded 28°C. The high-mass house performs significantly better than the equivalent lightweight house. However, a similar analysis for an upstairs bedroom showed only a marginal difference in performance. Figure 27.5 shows the equivalent living room results but includes the influence of the passive adaptation measures. The adapted high mass living room performs significantly better and will provide a good level of thermal comfort up to the 2080s. However, more analysis in this study demonstrated that for an upstairs bedroom there will be overheating problems by the 2020s even for the high mass, adapted house.

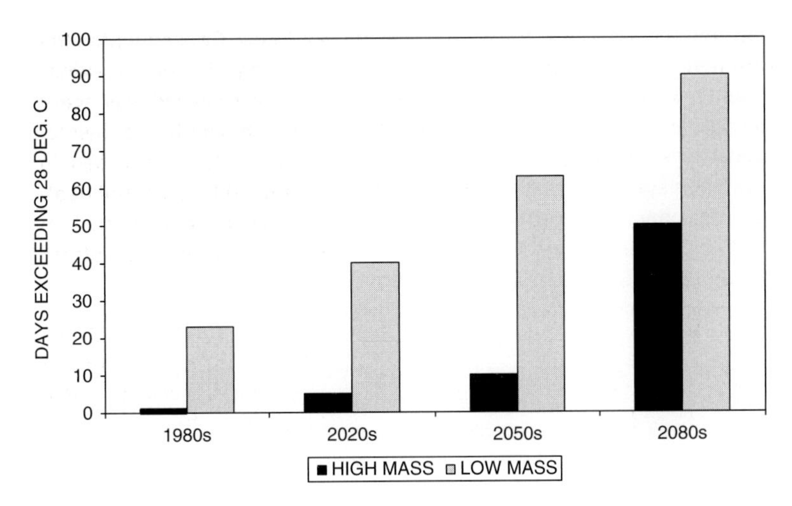

27.4

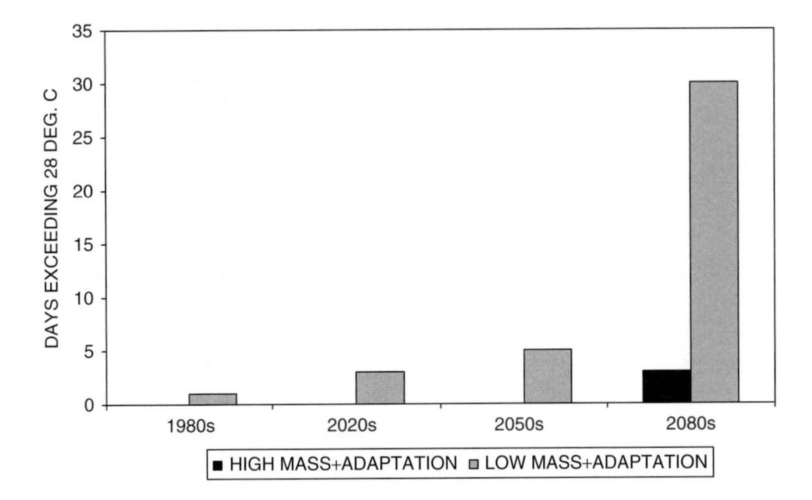

27.5

This type of finding is persuading some house designers to suggest that in future bedrooms should be located on ground floors with living areas at first floor level.

Designing for the rain effects of climate change

Climate change patterns for rain are expected, typically, to feature drier summers, wetter winters and more heavy rainstorms. More frequent and intense rainfall will lead to river flooding and the failure of urban drainage systems. Rising sea levels will add to flood risk for both coastal locations and low-level cities on or near rivers. The economic and social pressures for more development have led to many buildings being constructed on what were, historically, sacrificial flood plains. Natural drainage systems are disturbed and the consequence is more flooding. Climate change will probably make these flooding events more common and more severe. At the urban level, Sustainable Urban Drainage Systems (SUDS) are frequently employed for flood management. SUDS attempts to control and retard the run-off of surface water following rain storms though the use of gently sloping landscaped elements, soak ways to allow the rain to get directly back into the ground, permeable and porous pavements and car parks and sacrificial areas such as fields and ponds to store the flood water. Many of these approaches complement the adaptation strategies for urban cooling discussed previously. A detailed description of SUDS is given by CIRIA (2008). For an individual building, flood risk management seeks to minimise the risk of flooding and reduce the damage caused by flooding. Apart from creating physical barriers between the floodwater and the building, other risk-reduction approaches include decreasing the run-off of rain through harvesting of rainwater, providing permeable and/or drained ground surfaces and the use of green roofs (these suggestions are also part of a SUDS strategy). Green roofs, in particular, are seen as a potentially very powerful tool in adapting buildings to reduce climate change urban flood risk. Floodwater will penetrate a building not just through the obvious apertures in walls but also through cracks, defects and service penetrations in the building envelope, and so a high initial standard of construction, coupled with a rigorous maintenance and repair regime of the structure is important, particularly for buildings in known flood risk areas. All utility services, such as supply meters, electrical fittings and boilers, should be at least one metre above ground floor level, with pipes and cables dropping from first floor level. Drainage and sewer pipes should have one-way valves fitted to prevent the backflow of contaminated floodwater entering the building. A FEMA publication in the USA (FEMA 1999) provides a very detailed discussion of protecting building utilities from flood damage. Flood resistant finishes, such as plastics, vinyl, concrete, ceramic tiles and pressure-treated timber, should be used in place of carpets, chipboard, soft woods and fabric, and gypsum plaster should be replaced with a more water resistant material, such as lime plaster or cement render. To reduce the amount of repair after flooding it is helpful to fix plasterboards horizontally on timber framed walls rather than vertically and to replace mineral insulation within internal partition walls with closed cell insulation. Some of the most advanced ideas for making buildings flood resilient can be found in Holland, a country that is, even before climate change, typically 6m below sea level. One architectural solution is floating buildings that rise and fall with water levels. Examples of this approach are described by H_2OLLAND (2006).

Designing for the wind effects of climate change

The major ways in which buildings interact with the wind are in structural loading, wind speeds at pedestrian level and as a driving force for natural ventilation and cooling. Future scenarios for wind speed and direction are some of the most uncertain areas of climate change modelling and there is a great deal of uncertainty about prospective wind trends. However, it is believed that there will be an increase in the number and severity of storms. The most important wind feature is the once in 50-year design wind speed used in structural loading calculations. Given that buildings might stand for up to 100 years then it could be argued that structural building codes will need to review the design wind speeds and frequency of events to factor in safety margins in response to future climate change. Roofs are most at risk of damage in high winds, mainly due to a failure of the roof to be securely tied to its supporting walls and supports. Low pitched roofs are particularly susceptible to wind damage and a better choice might be a mansard roof, which has two slopes on each side, with the lower slope being almost vertical and the upper slope being almost horizontal. Other design features, such as buildings having a more aerodynamic form or minimum roof overhangs, may appear beneficial but would need to be tested to ensure that other problems are not created – for example, small overhangs might exacerbate flooding problems.

Designing for the subsidence effects of climate change

It is indicative of the global complexity of the issues that whilst climate change scenarios predict increased flood risk for some regions they also suggest that other areas will suffer from very dry seasons, water shortages and the risk of soils drying out. Reduced soil moisture levels have impacts on agriculture, flood control and buildings, where subsidence damage will become an increasing problem. UKCIP02 (2002) suggested that for different scenarios soil moisture will fall by between 20 per cent and 40 per cent by the 2080s. Subsidence is already a significant cause of building damage and climate change is only likely to make things worse. For existing buildings it is not viable to underpin original foundations in a way that will make them climate change resilient, and so the incidence of subsidence damage to buildings will increase during the coming decades. To make new and future buildings climate change resilient it will be necessary to change the design of foundations to make them stronger, stiffer and deeper in order to resist movement. New foundation technologies, such as pile-and-beam foundations, are described in an NHBC publication which also highlights the importance of careful tree planting management to avoid soil shrinkage and foundation damage by roots.

Conclusion

The growing impacts of climate change on the built environment over the next 50 years are likely to coincide with the impacts of energy shortages and price rises. The need for buildings to consume vast amounts of energy in order to service themselves is a relatively recent phenomenon, only starting from the beginning of the twentieth century. For millennia before then, buildings had to try and achieve comfort by modifying the prevailing climate using only passive or low energy systems incorporated in to their site, structure, materials and envelope design. Many of the design issues and solutions relating to climate change discussed in this chapter resonate with elements found in the vernacular architecture and urban layouts of other countries. It is too simplistic to say that since temperatures in London may one day resemble those already existing in, say, Lisbon then a linear design extrapolation can be made. However, there are lessons relevant to designing for climate change to be learnt from vernacular architecture, which offers a historical perspective on how, globally, built environments evolved in reacting to and coping with the challenges of changing climates.

Part **6**

Bibliography

CIBSE, *Climate Change and the Indoor Environment: Impacts and Adaptations*, CIBSE Technical Memorandum TM36, CIBSE (2005).

CIBSE, *Design for Improved Solar Shading Control*, CIBSE Technical Memorandum TM37, CIBSE (2006).

Morgan, C. and Stevenson, F. *Design and Detailing for Deconstruction,* SEDA Design Guides for Scotland: No. 1 (2005).

NHBC, *NHBC Standards, Part 4 – Foundations*, National House Builders Confederation (2007).

Webliogaphy

BRE Green Guide to Specification http://www.thegreenguide.org.uk/index.jsp (accessed 1 May 2008).

BREEAM www.breeam.org (accessed 1 May 2008).

CIRIA www.ciria.org.uk/suds (accessed 1 May 2008).

CLG Code for Sustainable Homes – technical guide (2008c) www.planningportal.gov.uk/uploads/code_for_sustainable_homes_techguide.pdf (accessed 1 May 2008).

CLG Greener homes for the future (2008a) http://www.communities.gov.uk/publications/planningandbuilding/codeleaflet (accessed 1 May 2008).

CLG The Code for Sustainable Homes – setting the standard in sustainability for new homes (2008b) http://www.communities.gov.uk/publications/planningandbuilding/codesustainabilitystandards (accessed 1 May 2008).

FEMA *Protecting building utilities from flood damage*, FEMA Report 348 http://www.fema.gov/hazard/flood/pubs/pbuffd.shtm (accessed 1 May 2008).

GBCA (2008) http://www.gbca.org.au/green-star/ (accessed 1 May 2008).

GBI www.thegbi.org (accessed 1 May 2008).

GPG *Ventilation and cooling option appraisal – a client's guide*, Good Practice Guide 290, BRECSU, Watford, www.carbontrust.co.uk (accessed 1 May 2008) .

H_2OLLAND Architecture with wet feet, http://www.h2olland.nl/ (accessed 1 May 2008).

Hacker, J.N. Belcher, S.E. and Connell, R.K. Beating the heat: keeping UK buildings cool in a warming climate, UKCIP Briefing Report, UKCIP www.arup.com/_assets/_download/download396.pdf (accessed 1 May 2008).

Hockerton Housing Project http://www.hockertonhousingproject.org.uk/ (accessed 1 May 2008).

iiSBE (2008) http://www.iisbe.org/iisbe/sbc2k8/sbc2k8-download_f.htm (accessed 1 May 2008).

LEED (2005) http://www.usgbc.org/DisplayPage.aspx?CMSPageID=220#v2.2 (accessed 1 May 2008).

LEED (2008) www.usgbc.org/ShowFile.aspx?DocumentID=4121 (accessed 1 May 2008).

Passive House Institute http://www.passivehouse.com/ (accessed 1 May 2008).

PassivHaus UK www.passivhaus.org.uk (accessed 1 May 2008).

TCPA *Climate change adaptation by design*, TCPA www.TCPA.org/publications.asp (accessed 1 May 2008).

UKCIP02 Chapter 4: *Future Changes in UK Seasonal Climate*, Chapter 4, *Climate Change Scenarios for the United Kingdom: the UKCIP02 Scientific Report*, Tyndall Centre pp. 51–2. http://www.ukcip.org.uk/index.php?option=com_content&task=view&id=353&Itemid=408 (accessed 1 May 2008).

University of Bath http://www.bath.ac.uk/mech-eng/sert/embodied/ (accessed 1 May 2008).

USGBC (2008) http://www.usgbc.org/DisplayPage.aspx?CategoryID=19 (accessed 1 May 2008).

Part 7
Case studies

Chapter **28**

Elizabeth Fry Building

Introduction

The Elizabeth Fry Building, at the University of East Anglia in Norwich, UK, represents a landmark in low energy buildings that used a combination of passive low energy design and mechanical supply of air through structural hollow core ceiling slabs. Designed by John Miller and Partners, the building was completed in 1995 at a cost of £2.9 million for a gross area of 3,250m^2. The building underwent a full programme of monitoring and user satisfaction surveys by the PROBE study (Anon 1998).

General description

The building is the last in a programme of development in teaching and accommodation at the western edge of the Norwich campus. It is arranged in four storeys along an east–west axis with the main entrance on the north side. The lower ground and ground floors are occupied by teaching rooms for general undergraduate use and conference activities with some catering facilities. The top two floors house cellular offices for academic and administrative staff together with postgraduate and resource rooms.

Building construction

The primary objective of the design team was to achieve low-energy comfort within the building. To this end, the design strategy combined the use of: the building structure (as an energy store), low pressure mechanical ventilation, heat recovery and openable triple-glazed windows. The structure of the building consists of an in situ reinforced concrete frame supporting precast concrete hollow core floors. Beneath the floor slab of the lower ground floor, specially constructed concrete chambers are used to circulate the air as part of the ventilation system.

For the low-energy comfort strategy to succeed, the building envelope needed to be highly insulated and well sealed. Double-skin concrete blockwork walls incorporating 200mm insulation were used throughout. Thermal bridging was reduced by means of nylon wall ties. The precast concrete roof has 300mm of insulation while 100mm of insulation is applied to the exposed floor soffits. With the use of low-E, argon filled triple glazing the building envelope achieves high levels of thermal insulation resulting in lower U-values as indicated in the table below.

All the floors have exposed structural ceilings made of precast hollow concrete slabs. These are used as ventilation ducts and at the same time their thermal mass helps reduce internal temperature fluctuations. The triple glazed windows incorporate an inner low-E argon filled sealed unit, mid-pane perforated metal Venetian blinds in the outer cavity, and external single glazing. In order to minimise cold bridging and air infiltration, the detailing of windows was carefully considered. These measures, together with window construction, contributed to reducing heat loss around windows in winter and heat gains through them in summer.

Ventilation

The design approach to ventilation is the use of a mixed mode, combining low-pressure mechanical supply with heat recovery and openable windows. The strategy involves the use of hollow core structural floor slabs as a ducting system to supply the air to various rooms and combine it with a heat recovery system during the heating season. This combination led to low energy use as the thermal mass of the floor would give a cooling effect in summer. During the heating season, the heat extracted from outgoing air is injected back into the incoming

Table 28.1 u-values of the various construction elements

Element	*Construction*	*U-value (W/m²K)*
Walls	Double skin blockwork, 200mm insulation	0.22
Exposed floors	Precast concrete, 100 mm insulation	0.16
Roof	Ventilated hollow core slabs, 300mm insulation	0.13
Windows	Triple glaze, low-E, argon filled	1.3

fresh air, thus reducing the heating load. The fresh air ventilation system operates only when the building is occupied, so that unnecessary heating loads are eliminated.

Heating

The heating system consists of three 24kW gas fired condensing boilers. The operating load of the boilers is variable according to demand. All three boilers are fired at start up, under the control of the building energy management system (BEMS) which determines the heating loads and turns off those not required. The heat output from the boilers is fed directly into the air-handling units which supply the air to the rooms via the ceiling hollow core slabs. These act as a sink to the heat generated internally (by occupants and equipment). In winter, this heat is supplemented by warm air from the ventilation system to keep the slabs at a temperature close to the room temperature. This combined with a highly insulated building, helps maintain comfort temperatures at lower heating loads.

Cooling

The hollow core ceiling slabs are once again the main feature that the cooling strategy relies upon. Since they are used as the delivery system for ventilation air (instead of conventional ducts), their thermal mass is used to good effect to do away with conventional mechanical cooling. During the summer, cool night time air is pushed through the slabs using fan power. The concrete slabs are cooled and act as a heat sink during the day resulting in eliminating the need for energy intensive air conditioning. Even on the hottest days in summer, the night time ventilation cooling can maintain the internal temperature under 25°C. The effect of the thermal mass of the slabs on the internal comfort conditions in summer is multifold:

- Internal heat gains from occupants, equipment and lighting are absorbed, thus contributing to a lowering of the internal temperature.
- Fresh air delivered through the hollow core will be cooled down before it is delivered to the rooms.
- Because air conditioning is not used, openable windows are used and occupants can open them if the need arises. This tends to have a positive effect on user satisfaction as occupants feel they have a certain level of control over their environment.

Lighting

The lighting strategy consists of the provision of daylight to rooms by means of single sided fenestration and a light well for the central circulation area. Windows occupy around 25 per cent of the area of external walls for offices. The use of controllable perforated Venetian blinds in the outer ventilated cavity of the triple glazing acts as a shading device. The outer pane of the triple glazing system is translucent to give diffuse light without the penalty of glare and high solar gains.

The atrium of the entrance foyer has a south sloping rooflight with motorised external shading devices controlled by means of a photoelectric control system. The end result is good daylighting conditions in the stairwells and entrance foyer. The only area where artificial light is required at most times is the central corridor between the two banks of rooms. Artificial lighting to the rooms consists of high frequency fluorescent lighting units concealed under the cornice of the ceiling. This indirect system of lighting comes with a penalty of reduced efficiency. Typical values for installed power densities are in the order of 15–30 W/m^2. These are higher compared to best practice office standard of 12 W/m^2 (Energy Consumption Guide 19 1998).

Energy performance

Different references give slightly different figures for energy consumption. Those quoted here are taken from the PROBE study (Anon 1998), which monitored the building for the first few years of its operation. The total electrical consumption at the Elizabeth Fry building is 61kWh/m^2/year. Lighting takes the biggest share at 26kWh/m^2/year followed by fan and pump power at 18kWh/m^2/year with the remainder used in catering and office equipment.

The gas consumption was put at 37kWh/m^2/year. This figure covers both heating and hot water systems. These figures give an annual total energy consumption of 98kWh/m^2. Comparison of the energy consumption for the Elizabeth Fry building with existing benchmarks is somehow not straightforward as the use of the building falls under two different categories: office buildings and academic buildings.

According to the ECON 19 guidelines for offices (Energy Consumption Guide 19 1998), the electricity consumption of the building falls between a type 1 (naturally ventilated, cellular office) and a type 3 (air conditioned office). What is even significant here is that the electricity consumption is half that of an air-conditioned office. When applying the EEO (1994) benchmark for educational buildings, again the electricity consumption at the Elizabeth Fry building is within the low consumption category (below 75kWh/m^2/year).

With regard to gas consumption, the EEO (1994) benchmark puts low annual gas consumption at below 185kWh/m^2/. Compare this building's figure of 37kWh/m^2/year and it is easy to see how low energy consumption is. For a detailed analysis of the building, the reader can be referred to http://www.learn.londonmet.ac.uk given the reference section.

User satisfaction

The building was the subject of a user satisfaction survey by the PROBE team (1998) and their results show high levels of satisfaction with various aspects of building performance and comfort. The final report concludes that the building is 'likely to become a role model for future building design and management'.

For under £900/m^2 the design and construction teams managed to produce a building that is a model for energy efficiency and scores highly among users. This makes it even more cost effective than a 'conventional' building and a delight to be in.

Chapter **29**

Notley School, Essex

Introduction

Notley Green primary school in Braintree, Essex, UK, was designed by Alfred Hall Monaghan Morris, through open competition and completed in 1997. The design was intended to be a prototype low energy sustainable school. The design team's objective to achieve a low energy building relied on the use of a highly insulated envelope, combined with natural ventilation, daylight and solar shading.

General description

The building has a triangular shape, with its points facing north-west, east and south. The layout of the single storey building is dominated by the multi-purpose hall at the north western corner of the triangle, with the classrooms at the opposite base of the triangle facing south east. The south-east–north-west section is characterised by a roof line that cants upwards allowing vertical roof lights to admit high level daylight and at the same time provide exhaust points for the natural ventilation system (see Figure 29.1).

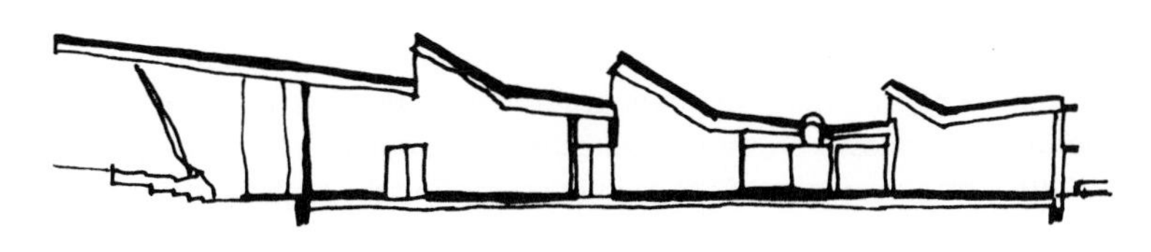

29.1

Construction

The one storey building has load bearing walls which support the roof and is supported by strip foundations. Internal walls are mainly of blockwork, while externally they are timber frame construction. These latter ones consist of 225mm timber stud frames lined with a double skin of plasterboard on the inside and a proprietary breather sheathing on the outside. The cavity in the frame is filled with Warmcell insulation, which is 100 per cent newspaper based recycled waste giving it low embodied energy. A back ventilated, low maintenance, tongue and groove cedar boarding is used as a cladding system. The external wall has a U-value of 0.21 W/m^2K.

The suspended ground floor slab consists of precast concrete planks spanning between the strip foundations and resting on a bed of engineering bricks. The planks are covered with a layer of screed, followed by insulation, screed where the underfloor heating pipes are buried, and finally the floor finish. This is either a timber finish or a carpet/linoleum one depending on room use. These two finishes give slightly different U-values; 0.38 W/m^2K and 0.37 W/m^2K respectively.

The roof structure consists of engineered timber I beams constructed of softwood flanges and a hardboard web. This gives them high strength combined with economy. These span between the load bearing walls at spans between 4 and 12m. The roof deck is a 15mm Douglas fir ply skin that acts as a stressed diaphragm transferring the roof loads to the load bearing walls. The deck is insulated internally using mineral fibre. The deck supports a proprietary green roof /sedum roof comprising a vegetation blanket, filters and drainage membranes. The combined roof construction has a U-value of 0.32 W/m^2K. Low-E double glazing windows are used throughout. These have a U-value of 1.6 W/m^2K.

Ventilation

The ventilation strategy consists mainly of the provision of fresh air by natural means. Only the kitchen and toilets use either assisted or mechanical extraction. Around 5–6 air changes per hour are provided for the toilet block using a passive stack system assisted fan power (Passivent). Air extraction from the kitchen is by means of a dual speed fan. The fan assisted natural ventilation system consists of three basic components that work in combination to provide the building with an adequate supply of fresh air. The side windows combined with high level clerestory motorised windows promote the necessary conditions for a continuous airflow. The side windows act as inlet points and the high level windows as exhaust ones. Having the rooflights facing away from prevailing wind direction gives the system even further exhaust pressure.

To deliver fresh air beyond the perimeter rooms, a 300mm diameter underground clay pipe is used in conjunction with an inlet louver on the external wall and fitted with a motorised damper, and a diffuser at delivery point (see Figure 29.2). The use of breathable external wall construction reduces the need for background ventilation to a minimum, as the risk of condensation, created by the high temperature drop across the insulating layer, is minimum.

Lighting and heating

The provision of daylight by means of side windows and rooflights is more than adequate. The latter ones ensure that daylight reaches the back of rooms. An average daylight factor of 4–5 per cent is typical in classrooms. The hall benefits from daylight coming through a continuous row of rooflights across its width. The daylight system is supplemented with luminaires mounted flush in the ceiling and using low energy compact fluorescent lamps. The lack of an automatic control system for the artificial lighting may have a negative effect on the efficiency of this low energy building.

The underfloor hot water heating system is fed by a gas fired, high efficiency condensing boiler with flow and return temperatures of 65 and 56 °C respectively. The building is subdivided into 22 control zones each of them is controlled by means of an adjustable thermostat. Having these control zones can make the heating system more efficient as it delivers only what heat is needed to any given space.

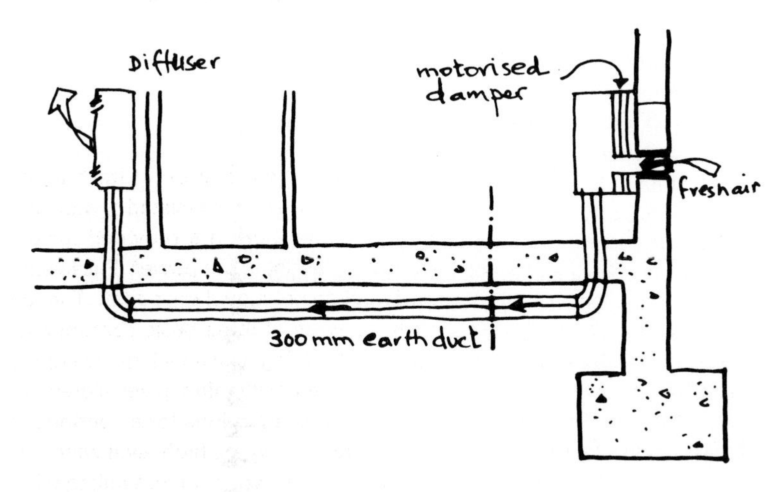

29.2

Low impact design strategy

The impact of materials used was considered whenever it was practical. The following is a list of materials where low impact was considered:

Table 29.1 Materials used and their impact

Material	*Application*	*Positive impact*
Engineered timber	Masonite beams	High strength material from re-used thin layers and low impact source
Insulation	External walls	From recycled waste paper
Wood fibre sheathing	External walls	From recycled waste
Compressed plastic bottles	Work tops	Recycled waste
Waste rubber (used tyres)	Entrance mats	Recycled waste
Sedum roof	Roof covering	Replace the green space taken by building

Furthermore the use of timber as a cladding and structural material enhances the embodied energy balance of the building.

Energy performance

The building was designed with a target energy use around 40–50 per cent of a standard building of the same type. Metered gas consumption was around 75kWh/m^2/year. This represents around 50 per cent of the national average consumption for the building type. Furthermore, using the national benchmark for educational buildings (EEO Yellow Book 1994), low annual consumption is anything below 185kWh/m^2/year. The Notley School gas consumption represents only 40 per cent of that benchmark.

Electricity consumption for the first year of operation was measured at 60kWh/m^2/ year. Although it is still lower than the upper level for low consumption according to national guidelines (EEO Yellow Book 1994), it is still higher than the national average consumption for schools. This is not necessarily due to any design failures, but rather to operational problems. First, the opening hours of the school have been extended to cover a daily shift from 6.30 until 18.00. On some nights this is extended even further to 21.00. This meant the lighting loads are increased drastically, particularly since the extra opening hours do not benefit from daylight. A second operational problem, which can easily be resolved, is the extract fans used in the toilet blocks. These have been running for 24 hours a day, 365 days a year. They were designed to run on a demand only basis. This latter problem has been remedied, and would certainly make a difference to the electrical load.

User satisfaction

In terms of overall score, the Notley School had a similar score to that of the Elizabeth Fry Building. Overall user acceptance was rated at just under 4.5 (on a scale of 1=bad to 7=good). Looking at the individual parameters that the questionnaire sought to evaluate, 7 out of 12 were rated above 4 (average), 1 was rated 4, and 4 were rated below 4.

The total cost of the building is given at ECU1.832 million. At the 1997 exchange rate, this would come around £1200/m^2 which would not be dissimilar to (if not less than) similar buildings completed around the same time. The building was completed within budget.

For a detailed analysis of the building, the reader can be referred to the London Metropolitan University website (see p.295) given in the bibliography to this section.

Chapter **30**

Small scale buildings

Introduction

To provide the reader with a flavour of what low impact low energy small-scale buildings are available, two different examples are presented in this section. The first one is a single pavilion type student residence, while the second one is a family dwelling.

Westminster Lodge, Dorset, UK

Westminster Lodge in Dorset, UK, is a purpose built students' residence serving Hooke Park College. The building was designed by Edward Cullinan Architects as a response to its site, a woodland area, and a live, hands on project to demonstrate what the college is about. The floor plan consists of four pairs of double rooms surrounding a central living/ dining area. The main feature of the building is the roof construction. This consists of a structural double lattice constructed from thinnings (young green saplings that are too slender for conventional use in construction). This is particularly relevant as the college's main aim is to research and demonstrate innovative ways of using timber technology.

Given that the local climate is characterised by cold winters and mild summers, the building was designed mainly for heating, hence the use of a highly insulated building fabric. The double lattice structure of the roof is insulated and covered with turf. The energy use is decreased further by means of both natural ventilation and daylight. The latter is facilitated by a centrally located skylight. It provides enough daylight to a point where no artificial lighting is needed in the communal central area during the day. According to Jones (1998), the building interior has a target monthly energy use (0.0686kW/h/m^2). This is equivalent to 14.3kWh/m^2 per year. Some 80 per cent of the load is taken by the heating system and the remainder used for lighting. The use of locally sourced timber from managed forests helped reduce the building's carbon footprint. This is further enhanced by supporting the building on stilts, thus preserving further green spaces, and using a green roof. The end result is a building that is in tune with its surroundings and with its green floating roof it feels as if it is coming out of the ground. Its low energy demand and locally sourced materials make it into a low impact building. Some of the low impact design strategies include the selection of materials to reduce both embodied and transport energy as well as the use of timber from managed sources.

The Autonomous Urban House, Nottinghamshire, UK

The house was designed by Robert and Brenda Vale, who are renowned in the UK for their environmentally sensitive designs. Although the house was completed in 1993, even by today's standards it has very low energy consumption. What makes it even more interesting is that it achieved this by means of low technology.

The building is a 2.5 storey detached house with a cellar, four bedrooms and two bathrooms, giving a habitable floor area of 169 m^2. The total floor area inclusive of the porch, cellar and conservatories amounts to 290 m^2.

The floor layout runs along a north–south axis, giving the house an east–west aspect. The ground floor is occupied by the bedrooms, while the living space is on the first floor. On the west side, a two-storey conservatory provides a well lit space and a means to harness heat from the sun (Figure 30.1).

Construction

Despite its external form and materials similar to those of the surrounding buildings, the house is different inside. It has a block and in situ concrete basement. The 2 × 100mm lightweight aerated concrete blocks act as permanent shuttering to the in situ reinforced concrete. This gives it a U-value of 0.3W/m^2K. The ground floor slab consists of a concrete beam and block system covered with screed and with 50mm cellulose fibre insulation sprayed on the soffit. The floor has a U-value of 0.6W/m^2K. External walls are constructed of clay bricks and an inner leaf of concrete blocks. The 250mm cavity is filled with mineral fibre insulation, which gives the wall a U-value of 0.14W/m^2K. The conventional external appearance of the roof hides its unconventional construction and the role it plays in raising the level of thermal insulation for the building. A 70mm structural soft wood decking with a polyethylene vapour barrier and I-beam rafters give support to 500mm of cellulose fibre insulation and clay pantiles. This construction has a U-value of 0.07W/m^2K. The triple glazed, krypton filled windows have a U-value of 1.15 W/m^2K.

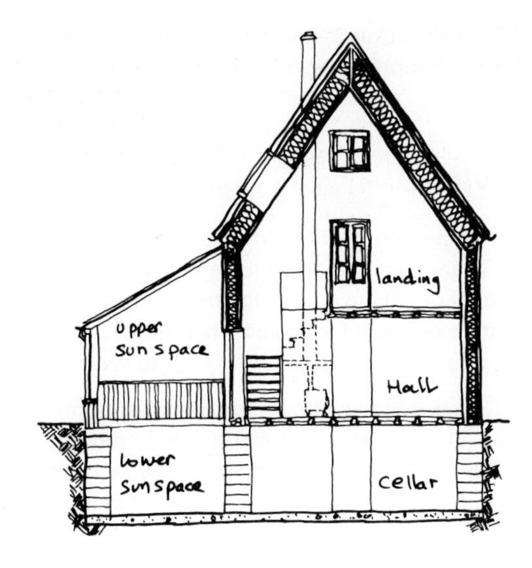

30.1

The low-E, double glazing system used in the conservatory yields U-values of 2.1 and 3.2 for vertical and sloping surfaces respectively.

Ventilation

The house makes use of mechanical ventilation with heat recovery using units located in the wet rooms (kitchen and bathrooms). Preheated air is taken from the conservatory and delivered to these rooms. The bedrooms have trickle vents in the window frames. These are opened at night.

Heating

Heat for the domestic hot water is provided by a heat pump that uses heat from the composting toilet as a primary source. The pump has a coefficient of performance of 3.5. This means that for every 1kWh of electricity used, the pump gives off 3.5kWh of heat. Space heating is provided by the passive solar gain from the conservatory. A 4kW wood stove with a ducted air supply is to supplement the solar heat gain. In order to maintain a minimum temperature of 18°C, the backup heating would need to provide 3kWh/m^2 a year.

Electricity

The house has an array of photovoltaic (PV) cells mounted on a wooden pergola in the garden. These are connected to the grid and have a capacity of 2.2kW. A backup battery is installed in the cellar to ensure continuity of water supply in the event of a power cut.

Water services

Rain water is collected on the roof and stored in 30 m^3 tanks located in the basement. The water is pumped to sand filters in the lower conservatory, then fed by gravity to a holding tank from which it is pumped to a tank in the loft, to be available as and when required. For drinking and cooking water, a further ceramic/carbon filtering system is used.

The house has its own sewage treatment plant, as it is not connected to the main sewer. The composting toilet has a holding compartment in the basement. This is vented by a 5W fan. The by-products are a permanent supply of garden fertilizer and grey water that enters a soakaway through a grease trap.

Energy consumption

Energy consumption was carefully monitored by the occupants. Prior to the installation of the PV system and the heat pump, the electricity used from the national grid was measured at 3072kWh/year. This load covered all the services except for the space heating which was by the wood stove. Given that the heated area is 169 m^2 this would mean an annual consumption of 18kWh/m^2 electricity and 4kWh/m^2 (ref.6) from wood totalling 22kWh/m^2 a year. This is still very low compared to conventional dwellings, particularly as this energy includes other services (sewage treatment, water treatment, etc.) which is not the case for conventional dwellings.

The installation of the PV array saw an output of 1,120kWh between July 1994 and May 1995 (Smith and Pitts 1997). Extrapolated over a whole year, this would mean an output equivalent to 1450kWh/year. The heat pump was estimated to reduce electricity usage to 1450kWh/year. This would eventually mean that for typical conditions, a house would have a net zero electricity input from the grid.

This building has demonstrated that much can be achieved in terms of low energy and low impact buildings. While on the outside, the house was no different in appearance from any of the dwellings surrounding it, internally it was conceived as an ultra low energy building. Its environmental credentials extend beyond the highly insulated envelope and passive solar heating. It does also deal with issues that reduce the environmental impact of buildings while providing comfortable and pleasant living space.

Chapter **31**

Vulcan House, Sheffield, UK

Introduction

Vulcan House is the new Home Office Headquarters in Sheffield. It was awarded a BREEAM Excellent rating in May 2006 and was the second highest rated BREEAM building in the UK at the time of the assessment. Architects Hadfield Cawkell Davidson worked with consulting engineers Mott MacDonald to develop a building that looks like a modern office development but which, in addition, delivers a very high level of sustainable performance. The Home Office wanted the building to demonstrate how it could help in achieving the government's target of becoming carbon neutral by 2012. At the same time, the Home Office wished to lease the building rather than own it, and so it asked developers to bid for the project, but set a very prescriptive green brief. Vulcan House demonstrates that it is feasible to construct an environmentally sustainable speculative office development provided the client can guarantee a long-term commitment.

Building form and structure

Vulcan House is sited in a central urban location on the banks of Sheffield's River Don and houses 1,100 staff. The building has a steel frame structure built on CFA piles with composite floors constructed of a metal-deck permanent formwork supporting a 150mm concrete layer. A total floor area of 13,650m^2 is spread over seven storeys. Vulcan House deliberately has a cube-like shape since, after a sphere, the cube form offers the largest internal volume for the smallest area of external surface. Environmental control issues are often dominated by what happens at the external façades of buildings and so minimising external surface area helps in regulating the internal environment. The exterior façades of the building include argon-filled double glazing, solar protective glass and opaque insulated ceramic panels. A light well penetrates vertically through the centre of the building to add extra daylight to the core of the open plan work areas, which are up to 15m in depth. Computer thermal simulations of the building using a year of local climatic data helped demonstrate that changing the orientation of the building could save 5 per cent on energy consumption and that the proportions of glazing on each façade should be 75 per cent on the north and east walls and 50 per cent on the south and west walls. A green roof is integrated in to the design to help regulate heat gain and loss and to increase the ecology of the site. The building is shown in Figure 31.1.

Building services

Vulcan House is, despite its high BREEAM rating, not naturally ventilated. Instead, the building uses mechanical ventilation with heat recovery and circulates air locally over short pipe runs rather than ducting air over large distances. This strategy helps reduce the energy needed to pump air from a typical value of 2.0W/litre/second down to 0.8W/l/s. The building was pressure tested prior to occupation for the possibility of air leaks and had an air permeability index of $7m^3/h/m^2$ at 50 Pa, which is significantly better than the current building regulations' required value of $10m^3/h/m^2$ at 50 Pa. The building is cooled by ammonia chillers rather than the more common air-conditioning plant which use hydrofluorocarbons (HFCs) as a refrigerant. This was because the global warming impact of 1kg of HFCs can be up to 1,900 times greater than 1kg of CO_2. A typical office multi-split air-conditioning system could contain around 30kg of HFC refrigerant, which will eventually leak

31.1

in to the atmosphere and need replacing. Conversely, ammonia does not have a global warming impact and is lighter than HFCs and so it is more energy efficient to pump around a cooling system. Natural and artificial lighting are integrated in a control scheme that is daylight and occupancy sensitive. In addition, floor to ceiling height was set at the generous value of 2.9m to encourage a good distribution of daylight across the office areas. Vulcan House also scored strongly in its BREEAM assessment for its water management strategy. Grey and rainwater recycling is used to flush toilets and water consumption is estimated to be 2.5m^3 per person per year compared with a Home Office target of 3m^3 and an annual use per person in 2003–2004 of 12.4m^3. An extensive metering system is in place to monitor monthly fuel, electricity and water consumption to allow comparisons to be made against predicted usage patterns.

Well being of people

Health and well being are BREEAM criteria and Vulcan House attempts to provide good levels of air quality and natural light. Ventilation rates are 20 per cent better than normal and the short pipe runs used in the localised ventilation system help reduce the risk of contamination. Low or zero volatile organic compound (VOC) paints were used throughout the building. All desks are either close to a window or have a view out and the lighting scheme is bright and attractive. Many low energy designs have failed in the past because building occupants did not understand how the building's systems and controls worked. In Vulcan House staff are given simple user manuals and guided tours before they start, to give them an understanding of the design principles in the building that will help them to save energy and water and reduce waste. In addition, part of the Home Office's CO_2 reduction strategy relates to reducing the number of vehicle journeys made by staff. The Home Office wants civil servants to commute by bus or tram instead of by car, and so it offers subsidised fares and route-planning advice. Driving to work is also being discouraged through a restriction of the number of parking places provided on site.

Part 7

Bibliography

Anon. Probe 14, Elizabeth Fry Building, *Building Services Journal* (1998).

EEO Yellow Book, *Introduction to Energy Efficiency in Further and Higher Education*, Department of the Environment, 6,94 (1994).

Energy Consumption Guide 19, *Energy Efficiency in Offices* (1998).

Jones, D.L. *Architecture and the Environment, Bioclimatic Building Design*, Laurence King (1998).

Olivier, D. and Willoughby, T. *Review of Ultra Low Energy Homes, Ten UK Profiles in Detail*, Report 39 Department of the Environment (1996).

Smith, P. and Pitts, A. *Concepts in Practice Energy, Building for the Third Millennium*, Batsford (1997).

Webliogaphy

When it's hip to be square, Building Services Journal (December 2007) www.bsjonline.co.uk (December 2007) (accessed 1 May 2008).

http://www.learn.londonmet.ac.uk/packages/euleb/en/home/index.html (accessed 1 May 2008).

NSC (March 2008) Super green building www.robinsons.com/documents/ww/Home%20Office,%20Sheffield.pdf (March 2008) (accessed 1 May 2008).

Index